A Global History of Sexuality

A Global History of Sexuality

The Modern Era

Edited by

Robert M. Buffington, Eithne Luibhéid,
and Donna J. Guy

WILEY Blackwell

Library of Congress Cataloging-in-Publication Data

A global history of sexuality : the modern era / edited by Robert M. Buffington, Eithne Luibhéid, and Donna J. Guy.
      pages cm
   Includes bibliographical references and index.
   ISBN 978-1-4051-2048-7 (cloth) – ISBN 978-1-4051-2049-4 (pbk.)   1. Sex–
History.   2. Sex customs–History.   I. Buffington, Robert M.
   HQ21.G586 2014
   306.7–dc23
                                        2013032340

A catalogue record for this book is available from the British Library.

Cover image: © IMAGEZOO / SuperStock
Cover design by Simon Levy Associates

Set in 10.5/13 pt Minion Pro by Toppan Best-set Premedia Limited
Printed in Malaysia by Ho Printing (M) Sdn Bhd

1   2014

Contents

Notes on Contributors

Katherine E. Bliss is Senior Associate with the CSIS Global Health Policy Center in Washington, DC. The author of books, articles, and policy reports regarding gender, sexuality, global health, and foreign policy, she is currently writing a book about public health and political surveillance in Mexico during the Cold War.

Robert M. Buffington is Associate Professor of Women and Gender Studies at the University of Colorado Boulder. His research focuses on the intertwined histories of gender, sexuality, and crime in modern Latin America, especially Mexico. His books include *Criminal and Citizen in Modern Mexico*, *Reconstructing Criminality in Latin America* (coedited with Carlos Aguirre) and *True Stories of Crime in Modern Mexico* (coedited with Pablo Piccato).

Sabine Frühstück teaches in the Department of East Asian Languages and Cultural Studies at the University of California, Santa Barbara. Mostly concerned with the history and ethnography of modern Japanese culture and its relations to the rest of the world, she has authored *Colonizing Sex: Sexology and Social Control in Modern Japan* and *Uneasy Warriors: Gender, Memory and Popular Culture in the Japanese Army*, and most recently coedited *Recreating Japanese Men*.

Jonathan Garcia is an Associate Research Scientist in the Department of Sociomedical Sciences at Columbia University. His research and publications focus on intersecting elements of lived experience (sexuality, gender, and class) that drive or hinder community-based responses to health issues (HIV, food security, and substance use) among racial-minority populations.

Donna J. Guy is Distinguished Professor of Humanities and History at Ohio State University. Her research interests include women's history, the history of sexuality, Latin American history, Argentine history, and economic history. She is the author of numerous books and articles including *Women Create the Welfare State: Performing Charity and Creating Rights in Argentina, 1880–1955*; *White Slavery and Mothers Alive and Dead: The Troubled Meeting of Sex, Gender, Public Health and Progress in Latin America*; and *Sex and Danger in Buenos Aires: Prostitution, Family, and Nation in Argentina*.

Eithne Luibhéid is Associate Professor of Gender and Women's Studies at the University of Arizona. Her research explores the intersections between sexualities, racialization, and migration in transnational contexts. She is the author of *Pregnant on Arrival: Making the "Illegal" Immigrant* and *Entry Denied: Controlling Sexuality at the Border*, and coeditor of *Queer Migrations: Sexuality, U.S. Citizenship, and Border Crossings*.

Laura McGough is a consultant based in Accra, Ghana. With a PhD in history from Northwestern University and postdoctoral work in STDs at Johns Hopkins University, she has taught at several universities, including the University of Ghana. She is the author of *Gender, Sexuality and Syphilis in Early Modern Venice* and several articles on STDs and public health.

Richard Parker is Professor of Sociomedical Sciences and Anthropology and a member of the Committee on Global Thought at Columbia University in New York City, where he also directs the Center for the Study of Culture, Politics and Health. He is the founder and Co-Chair of Sexuality Policy Watch (http://www.sxpolitics.org) and the author of numerous books and articles.

Hai Ren is Associate Professor of East Asian Studies and Anthropology at the University of Arizona. His current work focuses on the sociocultural effects of globalization on everyday life. His books include *Neoliberalism and Culture in China and Hong Kong: The Countdown of Time* and its sequel, *The Middle Class in Neoliberal China: Governing Risk, Life-Building, and Themed Spaces*.

Mytheli Sreenivas is Associate Professor of Women's Studies and History at The Ohio State University. She has research interests in women's history, the history of sexuality and the family, colonialism and nationalism, and the cultural and political economy of reproduction. Her book, *Wives, Widows, Concubines: The Conjugal Family Ideal in Colonial India*, was awarded the Joseph Elder Prize from the American Institute of Indian Studies. Her current project examines the cultural history of population and reproduction in modern South Asia.

Acknowledgments

First and foremost, we thank our Wiley Blackwell editor, Tessa Harvey, for her enthusiasm, patience, and support throughout the long and arduous gestation of this book. Without her, it would never have happened.

We also thank the terrific editors and staff at Wiley Blackwell—especially Georgina Coleby, Sally Cooper, Julia Kirk, Anna Mendell, Isobel Bainton, Gillian Kane, Caroline Hensman, and Hazel Harris—for their hard work and invaluable advice along the way.

For help with translation, we thank our colleagues Deepti Misri, Hai Ren, Marjoleine Kars, and Donna Goldstein. Any translation errors are the fault of the editors.

For logistical support and good cheer, we thank the wonderful staff at the University of Colorado Boulder, Women and Gender Studies Program: Alicia Turchette and Valerie Bhat.

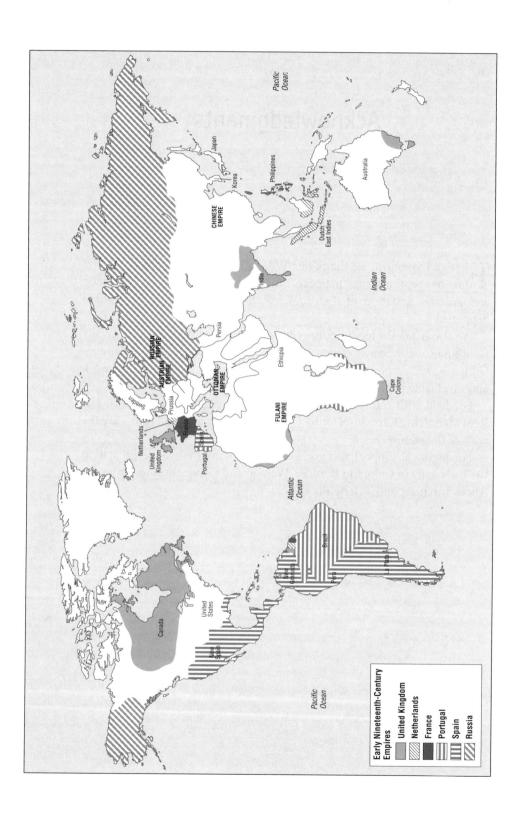

Early Nineteenth-Century Empires

- United Kingdom
- Netherlands
- France
- Portugal
- Spain
- Russia

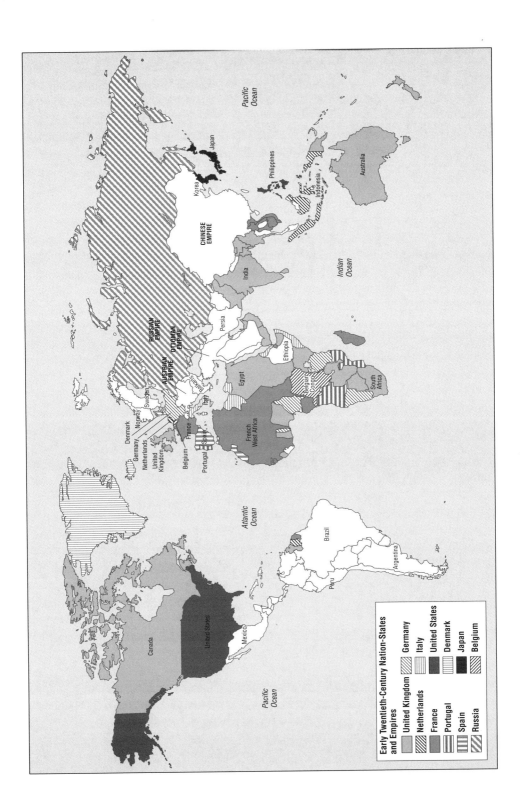

Early Twentieth-Century Nation-States and Empires

United Kingdom
Netherlands
France
Portugal
Spain
Russia
Germany
Italy
United States
Denmark
Japan
Belgium

Nation-States c. 2000

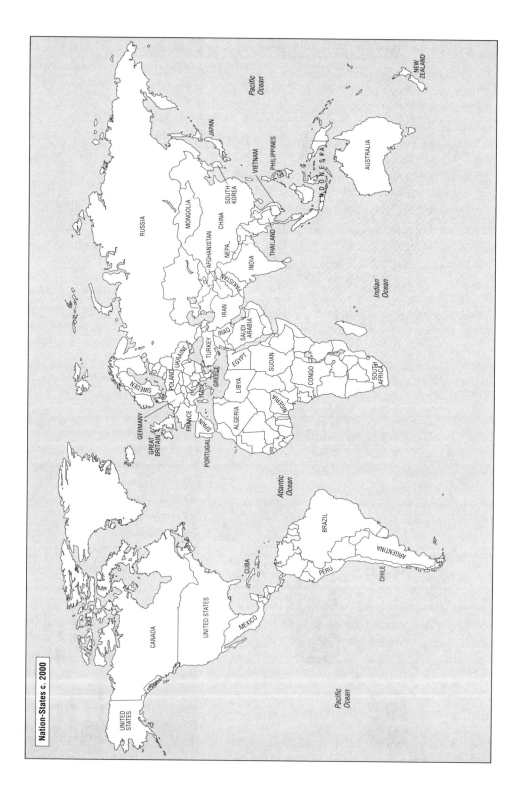

1

Introduction

Robert M. Buffington

Although questions about sex and sexuality preoccupy almost everyone these days, we are offered few intellectual strategies for incorporating our concerns and obsessions into a larger historical context. This is especially true when historical perspective takes on global proportions. In the contemporary world, our own sexuality and our sense of the sexualities of others color all aspects of contemporary life, from interpersonal relations to foreign affairs. We literally cannot imagine our world or make sense of our place in it without referencing sexuality. Those of us who write and teach history thus have an obligation to help our readers and students understand how sexuality "works"—to help them understand how our most intimate concerns intersect with complex global and historical processes. This obligation (which is also a pleasure) is the driving force behind *A Global History of Sexuality*. To that end, the book seeks to provide not a titillating catalog of past sexual practices (although sex is clearly an important part of our story) but rather an accessible synthesis of the best recent research into what sexuality has meant across the past three centuries in the everyday lives of individuals; in the imagined communities formed by the powerful bonds of shared religion, ethnicity, language, and national citizenship; and on the turbulent global stage of cultural encounter, imperialist expansion, transnational migration, and international commerce.

Humans have obsessed about sex and it implications for reproduction, morality, intimacy, social stability, and so on since the beginning of the

A Global History of Sexuality: The Modern Era, First Edition.
Edited by Robert M. Buffington, Eithne Luibhéid, and Donna J. Guy.
© 2014 Robert M. Buffington, Eithne Luibhéid, and Donna J. Guy.
Published 2014 by Blackwell Publishing Ltd.

historical era (and certainly long before that), but the history of sexuality—
as a recognizable subfield of the discipline of history—is relatively recent.
This is not to suggest that until the late twentieth century scholars had
avoided the subject out of academic prudishness, fear of ridicule, lack of
interest, or because they considered it trivial. Indeed, an influential generation of late nineteenth and early twentieth-century (mostly) European "sexologists" went to great lengths to collect and synthesize everything they
could find on past and present human sexual attitudes and behaviors. Some
scholars used this impressive body of historical evidence to demonstrate
considerable variations in human sexual expression across time and across
cultures—at times with the worthy goal of promoting greater understanding and tolerance of sexual difference in their own societies and at other
times in order to articulate racist colonial norms that justified and reinforced social inequalities. Despite their efforts to document human sexual
diversity, early sexologists had little interest in analyzing the particular
historical and social conditions that had produced these diverse expressions (Phillips and Reay 2002, p. 13; Cocks and Houlbrook 2005, p. 4).
Moreover, the rising tide of psychoanalytic thought, especially founding
father Sigmund Freud's insistence on ascribing sexual behavior to universal
human "drives" and "taboos" that transcended cultural and historical differences, further discouraged scholarly inquiry into the historical particu-
larities of human sexuality.[1]

Throughout the 1960s and afterward, most scholars in the social sciences
and humanities—anthropologists, sociologists, historians, literary critics,
etc.—followed the lead of sexologists (collecting examples of sexual customs) or psychologists (finding evidence of universal drives and taboos) or
some combination of the two approaches. Although studies of sexuality per
se remained marginalized in many disciplines, anthropologist Kath Weston
argues that:

> from the beginning, assumptions about sexuality infused social science con-
> cepts such as normality, evolution, progress, organization, development and
> change. Likewise, judgments about sexuality remain deeply embedded in the
> history of scholarly explanations for who acquires power, who deserves it,
> and who gets to keep it. The same can be said for a multitude of theories
> about cognition, reciprocity, gender, race, and many other stock concepts in
> social science. (Weston 1998, p. 20)

Although historians typically operate at the humanistic edge of the social sciences, in this instance, their reliance on the "sexuality infused social science

concepts" identified by Weston for the social sciences in general supports a similar interpretation of their work.

By the early 1970s, the intellectual tide had begun to turn as "social constructionists" such as philosopher–historian Michel Foucault developed compelling critiques of "essentialist" notions of human sexuality and noted its central role in producing and maintaining social inequalities of power and privilege. Social constructionist critics rejected the essentialist idea

> that beating at the centre of [the varieties of sexual experience] was a core of natural sexuality, varying in incidence and power, no doubt, as a result of chance historical factors, the weight of moral and physical repression, the patterns of kinship, and so on, but nevertheless basically unchanging in biological and psychological essence. (Weeks 2000, p. 30)

Instead, they insisted that human sexuality at any given moment in time was the product of distinct and changeable social circumstances, especially discourses around sexuality, which determined the "nature" of all sexual experience. This emphatic rejection of an essential human sexual nature had political repercussions, including for sexual rights advocates who feared that the denial of the natural roots of sexual differences would undermine their efforts to promote sexual variation as "normal" and thus worthy of protection rather than persecution (through efforts to reprogram homosexuals for example). And some scholars objected to what they considered an unwarranted denial of biological factors in sexuality, arguing that basic sexual orientations such as hetero, homo, and bisexuality, firmly grounded in human biology, have characterized all societies, albeit under different names (Cocks and Holbrook 2005, pp. 9–10).

In response to these objections, sexuality scholars (including historians) have begun to challenge the sharp binary that characterized the essentialist–social constructionist debate, arguing that the physiological aspects of human sexuality shape its social construction and vice versa in a continual spiral between natural influences on one hand and cultural influences on the other. Nonetheless, most historians of sexuality would agree that social constructionist scholarship on human sexuality provided the intellectual foundation for most subsequent histories of sexuality and for its recognition as a viable, important, and vibrant subdiscipline of history. While the authors included in this book have gone to considerable trouble to avoid a doctrinaire approach to the subject—as the very different histories of sexuality reflected in each chapter will attest—we are still deeply indebted to the work of social constructionists. In his 2000 book, *Making Sexual History*, historian–sociologist Jeffrey Weeks summarized the basic elements of a social constructionist approach with "five broad categories of social relations, which are both constructed around and in turn shape and reshape sex and gender relations":

> First, there are the kinship and family systems that place individuals in relationship to one another, and constitute them as human subjects with varying needs and desires, conscious and unconscious. Second, there are the economic and social organizations that shape social relations, statuses and class divisions, and provide the preconditions and ultimate limits for the organization of sexual life. Third, there are the changing patterns of social regulation and organization, formal and informal, legal and moral, populist and professional, religious and secular, unintended consequences as well as organized and planned responses. Fourth, there are changing forms of political interest and concern, power and policies. Finally, there are the cultures of resistance which give rise to oppositional subcultures, alternative forms of knowledge and social and sexual movements. (Weeks 2000, p. 132)

Nearly fifteen years later, these five general categories of social relations continue to ground most histories of sexuality, including those in this book.

What distinguishes this present volume from previous histories of sexuality is its synthetic approach to the *global* history of sexuality. By and large, the most influential histories of sexuality that have come out in recent years have focused—as Foucault did—on the West, defined as beginning with Greco-Roman antiquity and continuing to the present day. Many of those histories have taken even more narrow regional, national, and local approaches. Other parts of the world have sometimes entered the historical frame as Western attitudes toward sexuality spread through imperial conquest. And edited volumes of scholarly essays that include non-Western case studies in the history of sexuality have appeared with increasing frequency. Still, we believe that this book represents the first attempt to produce a truly global history of sexuality in the modern era aimed primarily at a general audience.

Writing a global history of sexuality that would be accessible to a general readership involved making choices, some of them quite complicated. One of the most difficult to resolve was the book's title. Given the breadth of the subject matter, the decision to avoid the authoritative "the" in favor of the more modest (and truthful) "a" was simple. Everyone involved in this project has struggled mightily to synthesize and frame the material as clearly and conscientiously as possible, but none of us would contend that our respective chapters or this book as whole represent *the* global history of sexuality.

If the decision to write *a* global history was easy, decisions about the rest of the title were more tricky. Our collective debt to *The History of Sexuality: Volume 1*, philosopher and historian Michel Foucault's (1978) seminal study of sexuality in modern Western societies, will be obvious to fellow academics, and is openly acknowledged in several chapters. So it made sense to add "global" to his famous title both as an act of homage and to point out the difference between our project and his. But the debt runs deeper than a borrowed title. Like Foucault, we have taken the eighteenth-century rise of the nation-state in the "West" and elsewhere as our starting point—even through Foucault himself went on to write histories of sexuality in ancient Greece and Rome, and despite convincing arguments from fellow historians for including the histories of premodern sexualities (Foucault 1998, 1990; Canaday 2009, pp. 1253–4).

The obvious reason to start with the eighteenth century was to keep things manageable in terms of length for our readers and in terms of conceptual framework for our authors. Less obvious to those unacquainted with Foucault's periodization, but crucial to the conceptualization of this book, is the profound sea change in the meanings ascribed to sexual behavior that occurred, especially but not exclusively in the "West," during this period. In *The History of Sexuality*, Foucault illustrates this radical shift with an apparently innocuous anecdote about a simple-minded French farmhand who is arrested by local authorities on reports that "he had obtained a few caresses from a little girl, just as he had done before and seen done by the village urchins round about him." In answer to the rhetorical question "What is the significant thing about this story?" Foucault responds:

> The pettiness of it all, the fact that this everyday occurrence in the life of village sexuality, these inconsequential bucolic pleasures, could become, from a certain time, the object not only of a collective intolerance but of a judicial action, a medical intervention, a careful clinical examination, and an entire theoretical elaboration. (Foucault 1978, p. 31)

The chapters that follow, then, explore in different ways and in different contexts (individual, cultural, institutional, etc.) "a constant optimization and an increasing valorization of the discourse of sex . . . meant to yield

6 *Robert M. Buffington*

multiple effects of displacement, intensification, reorientation, and modification of desire itself," a process that began in earnest in the eighteenth century and has yet to run its course (Foucault 1978, p. 23).

In sum, beginning sometime in the eighteenth century in the "West" and occurring at different times and in different ways in other parts of the world, the formation of the "modern" nation-state, in particular new notions of national belonging and citizenship, led to an increased focus on sex that produced what Foucault calls "multiple effects." Societies became structured in large part through sexual and intimate norms, which were not everywhere and always the same yet almost invariably privileged sexuality channeled into childbearing within male–female marriage among the dominant group while generating continually changing specifications of "perversions" and dangers against which society had to guard. The radical shift theorized by Foucault, with its "constant optimization and . . . increasing valorization of the discourse of sex," has meant that in modern times concerns about sexuality have become central to apparently nonsexual domains of social life (displacement), become more acute in all domains of social life (intensification), taken on new meanings (reorientation), and changed the ways in which we experience desire (modification). As anthropologist Gayle Rubin points out, sex "at any given time and place" has always been in some sense political, "but there are also historical periods in which sexuality is more sharply contested and more overtly politicized" than others (Rubin 1984, p. 267). Our premise is that the eighteenth century marks the beginning of just such a historical period—and so our story starts there. At the same time, the production of sexuality in the West was inseparable from European colonial projects in Africa, Asia, and the Middle East. Anthropologist Ann Stoler reminds us that imperial governance required "natural" social categories such as colonizer/colonized, European/non-European, white/nonwhite, categories that were secured, contested, and remade "through forms of sexual control" that linked colonial projects with nation building at home (Stoler 2002, pp. 42–7).

With regard to the book's title, the most difficult decision of all involved the apparently innocuous word "global." In recent years, scholars have hotly debated the proper term for histories that "break out of the nation-state or singular states as the category of analysis, and . . . eschew the ethnocentrism that once characterized the writing of history in the West" (Bayly et al. 2006, pp. 1441–2). That debate has produced at least five viable candidates—comparative, international, world, global, and transnational history—each of which has taken on different methodological and ideological connotations. Our problem was that, in the methodological sense at least, every chapter in this book engages to a greater or lesser extent with each of the five frameworks: each chapter includes explicit comparisons between countries and regions, each addresses international relations among nation-states, each takes a world view, each explores global processes, and each examines "flows" of capital, people, technology, media, and ideas (Appadurai 1996).

For our purposes, the methodologies of comparative and international history seemed too narrowly focused on comparisons or relations between nation-states to describe the book as a whole. And world history seemed too vague. That left us with global and transnational history, methodologies that emphasize "flows" that circulate within and across national boundaries and geographical regions in ways that undo and remake multiple inequalities. Despite their conceptual similarities, the two terms have gotten caught up in ideological debates among scholars and policymakers over the neoliberal policies that have dominated the world economy since the end of the Cold War. Those who promote globalization—the preferred stand-in term for neoliberal economics—for its undeniable capacity to generate immense wealth despite serious negative "side effects" have rendered the term "global" untenable for many activists and critics, including in academia (Grewal and Kaplan 1994; Parisi 2011). Moreover, some scholars argue that global history by definition ignores regional transnational flows that "do not claim to embrace the whole world" (Bayly et al. 2006, p. 1448; see also Alexander and Mohanty 1997).

Although we share these concerns, we have opted to describe this project as a global history for three reasons. First, the book is indeed global in scope even through many of the case studies deal with regional rather than global flows. Second, we want to ensure the widest possible audience for what we think is a very important and timely topic, and the term global, despite its unfortunate appropriation by globalization proponents, seems less polemical and for that reason more welcoming to uninitiated readers than the more academic-sounding transnational. Third, as the alert reader will quickly discover, we (and our authors) have also struggled to find the proper terms to distinguish political, economic, social, and cultural inequalities among countries and regions around the world. In this instance, most of us settled on Global North and Global South—despite the obvious geographical problems presented by relatively wealthy southern-hemisphere countries such as Argentina, Australia, Singapore, and Taiwan—in order to avoid the value judgments inherent in comparisons between First, Second, and Third World countries and between developed, developing, and under-developed countries.

The seven densely packed chapters that follow raise any number of important themes in the global history of sexuality. All of them, however, are organized around four interrelated processes: *the formation of sexual identities* around notions of femininity, masculinity, normality, and abnormality; *the regulation of sexuality by societal norms* including patriarchy, heterosexuality, racism, religious beliefs, and customary practices; *the regulation of sexuality by institutions* such as family, community, organized religion, law, and the state; and *the intersection of sexuality with global/ transnational processes* such as cultural exchange, biological transmission, trade, migration, and imperial expansion. To illustrate and complicate these general processes, each chapter provides a range of case studies, integrated into the larger narrative in some chapters and analyzed in distinct subsections in others. These case studies are intended to help the reader see the different ways that the general processes outlined above play out at different times and in different places around the world.

Our global history of sexuality begins with Sabine Frühstück's chapter on SEXUALITY AND THE NATION-STATE. Chapter 2 builds on the well-established claim that nation-building efforts around the world have been permeated with sex talk, and that sex talk has been permeated with concerns about nation building—both at home and abroad. Although the general contours of this link between sexuality and modern nation-state formation look much the same all over the world, a closer look at the cases of Japan, the United States, and South Africa reveals important and often unexpected variations on a common theme. In early twentieth-century Japan, for example, nation building prompted an obsession with all things modern (including the perceived need to modernize sexual attitudes and behaviors) and a rejection of backwardness (including traditional sexual attitudes and behaviors) whether at home or in the colonies of the nascent Japanese empire. While never blindly in thrall to Western ideas, Japanese policymakers, scientists, and educators nonetheless understood the vital importance of intellectual exchange with their counterparts elsewhere, and thus produced a "sexual regime" as modern, yet recognizably Japanese, as any in the world. The intersection of racial difference and sexual deviance was mostly a colonial concern for Japanese social engineers. For their US counterparts, however, this troublesome intersection was at the heart of national "reconstruction," especially during the late nineteenth and early twentieth centuries as the country struggled to recover from a devastating civil war, settle its western territories, assimilate foreign immigrants, and make sense of unruly colonial subjects in faraway places such as Puerto Rico and the Philippines. Whether validated by religious morality, manifest destiny, social Darwinism, or eugenic science, interlinked notions of white racial supremacy and moral superiority (defined as sexual continence) have provided the ideological underpinnings of the national "imagined community" up until the present day. In contrast to Japan and the United States, nation building in late twentieth and early twenty-first-century South Africa has centered on controversies over sexual and racial inclusiveness. Setting the new nation apart from its segregationist, white-supremacist past meant constructing an imagined community grounded in multicultural, multiracial, and multisexual tolerance. Progressive legislation advanced by a self-consciously modern state, however, has not necessarily translated into widespread cultural acceptance of same-sex marriages or nonnormative sexual identities, although it has altered (but not supplanted) "traditional" sexual categories.

The focus shifts from modern nation-states to modern empires in Chapter 3, SEXUALITY AND MODERN IMPERIALISM. In this chapter, Mytheli Sreenivas analyzes the central importance of sexual encounters and sexual intimacies—some coerced, others consensual, most contentious (especially for colonial authorities)—to the forging and maintenance of modern empires. In order to make sense of these encounters and intimacies, Sreenivas teases out three distinct themes in imperial understandings and governance of colonial sexualities: the intersection of sexuality and race in the imperial imagination, colonial authorities' efforts to regulate intimate relations between colonizer and colonized, and imperial interventions in the sexualities of colonized populations. To illustrate these themes, the chapter draws from a range of imperial experiences including the Dutch in the East Indies, the British in India and Africa, the French in Indochina (Vietnam), the Germans in Southwest Africa (Namibia), and the United States in Puerto Rico and the Philippines. In each instance, imperial understandings, regulations, and interventions with regard to everything from prostitution to concubinage, interracial marriage, and nonnormative sexual practices impacted groups and individuals in the metropole as well as in the colonies. And in each case, they met with a combustible mixture of acceptance, negotiation, and resistance that transformed sexualities all over the world.

With Chapter 4, the historical narrative shifts from links between sexuality and political structures—as embodied in nation-states and empires—to the multifaceted problem of sexually transmitted diseases. Laura

McGough and Katherine Bliss's historical overview of SEX AND DISEASE FROM SYPHILIS TO AIDS exposes the ways in which the biological becomes political (and vice versa) through moral panics around the transmission of these two deadly epidemic diseases, associated in the popular, scientific, and official imagination with sexual promiscuity and social degeneration. As the chapter makes clear, the stigma and shame prompted by sexually transmitted diseases "are embedded in wider social processes of power, domination, and social inequality" that often take the shape of public health campaigns aimed at marginalized populations including prostitutes, foreigners, the poor, and racial/ethnic minorities. Sexually transmitted diseases (STDs) have been around since the beginning of recorded history (and before), but state-directed public health campaigns to prevent their spread are a relatively new phenomenon that accompanied the rise of the nation-state and then spread quickly throughout the world either through direct colonization or as imported "technologies of power" purporting to represent the latest advances in medical science. A wide range of examples from Europe, Sub-Saharan Africa, Asia, North America, and Latin America illustrate the global impact of epidemic STDs, the moral panics they induced, and the scientific-bureaucratic technologies developed to counter their deadly effects. Two concluding case studies of successful HIV/AIDS-prevention initiatives in Brazil and Uganda remind us that, despite the checkered history of state-driven public health campaigns and their complicity in perpetuating social inequalities, they do sometimes help prevent the spread of epidemic diseases.

Chapter 5, SEXUALITY AND INTERNATIONAL MIGRATION, examines a different sexualized global flow, the movement of people across national borders, including from poorer countries in the Global South to wealthier countries in the Global North. As Eithne Luibhéid explains, sexuality has been "a crucial site where the interplay between agency, subjectivity, and structural hierarchies of power get contested and remade through struggles over migration possibilities." These powerful links between sexuality and migration intensified with the rise of modern states and their obsession with delineating and policing fixed national borders. Although prompted by a wide range of circumstances, migration across national borders has involved an intensive selection process that favors immigrants deemed "desirable" by the host country and seeks to exclude those deemed "undesirable." In most instances, politicians, immigration officials, prospective employers, and other interested parties have preferred immigrants who conform to an "idealized heterosexual marriage norm . . . crosscut by racial, cultural, class, and gender hierarchies"—a preference expressed in various ways, including through family-reunification immigration policies, labor preferences for married men, fears of hyperfertile women, and the exclusion of LGBTQ folk. In the face of these pressures, Luibhéid demonstrates that "migrants continually remake their identities, cultures and communities including through challenging—or hewing to—sexual norms in their own and other communities."

Chapter 6 explores the most explicitly sexual of all global flows, SEX TRAFFICKING. Robert Buffington and Donna Guy open the chapter with a brief history of media-driven moral panics over sex trafficking from the anti-white slavery campaigns of the late nineteenth and early twentieth centuries to their latest incarnation in early twenty-first-century global initiatives to end "modern-day slavery." In the pages that follow, the authors attempt "to navigate the distortions put forth by politicians, law enforcement, journalists, and antitrafficking organizations (including the United Nations) in order to produce a historical overview of sex trafficking in the modern era that is as complicated, perplexing, and disturbing as the phenomenon itself has always been." Case studies of three long-standing sex trafficking routes—Nepal to India, the Philippines to South Korea, Central and Eastern Europe to Western Europe and the Americas—reveal the complex interplay of local, regional, national, and global forces that produce sex trafficking, in particular historic economic disparities between sending and receiving countries. Of note, especially in the first two cases, is the prominent role of imperial governance and "friendly" military occupations in fostering the conditions under which sex trafficking has flourished. The third case highlights the potent mix of contemporary geopolitics combined with a long history of political and economic instability that has driven the latest wave of sex trafficking out of Central and Eastern Europe.

Chapter 7, on SEXUALITY AND MASS MEDIA, shifts our attention from the transnational movement of peoples through immigration and trafficking to the global circulation of sexual culture via mass media. In this chapter, Hai Ren explores three central themes in the relationship between sexuality and mass culture: the way media shapes understandings of sexuality around the world; the way it helps "to regulate sexuality as normal or abnormal, permissible or prohibited, and pleasurable or risky"; and the way "powerful links between sexuality and mass culture on a global scale work to affirm some sexual norms and moralities while challenging others." These themes play out in distinct ways in four case studies drawn from different historical periods, different parts of the world, and different media. The first case looks at early twentieth-century advertisements for cosmetics and toiletries directed at "modern girls" in North America, Latin America, Africa, and Asia. The second case involves mid-twentieth-century sex education debates provoked by widely disseminated advice columns in the United States. The third examines the youth culture that developed around manga comic book art, especially the "beautiful fighting girl" figure, in post-1960s Japan. The fourth analyzes the controversies surrounding social media, including "sexting," in contemporary China. Taken together, these four cases reveal the profound impact that mass media has had on the ways in which modern societies have represented, understood, and regulated human sexuality.

Chapter 8, SEXUALITY IN THE CONTEMPORARY WORLD: GLOBALIZATION AND SEXUAL RIGHTS, examines the contentious sexual politics of the late twentieth and early twenty-first centuries, especially the growing global prominence of local, national, transnational, and international sexual rights movements. In this chapter, Richard Parker, Jonathan Garcia, and Robert Buffington argue that the struggle to define sexual rights as part of our essential political, economic, and civil rights is especially important in the contemporary world because sexual norms are increasingly understood to play a role as central as gender, race, ethnicity, poverty, and class discriminations in circumscribing human rights around the world. To highlight the complex interplay between international initiatives that advocate for "universal" (if sometimes hotly contested) sexual rights and local social movements that operate on behalf of specific constituencies, the chapter includes case studies on four grassroots organizations from the Global South: Criola, a black women's group in Rio de Janeiro, Brazil; Inner Circle, a Muslim queer rights group in Cape Town, South Africa; Durbar Mahila Samanwaya Committee (DMSC), a collective for female, male, and transgender sex workers in Kolkata, India; and El Closét de Sor Juana, a lesbian activist group in Mexico City. In all four instances, the authors argue, local groups formed in response to local issues have leveraged religious and secular discourses of sexual rights to legitimize their advocacy efforts in their home communities *and* to link their local struggles to national and international initiatives aimed at large-scale social transformation.

So where do these seven interlaced histories of modern sexuality leave us? In his *History of Sexuality*, Foucault famously insists that for historians:

> The central issue . . . is not to determine whether one says yes or no to sex, whether one formulates prohibitions or permissions, whether one asserts its importance or denies its effects, or whether one refines the words one uses to designate it; but to account for the fact that it is spoken about, to discover who does the speaking, the positions and viewpoints from which they speak, the institutions which prompt people to speak about it and which store and distribute the things that are said. (Foucault 1978, p. 11)

Foucault's charge to *account* for sex as a "discursive fact"—as an undeniable reality of social life despite its myriad and mercurial meanings—is something each author has taken to heart with full knowledge that we too are contributing to the obsessive "putting into discourse of sex" that continues to characterize our world (Foucault 1978, pp. 11–12).

Acknowledgments

Special thanks to Eithne Luibhéid for her invaluable help with the several incarnations of this introductory essay.

Note

1   Freud and his followers also posited an evolutionary trajectory for human sexuality that culminated in heterosexual desire expressed through intercourse and branded other forms of sexual expression as perverse, immature, or atavistic (primitive). The work of sexologists in England, Germany, Japan, and the United States is discussed at length in Chapter 2.

References

Alexander, M.J. and Mohanty, C.T. (1997) Introduction: Genealogies, legacies, movements, in *Feminist Genealogies, Colonial Legacies, Democratic Futures.* Routledge, New York, pp. xiii–xlii.

Appadurai, A. (1996) *Modernity at Large: Cultural Dimensions of Globalization.* University of Minnesota Press, Minneapolis.

Bayly, C.A., Beckert, S., Connelly, M, et al. (2006) AHR conversation: On transnational history. *American History Review*, 111 (5), 1441–64.

Canaday, M. (2009) Thinking sex in the transnational turn: An introduction. *American Historical Review*, 114 (5), 1250–7.

Cocks, H.G. and Houlbrook, M. (2005) Introduction, in *The Modern History of Sexuality* (ed. M. Houlbrook and H.G. Cocks). Palgrave MacMillan, New York, pp. 1–18.

Foucault, M. (1978) *The History of Sexuality, Volume 1: An Introduction* (trans. R. Hurley). Vintage, New York.

Foucault, M. (1988) *The History of Sexuality, Volume 3: The Care of the Self* (trans. R. Hurley). Vintage, New York.

Foucault, M. (1990) *The History of Sexuality, Volume 2: The Use of Pleasure* (trans. R. Hurley). Vintage, New York.

Grewal, I. and Kaplan, C. (1994) Introduction: Transnational feminist practices and questions of postmodernity, in *Scattered Hegemonies: Postmodernity and Transnational Feminist Practices*. University of Minnesota Press, Minneapolis, pp. 1–35.

Parisi, L. (2011) Transnational, in *Rethinking Women's and Gender Studies* (ed. C. Orr, A. Braithwaite, and D. Lichtenstein). Routledge, New York, pp. 310–27.

Phillips, K.M. and Reay, B. (2002) Introduction, in *Sexualities in History: A Reader*. Routledge, New York, pp. 1–23.

Rubin, G. (1984) Thinking sex: Notes for a radical theory of the politics of sexuality, in *Pleasure and Danger: Exploring Female Sexuality* (ed. C. Vance). Routledge, New York, pp. 267–319.

Stoler, A.L. (2002) *Carnal Knowledge and Imperial Power: Race and the Intimate in Colonial Rule*. University of California Press, Berkeley.

Weeks, J. (2000) Sexuality and history revisited, in *Making Sexual History*. Polity Press, Cambridge, pp. 125–41.

Weston, K. (1998) The bubble, the burn, and the simmer: Introduction: Locating sexuality in social science, in *Long Slow Burn: Sexuality and Social Science*. Routledge, New York, pp. 1–28.

Suggested Reading

AHR Forum (2009) Transnational sexualities. *American Historical Review*, 114 (5), 1250–353.

Foucault, M. (1978) *The History of Sexuality, Volume 1: An Introduction* (trans. R. Hurley). Vintage, New York.

Halperin, D.M. (2004) *How to Do the History of Homosexuality*. University of Chicago Press, Chicago.

Harris, V. (2010) Sex on the margins: New directions in the historiography of sexuality and gender. *Historical Journal*, 53 (4), 1085–104.

Houlbrook, M. and Cocks, H.G. (2005) *The Modern History of Sexuality*. Palgrave MacMillan, New York.

Nye, R.A. (1999) *Sexuality*. Oxford University Press, Oxford.

Phillips, K.M. and Reay, B. (2002) *Sexualities in History: A Reader*. Routledge, New York.

Rupp, L.J. (2001) Toward a global history of same-sex sexuality. *Journal of the History of Sexuality*, 10 (2), 287–302.

Weeks, J. (2000) *Making Sexual History*. Polity Press, Cambridge.

2

Sexuality and the Nation-State

Sabine Frühstück

Sexing the Nation, Nationalizing Sex: An Introduction

A 1906 article in the *Far East News* reported the arrest of thirty-year-old
Kazutoshi in Dalian, Manchuria. Kazutoshi turned out to be of greater
interest to the authorities than a common thief would have been. He was
discovered to be "a cripple," part male and part female. After classifying
him a "strange double-sexed person," government officials probed into his
past. They discovered that Kazutoshi had been born with the name Fuji—
and as a woman. The tale appeared in the newspaper under the title, "A
Woman Found to Have Testicles" (Algoso 2011).

Kazutoshi's story evoked a number of binaries (opposing categories
that define each other through contrast)—man/woman, heterosexual/
homosexual, normal/pathological—that had become indicative of a modern
understanding of sexuality by around 1900. This chapter traces the emergence of this modern understanding of sexuality and its relation to
politics—in particular, the politics of nation building. It builds on the well-
established assumptions that nation-building efforts the world over have
been permeated with sex talk, and that sex talk has been permeated with
themes rooted in the way the people view nation-states—both their own
and others. As early as 1982, pioneer historian of sexuality George L. Mosse
was insisting that scholars could no longer treat the nation and sexuality
as discrete and autonomous constructs but must instead consider them

A Global History of Sexuality: The Modern Era, First Edition.
Edited by Robert M. Buffington, Eithne Luibhéid, and Donna J. Guy.
© 2014 Robert M. Buffington, Eithne Luibhéid, and Donna J. Guy.
Published 2014 by Blackwell Publishing Ltd.

two of the most powerful, intertwined discourses shaping contemporary
notions of identity (Mosse 1982; Parker et al. 1992, p. 1). This chapter illuminates this claim through the examples of three distinct nation-states—
Japan, the United States, and South Africa. As we will see, in each case,
notions of modernity and what it meant to be a *modern* nation-state were
tied to establishing and maintaining the binaries that Kazutoshi's case
evoked: man/woman, heterosexual/homosexual, normal/pathological.

Of course, neither "sexuality" nor "nation" is a simple notion. Although
many of us accept nation-states as part of the "natural" order (like sexuality), neither nations nor states have existed at all times and in all circumstances.[1] Moreover, postcolonial theorists such as Homi Bhabha (1990)
have insisted that no single model can adequately represent the myriad and
contradictory forms taken by nation-states in the modern era. Nevertheless, we can fruitfully examine the interaction of nation building and the
construction of modern sexualities in a wide range of possible configura-
tions even if crafting a *global* historical narrative necessarily entails acknowledging differences and similarities in how various nation-states around
the world have framed that interaction. Among other things, the nation-
building process has often meant pitting scientific truths against religious
beliefs, changing both in the process. Government officials cum public
health experts have employed science speak and the "language of truth" in
order to colonize ever more spheres of human life, including sex, and to
manage ever smaller details of citizens' everyday existence. They have justified this intrusion in large part by invoking the rhetoric of liberation from
the yoke of tradition, religion, and superstition—from an undesirable pre-
civilized or premodern state of being. Modern life including sexual behavior, they have insisted, must be measured, counted, considered comparatively,
reformed and, in some places, revolutionized.

Like nation, the concept of sexuality has a history. Once "sex" signified
a vague amalgamation of biology, nature, and culture. In modern times,
"sexuality" has become popularly understood as the biological marker
of a supposedly essential identity, an inherent characteristic distinct from
"gender" that has taken on the cultural traits that come from education,
training, self-mastery, and daily performance (Butler 1990). Understanding
sexuality as the "natural" source of human life and social renewal, scientists,
reformers, and government officials everywhere have made it a principal
target in their efforts to know, manage, and control national populations—a
"linchpin of modernity" (in Michel Foucault's terms) in the nation-building
project.

Figure 2.1 Nazi pro-motherhood poster depicts an Aryan-looking mother breastfeeding her baby while her husband plows in the background. The slogan reads "Support the Relief Organization, Mother and Child," a social welfare institution for single and low-income mothers set up by the Nazi Party in 1934. Propaganda Minister Joseph Goebbels considered the organization (and healthy mothers and children) an essential component of Nazi population policy—and thus crucial to Germany's future. *Source*: © Mary Evans Picture Library / Alamy.

Figure 2.2 Indian family planning poster, 1996. The sign reads: "For a healthy family, wait for three years before your second child. You can get these family planning methods from government health workers, hospitals, and health centers for free." The images at the top of the poster depict various forms of contraception. The inclusion of a female child represents government efforts to address male-preference in many Indian families, which has led to a significant imbalance in the ratio between men and women. *Source*: SIFPSA (State Innovations in Family Planning Services Agency).

Figure 2.3 One-child-policy tile mural in Nanchang, Jiangxi province, China, 2013. The text at the top of the mural says "flower of happiness," a reference to the little girl. As in the Indian example (Figure 2.2), the inclusion of a female child represents government efforts to address male-preference. *Source*: © Lou-Foto / Alamy.

Examples abound: Military administrators around the world have routinely investigated conscripts' patterns of STD infection. Military physical
exams have revealed which male bodies were fit and which unfit for that new
mode of service to the nation-state, modern war. Public health officials have
regulated prostitution along a continuum ranging from segregation to prohibition. A range of reproductive-rights activists, including socialists, feminists, doctors, and other health experts, have agitated for the legalization of
abortion and various means of birth control. Medical professionals, religious leaders, and concerned parents have fiercely debated the issue of vir-
ginity as a hindrance to or expression of women's rights. The list goes on . . .

This desire to know the "truth" about sexuality and use that knowledge
for nation building and nationalist ends has also driven interest in knowing
more about nonconforming *others*, most prominently gender benders, her-
maphrodites, those physically attracted to their own sex, and individuals
variously labeled "perverts," "deviants," "indeterminates," "third sex," or
"degenerates." Some investigators have focused their search for "others"
elsewhere than on their own national sexual cultures.[2] These explorations
are frequently double edged. While early Western ethnographers of sexualities often used their findings to reconfirm preconceived notions of other
sexual cultures' primitivism and backwardness, many also employed their
insights regarding other sexual cultures to criticize Euro-American puri-
tanism, rigidity, and hypocrisy. Regardless, the production of sexual knowledge has connected like-minded activists, policy makers, social reformers,
and ordinary men and women across national borders, which has led to
new understandings and misunderstandings about sexuality. Someone as
radically progressive as physician and sexologist Magnus Hirschfeld, for
instance, exoticized peoples around the world while, in the same breath,
proposing in 1933 that "genuine love of people, love of whatever sort,
mutual, nurturing love is the one and only bridge to overcoming existing
differences and contradictions between person and person, people and
people, and land and land" (Hirschfeld 2006, p. 436). As we will see, the
intrinsically political character of the production and circulation of sexual
knowledge has remained a central feature of the global story of sexuality
and the nation-state.

The production and circulation of sexual knowledge have been intimately intertwined not just with internal nation building but also with
overseas expansion—a process that further consolidated nation building at
home. In many parts of the world, the formation of nation-states from the
eighteenth century forward was a nationalist, militarist, and colonialist

pursuit that necessarily intersected with sex. Imperialist projects by Britain in India, European powers in Africa and around the world, and Japan in Asia, to name but a few, spurred the production of new models of citizenship grounded in new sexual regimes, often imposed by violence, be it the mass rape of women as troops advanced or retreated, or hate crimes against people of nonnormative sexual and gender identities. These new forms of citizenship—whether developed at home or abroad or in both places at once—were rooted in beliefs about the significance of national origin and predicated on ideals of social respectability, social reproduction, public hygiene, and the bourgeois family. And national and colonial authorities alike disseminated ideas about the duties and rights of citizenship through new modes of cultural transmission, including public education, mass conscription of young men, expanding print media, and improved technologies of communication and transportation.

This chapter illustrates a number of these complex relationships and crosscurrents between nation building and sexual regimes. As the story shifts from one locale where the nation-state took hold of sex to another, it is crucial for the reader to remain aware of differences and similarities, patterns and aberrations, normativities and transgressions. The journey begins in Japan, a key player in the intertwined history of sexuality and the modern nation-state. Japanese culture has a rich sexual tradition and *ars erotica* (erotic arts) that spanned several centuries prior to the restoration of the Meiji emperor in 1868, which initiated several decades of rapid modernization (Screech 2009). By the end of the Meiji period in 1912, Japan had assumed the role of broker of sexual knowledge between Europe (particularly Germany) and Asia (particularly China).[3] A late and successful modernizer, Japan also became an anticolonial colonizer. Prominent members of the country's elite fashioned Japan as the engine that would bring modernity and science to Asia. At the same time, they promoted Japan as the legitimate, fatherly leader of the fight against the encroachment of Western imperialism. Similar to imperialist nation-states elsewhere, Japanese efforts at nation and empire building coincided with processes of knowledge production that created a series of "sexual questions." These efforts will be discussed in the first case study.

In the second case study, the discussion shifts to the United States. While early twentieth-century Japanese nation builders imagined their country to be racially (if not ethnically) homogeneous, a bloody civil war and contentious Reconstruction in the second half of the nineteenth century compounded by massive foreign migration in the late nineteenth and early twentieth centuries ensured that the United States would continue to be imagined in racial and ethnic terms. And those terms proved unimaginable without a strong sexual subtext, which tied nonnormative sexual identities to nonwhite populations or washed them out of the national narrative altogether (Somerville 2000).

The third case study takes up some fascinating links between sexuality and race in contemporary South Africa. Although of long-standing interest to ethnographers who study sexual behavior, recent scholarship on sexuality in South Africa after the end of apartheid (legally sanctioned racial segregation) in the early 1990s challenges our assumption about how concepts such as sexuality and the modern nation-state travel across national and cultural boundaries. This case study thus explores the contrast between postapartheid South Africa's relatively progressive laws on sexuality and the everyday discrimination, including violence, faced by people whose sexuality fails to conform to social norms.

Brokering Sexual Modernity/Modern Sexuality: Japan

The restoration of the Meiji emperor in 1868 marked the beginning of serious efforts to modernize the Japanese state. These modernization efforts included the establishment of new institutions charged with the discovery, documentation, control, and management of sexuality. The impact of these institutions on sexual behavior in Japan serves as a vantage point from which I will pursue two intertwined arguments. First, that a variety of experts (social reformers, feminists, government officials) and state agencies (health administration, police, military) strategically tied new ideas, norms, and policies regarding sex to the pursuit of modernity in general. Second, that the establishment of a modern notion of sexuality relied on the international circulation and appropriation of ideas, norms, and policies regarding sex.

The advent of the modern state in Japan facilitated the collection of information that subsequently changed official and (to a certain extent) popular views of sexuality and sexual behavior. The 1872 introduction of the mandatory military physical exam for all males, for instance, became the medico-legal framework for learning about and categorizing human populations into a series of types and identities, labeling some conscripts as suitable for military service and others as effeminate, syphilitic, and hysterical or neurasthenic. Likewise, school health examinations within the new context of mandatory elementary schooling for boys and girls facilitated the "discovery" of the masturbating child and the neurasthenic youth.[4] From the 1890s onward, new legislation and control mechanisms regarding childbirth and registration made it much harder for midwives and pregnant women to perform an abortion or practice infanticide. And mandatory reporting brought a broad range of sexual activities—pregnancy, birth, venereal disease, the decision to enter the sex trade—under official scrutiny. The Japanese state even set up special bureaucracies to monitor these activities, such as the hygiene police, a division of the special police forces, and other similar state agencies in Japan proper, along with counterparts throughout the Japanese empire, which by the 1930s included Korea, Taiwan, Manchuria, and several Pacific islands.

As the empire expanded across eastern and southeastern Asia, Japanese authorities sexualized, nationalized, and modernized their new colonial

Figure 2.4 A 1926 Japanese advertisement for "Victoria" sanitary napkins from the magazine *Tsūzoku Igaku* (Popular Medicine). Sanitary napkins were seen as a huge improvement over the loincloth that Japanese women had previously used.

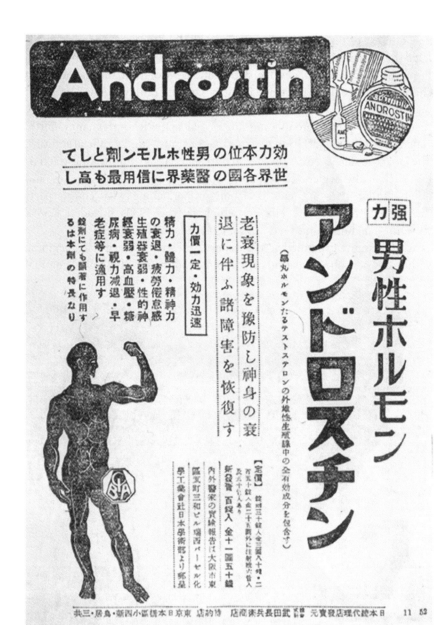

Figure 2.5 A 1937 Japanese advertisement for the male hormone Androstin from *Tsūzoku Igaku* (Popular Medicine). The hormone promised to counter the effects of aging and enhance sexual functioning in men.

subjects in a variety of ways (Frühstück 2003). In their efforts to modernize the empire, Japanese scientists studied prostitution and venereal disease in Korea, tested the latest contraceptive methods on women in Taiwan, identified "perversions" in parts of Asia that were yet to be modernized, and proposed crossethnic mass marriages. Like Western colonialists, they were enthralled by the (often imagined) sexual practices and customs of the other Asians they studied and documented. The information and knowledge they produced fed an ongoing debate about whether to promote pan-Asian solidarity or Japan's sense of racial and cultural superiority. Nostalgia for Japanese traditions—some only imagined, others imagined lost—both nourished and was nourished by the production of this knowledge. In the process, sexuality, especially as a marker of civilizational status, became overtly political.

Designed to police pregnancies, abortions, and prostitution, the control apparatus was oppressive wherever it reached. Consider, for instance, the risk of discovery in the case of an illegal abortion or infanticide, a discovery that could lead to years in prison. Imagine the dilemma of a seriously ill prostitute who was legally barred from working but pressed to do so by a greedy brothel owner. Envision soldiers threatened with military discipline because syphilis had rendered them too ill to fight.

At the same time, the sexual control apparatus was also productive. It accumulated massive amounts of data that policymakers used to formulate debates, implement policies, and make claims about normative sexual behavior. The "modern" obsession with data had important ideological effects. Nation building in Japan and elsewhere went hand in hand with claims about the importance of institutional rationality and scientific management, and the perceived need to push back against religious and superstitious beliefs (Muta 1996; Frühstück 2003; Silverberg 2009). The rise of statistical thinking in the late nineteenth century also helped to establish some sexual behaviors as normative while marginalizing others as pathological or criminal. This compulsion to normalize some sexual behaviors and marginalize others continued into the twentieth century, sometimes exceeding government control, as individual scholars and social reformers began to make significant contributions to the "discovery" of sex and sexuality, reiterate the need for scientific study, propose their versions of modern *Japanese* sexuality, and engage with researchers and reformers around the world, from Magnus Hirschfeld in Berlin to Margaret Sanger in New York. By the early twentieth century, then, a range of different actors were involved in the pursuit of the truth about sex and its social management. For all their methodological and instrumental differences, governmental officials, scholars, and social reformers were connected by a common desire to understand, document, and regulate the sex lives of the Japanese populace and those under Japanese imperial rule, including Koreans, Taiwanese, and Chinese. And all parties sought to link sexuality research to their visions of the past, present, and future of the Japanese nation.

Take Yamamoto Senji (1889–1929), for instance, a prominent biologist, socialist, and member of the Unitarian Church. Yamamoto researched sexual experiences and practices in an innovative interview format that anticipated the much better known US-based Kinsey Reports (discussed in the following case study). By cataloging and quantifying sexual experiences and practices, he attempted to capture the richness and variety of actual sexual experiences in a manner reminiscent of earlier European sexologists such as Richard von Krafft-Ebing, Havelock Ellis, and Magnus Hirschfeld. At the same time, unlike doctors of the Japanese medical establishment, Yamamoto was a scientist *and* social reformer willing to challenge conventional scientific wisdom. For example, upon finding that more than 90 percent of the male university student respondents to his surveys had engaged in masturbation, he proposed that the practice was normal—in the face of public condemnation of masturbation as the source of a softening brain, weak spine, sexual neurasthenia, and a host of other severe mental and physical illnesses. Time and again he argued that, if the practice was commonplace in human populations, it must be physiologically and perhaps even psychologically normal. And, if a given sexual behavior or phenomenon could be established as normal, it should be accepted, not condemned.

In addition to being a pioneer sexologist and member of parliament for the left-leaning Labor-Farmer Party, Yamamoto was also a fierce proponent of legalized abortion and birth control, which he saw as important tools of class struggle because they improved quality of life for the underprivileged. So when the Japanese state and its agencies promoted Japanese emigration and pursued expansion into Asia using the excuse that the Japanese "lacked space"[5]—all the while propagating pro-birth slogans such as "procreate and multiply for the good of the country"—Yamamoto pushed for fewer children per family as a foundation for international peace and as a tool to undercut Japanese imperialist expansion.

Given the energetic exchanges then taking place between Japanese, German, and British medical experts, it is unsurprising that Yamamoto was familiar with the work of his European colleagues.[6] Moreover, Japanese sex researchers and social reformers such as Yamamoto brought international figures such as American social reformer Margaret Sanger (1879–1966) to Japan. A prominent birth control activist, eugenicist, sex educator, and nurse, Sanger had founded the American Birth Control League (later renamed Planned Parenthood) in 1921. The following year, in a speech at New York's Carnegie Hall (Sanger 1922), she reported that the Japanese government had at first refused to let her set foot on Japanese soil but eventually relented, allowing her into the country to give five speeches on birth control.

Although eager to stay current with the latest advances in the sexual sciences, Yamamoto and his Japanese colleagues did not blindly adopt the views of Sanger and other international activists, especially when they perceived their calls for sexual reform to be patronizing, orientalizing, or racist. Then as now, global debates around sex and sexuality remained entangled in hierarchical notions of civilization, progress, national character, and race. For instance, Dr. Friedrich Salomon Krauss (1859–1938), an Austrian pioneer of sexual ethnology who had traveled from Vienna to Tokyo to collect material for a 1907 book on *The Sex Life in Beliefs, Morals, Customs and Common Law of the Japanese* (*Das Geschlechtsleben in Glauben, Sitte, Brauch und Gewohnheitsrecht der Japaner*), adopted the always condescending, sometimes admiring, perspective typical of European folklorists and ethnologists of East Asia, when he observed that:

> the Occidental looks at Japan through Occidental glasses: He sees moral degeneration where there is in naked reality nothing but unmediated joy of life and irrepressible joy for sexual matters combined with a lack of any kind of hypocrisy. (Krauss 1911, p. 10)

On one hand, ethnographers such as Krauss directed their observations on "the joy of life" in Japan and other "foreign" cultures at the restrictive sexual order at home in Western Europe or the United States. On the other, they used ethnic others including the Japanese to generate and reinforce white Western sexual norms while at the same time identifying new groups of nonwhite, non-European peoples who might benefit from the lifting of outmoded taboos on sexual behavior—an act of sexual liberation that outside observers expected would make non-European peoples happier,

more natural, and less self-conscious or at least help them overcome supposedly violent and uncivilized sexual practices.

The racist implications of these judgments were obvious at the time. And
early twentieth-century Japanese intellectuals often dismissed the Oriental-
ist perspective of Western ethnographers such as Krauss in order to claim
for Japan an equal status within the hierarchical order of world civilizations.
For example, in his 1906 book *Our Fatherland Japan* (*Unser Vaterland
Japan*), influential bureaucrat and statesman Nitobe Inazô noted that:

> It is a general perception of foreign tourists (many of whom are *learned
> gentlemen*) that Japanese life lacks morality just as its flowers lack a scent.
> What a sad confession of the moral and intellectual imagination of these
> tourists themselves! (cited in Krauss 1911, p. 13, emphasis added)

Although different scholars reached different conclusions, the new
sexual science had radically changed the study of sexual practices and
attitudes around the globe within only a few decades. Western European
sexologists such as Krafft-Ebing in Austria, Ellis in England, and Hirschfeld
in Germany garnered most of the initial international attention, but by the
1910s and 1920s East Asian scholars were playing a central role. Among
the most prominent were Yamamoto Senji and Yasuda Tokutarô in Japan,
and intellectuals of the May Fourth New Culture period (1915–37) in
China, who translated sexology and sex educational texts from Europe,
Japan, and the United States and introduced them to Chinese readers
(Rocha 2010).

In the early years, these intellectual exchanges took place almost exclusively among male scientists and policymakers. Beginning in the 1920s,
however, women's voices became increasingly prominent, especially on
issues such as love, motherhood, sexual freedom, birth control, and female
suffrage. As happened with their male counterparts, the most influential
female figures on the international stage were Westerners, such as Margaret
Sanger and Swedish suffragist, educator, and writer Ellen Key. But Japanese
women such as Yamada Waka, Hiratsuka Raichō, Yamakawa Kikue, Yosano
Akiko, and Yasuda Satsuki participated as well, often speaking out in favor
of progressive feminist measures such as a woman's right to abortion and
birth control. These early Japanese feminists developed their ideas in dialogue with their Western counterparts but struggled to achieve consensus
on the appropriateness of Western concepts of autonomy, emancipation,
and equality for women in Japanese culture and society. For example, in a

debate over whether or not pregnant women and mothers should expect state support, renowned poet Yosano Akiko dismissed what she perceived as a Western feminist stance in favor of state support for women during pregnancy and birth, arguing that it would undermine women's limited independence by valuing them only as mothers. In contrast, fellow feminist Hiratsuka Raichō strongly advocated for state protection for women and forced sterilization for men with venereal diseases.[7] Despite major differences of opinion, however, Japanese feminists generally treated sexuality as a domain of restriction and danger for women rather than as a source of self-exploration and pleasure.

Prostitution was another hotly debated sexual issue with substantial social and political implications. As early as 1900, members of the emerging abolition movement in Japan denounced both rural fathers for selling their daughters to brothels and the state for tolerating, if not supporting, the practice. They demanded better health services for prostitutes and ways for them to leave the "water trade" (the traditional euphemism for Japan's nighttime entertainment business). Japanese abolitionists initially debated the question of how to do away with prostitution; later, when that proved impossible, they argued over ways to better control prostitutes in order to protect the health of Japan's men and their "innocent wives and children." By 1940, most critics of prostitution came to agree that it was better, perhaps necessary, to sacrifice a few women in order to keep the social order from collapsing, to protect "innocent" women from male sexual violence, and to keep up soldiers' morale in the homeland and on the front. This Japanese debate and similar attitudes elsewhere encouraged the development of a variety of sexual slavery systems, ranging from so-called "comfort stations" for Imperial Japanese Army troops to Wehrmacht brothels all over Europe and rape camps within the concentration camps of the Nazi regime (Yoshimi 2000; Soh 2008; Harris 2010; Hedgepeth and Saidel 2010).

As this reference to Nazi Germany suggests, the era of "erotic grotesque nonsense" in 1930s Japan mirrored "the stimulation of affect and sensation to bind the people to fascist regime[s]" in Italy, Spain, the Third Reich and perhaps elsewhere as well (Herzog 2005, p. 10; see also Silverberg 2009). Only a handful of years after Hirschfeld's two-volume magnum opus, *Sittengeschichte des Weltkrieges* (The Sexual History of the World War), was published in 1930, the great project of progressive sexology came to an end as military regimes began to replace liberal democracies in many countries around the world. The byline on the book's title page nonetheless hailed the author as the principal creator of "the Sexual Sciences." Indeed, the litany of academic honors showered on Hirschfeld expressed in no uncertain terms the achievements of sexual research in Weimar (pre-Nazi) Germany: human sexuality was no longer to be understood through long-held beliefs but rather through scientific study, and it was no longer to be regulated by local communities but by government agencies. While many scientists, medical doctors, and other sociosexual reformers including Hirschfeld and Yamamoto had worked hard to protect sexual behavior from state intrusion, others had been equally keen to assist the state in its quest to organize, manage, and control sexual behavior. Regardless, the uneasy relationship between the sexual sciences and the state—cozy for some, contentious for others—would take a more ominous turn during the 1940s and 1950s, not just in authoritarian states such as Japan and Germany but also in liberal democracies such as the United States.

Racializing Sexuality/Sexualizing Race: The United States

The history of sexuality in the United States is inseparable from the internal politics of race and ethnicity. As historians John D'Emilio and Estelle Freedman explain:

> Ever since the seventeenth century, European migrants to America had merged racial and sexual ideology in order to differentiate themselves from Indians and blacks, to strengthen the mechanisms of social control over slaves, and to justify the appropriation of Indian and Mexican lands through the destruction of native peoples and their cultures. In the nineteenth century, sexuality continued to serve as a powerful means by which white Americans maintained dominance over people of other races. Both scientific and popular thought supported the view that whites were civilized and rational, while members of other races were savage, irrational, and sensual. These animalistic elements posed a particular threat to middle-class Americans, who sought to maintain social stability during rapid economic change and to insure that a virtuous citizenry would fulfill the dream of republicanism. At a time when middle-class morality rested heavily upon a belief in the purity of women in the home, stereotypes of immoral women of other races contributed to the belief in white superiority. In addition, whites feared the specter of racial amalgamation, believing it would debase whites to the status of other races. (D'Emilio and Freedman 1988, p. 86)

As D'Emilio and Freedman suggest, this potent mix of white racial and moral supremacy could take many forms. On the western frontier it appeared in Christian missionary efforts to teach Native Americans sexual restraint, including the proper "missionary" position for intercourse between married men and women, and to convince Chinese migrant workers to abandon polygamous marriage in favor of monogamy (D'Emilio and Freedman 1988, p. 92–3). When missionary efforts failed to convert "heathen" peoples to white Christian ways (often before they were tried), soldiers and settlers sometimes resorted to sexual violence against women of color as a means of retaliation, intimidation, and perhaps even genocide. In later years, medical experimentation, including forced sterilization, served similar ends (Smith 2005).

In the South, the institution of slavery conditioned sexual and racial relations in different ways than in the free states. However, the underlying dynamics of white men's racial, sexual, and gender privilege took a similar form as "southern moralists condoned white men gratifying their lust, as long as they did so discreetly with poor white or black women" (D'Emilio and Freedman 1988, p. 95). Some interracial and cross-class relations were consensual; many were not. With the end of slavery, sexual violence became a "weapon of terror," used to intimidate blacks and keep them from assuming social and political equality with whites. White supremacists deployed this weapon against black women and men alike whether by raping black women with impunity or lynching black men accused of raping white women. In the years following the Civil War, fear of race mixture or "miscegenation" led southern states to pass new laws to prevent interracial marriage (D'Emilio and Freedman 1988, p. 106).

By the turn of the twentieth century, fear of social degeneration through miscegenation had spread throughout much of the country. Inspired by social Darwinism and a desire to better the human race through eugenics (selective breeding), physical anthropologists, medical experts, and policy makers alike worried that race mixture would undo the centuries of racial "progress" that had culminated in white European and North American civilization. To counter its negative effects, they developed elaborate racial taxonomies with classifications such as mulatto, Malay, Mongolian, and Negro, which they used to determine suitable marriage partners. These purportedly scientific taxonomies produced multiple effects. As historian Alexandra Stern has argued, "the solidification of . . . racial hierarchies was integral to the entrenchment of Jim Crow segregation after

Reconstruction and the rise of Sinophobia and anti-Asian discrimination, and it helped to rationalize colonial ventures in Latin America and the Pacific" (2005, p. 13). Although genocidal Nazi eugenic policies during World War II discredited a field tainted by what critics have called "scientific racism," researchers working in the newly christened field of "social biology" turned toward genetic marital counseling at home and "retooled eugenics with the export of Western-led modernization to the Third World" (Stern 2005, p. 4).

While racial and ethnic politics have been central to the story of sexuality and the nation-state in the United States, other factors have played a role as well—although they usually took on racial overtones in the process. Just as racial and ethnic minorities supposedly embodied a degenerate sexuality against which whites defined themselves, other "deviant" groups also threatened to undermine the social order. Concern about nonnormative sexualities, especially homosexuality, became especially acute in the latter half of the nineteenth century as fears about sexual deviance previously confined for the most part to the private sphere began to enter public discourse and public policy. As noted earlier, the twin themes of westward expansion and modernization saturated the foundation narrative of the United States from the beginning. By 1900, conventional national histories related how transplanted white Europeans had become Americans by moving triumphantly westward, taking possession of the wilderness, and subduing savagery. Nonnormative sexualities had no place in this story—at least for its principal (white) protagonists.

This widely accepted reading of America's frontier past as the heyday of white, heterosexual patriarchy might have appealed to the national imaginary but the historical reality was quite different. In stark contrast to this comforting foundational fiction—which proved its lingering discursive power in the controversy over the rugged cowboy lovers in Ang Lee's 2005 film *Brokeback Mountain*—we know from recent historical research that Western migrants and long-term residents often changed their gender and sexual identities for any number of reasons. These changes meant different things to different people (and in different cultural settings). As historian Peter Boag notes, the decision to change their gender or sexual identity "simply felt natural to some men and women, while women sometimes found it useful to dress as men in order to travel safely or make a decent income" (Boag 2011, pp. 7–8).

Turn-of-the-century sexologists had no trouble with the frontier myth of American triumphalism but worried that the onset of modernity in

Figure 2.6   Martha Jane Burke, better known as Calamity Jane, seated with a rifle. Calamity Jane was a scout in the American Indian Wars and a famed Western markswoman. Her unabashedly "butch" public image suggests that gender identities were not nearly as stable (or closeted) as the myth of the Western frontier would lead us to believe. Undated photograph. *Source*: © Bettmann / Corbis.

Eastern cities was undermining traditional gender roles, producing a condition they labeled "sexual inversion" in which men behaved as women and women behaved as men (Boag 2011, pp. 5–7; Somerville 2000, p. 3). As noted in the previous section, European sex researchers such as Hirschfeld, von Krafft-Ebing, Ellis, and others had shown a pronounced interest in nonnormative sexualities, including several different types of same-sex sexual behaviors. Scientific interest was accompanied by a growing public acknowledgment among educated Europeans that many people were attracted physically and emotionally to members of their own sex. And, in Europe at least, both sexologists and the educated public agreed that these types of sexual "deviance" were likely a product of the challenges that rapid urbanization presented to "traditional" lifestyles. This urbane frankness about the variability of human sexuality was not typical of attitudes in the United States at the time. While members of the American medical establishment had some knowledge of the latest advances in late nineteenth-century European sexology, for the most part they did not research sexual topics until later in the twentieth century, unless it was to expose the potential health threats posed by extramarital sex. Likewise, public discourse on sexuality carefully emphasized the benefits of chastity and abstinence by portraying the horrors of venereal diseases rather than dwelling on "unpleasant" topics such as sexual deviance. In the United States, these relatively conservative views on sex education and sexuality did not change much until after World War II.

Despite a prolific scientific and public discourse on sexuality in the United States characterized by fearmongering, disapproving reticence, and suggestive obfuscation, historical evidence suggests that by the 1920s many American cities had vibrant urban subcultures built around alternative sexualities. For example, University of Chicago graduate students working under one of the first American sociologists to carry out extensive research on homosexuality, Ernest W. Burgess, "discovered" an active gay community of cabarets and nightclubs on the Near North and South Sides of Chicago in the late 1920s and early 1930s (Heap 2003, p. 467). By 1930, a local magazine noted that as many as thirty-five "pansy parlors" had opened in just six months in Towertown, the neighborhood adjacent to the old Chicago Water Tower (Heap 2009, p. 88). The emergence of Chicago's gay subculture was closely tied to an explosion of popular culture in the city's growing racial and ethnic communities and the fashionable slumming on the part of adventurous white middle- and upper-class bohemians that accompanied both phenomena. After a series of 1938 visits to the Cabin

Inn, a popular interracial ("black and tan") cabaret famous for its "painted boys," a University of Chicago graduate student reported that "every night we find the place crowded with both races, the black and the white, [and] both types of lovers, the homo and the hetro [sic]" (cited in Heap 2009, p. 95). According to historian Chad Heap:

> By 1938, Chicago sociologists' association of homosexuality with particular urban spaces was so complete that Professor Burgess could expect students in his social pathology course to provide an affirmative answer to the true-false exam question, "In large cities, homosexual individuals tend to congregate rather than remain separate from each other." (Heap 2003, p. 467)

World War II and the military draft brought together thousands of men from rural prairie states and seaside cities, exposing them to a range of new sexual experiences and possibilities, including sexual relations with other men (Bérubé 1990; Jarvis 2010, pp. 72–85). World War II also provided opportunities for women to live and work in all-women's environments outside the purview of their families and communities. Efforts to police against "mannish" women in the Women's Army Corps, and to enforce standards of white, middle-class feminine respectability among the ranks, reflected anxieties over shifting gender hierarchies, as these intersected with racial and class inequalities in the context of rapid social change. Leisa Meyer suggests that "while butch women were particularly likely to be targeted as lesbians . . . their visibility also served as both an anchor and rallying point for the formation of lesbian communities within the corps" (Meyer 1996, p. 9).

When economic prosperity returned to the United States after World War II, interest in sexuality research revived as well. At the forefront of this postwar revival was a team of researchers headed by Indiana University sexologist Dr. Alfred Kinsey and their soon-to-be-world-famous Kinsey Reports on *Sexual Behavior in the Human Male* (1948) and *Sexual Behavior in the Human Female* (1953).[8] Based on over eleven thousand confidential interviews with American men and women, the Kinsey Reports attempted "to accumulate an objectively determined body of fact about sex which strictly avoids social or moral interpretations of the fact" (Kinsey et al. 1948, p. 5). A zoologist by training, Kinsey approached the study of human populations with fewer preconceived notions (about sex) and less reticence than most of his predecessors. And, although his critics pointed out the "subjective" nature of his interview data, its massive volume and the study's

Figure 2.7   Erotic photograph of two sailors kissing taken by an anonymous photographer in the 1940s. *Source*: The Kinsey Institute for Research in Sex, Gender and Reproduction, KI-DC: 44270 (copyright holder unknown).

matter-of-fact tone tended to overwhelm their objections. The Kinsey Reports' widely reported findings provoked intense controversy within and outside the scientific community. For many, its "revelations"—that 37 percent of men and 13 percent of women had experienced orgasm with a partner of the same sex, that nearly 46 percent of men had had a sexual experience with another man, that 10 percent of men and 6 percent of women were predominantly homosexual, that 11 percent of men had anal sex with their wives, that 92 percent of men and 62 percent of women had masturbated—were not just controversial but deeply shocking (Kinsey Institute 2013). For others, the Kinsey data provided long-overdue vindication after decades of American hypocrisy, prudery, and denial. Whatever the reaction, American understandings of sexuality changed dramatically after the publication of the Kinsey Reports.

With regard to homosexuality, Kinsey's analysis—supported by his unprecedented data set—reinforced the contention of earlier sexologists that same-sex attraction was common (and thus "natural") in human populations, sometimes manifesting as a youthful phase and at other times as a lifetime trait. As explained in *Sexual Behavior in the Human Male*, "males do not represent two discrete populations, heterosexual and homosexual. The world is not to be divided into sheep and goats . . . the living world is a continuum in each and every one of its aspects" (Kinsey et al. 1948). Moreover, the Kinsey Reports dispelled once and for all the myth that homosexuality was an urban by-product of modern life with the discovery that rates of same-sex behavior among men in rural communities, especially in the West, were higher than in cities (Boag 2011, p. 3). Perhaps most important, the work of postwar sexologists such as Kinsey and his colleagues put a definitive end to the "sexual inversion" model developed by turn-of-the-century European sexologists, replacing it with a more psychologically nuanced understanding of same-sex behavior that has (somewhat ironically) given rise to modern notions of homosexual identity (Laqueur 1992, 2004).

Even though scientific and popular understandings of human sexuality have shifted in the past few decades, the American preoccupation with homosexuality has remained a constant. As with race and ethnicity, the reason for this ongoing obsession is tied directly to the foundational fictions that continue to define the nation-state. As historian Jennifer Terry explains:

Because of the various ways that homosexuality has been figured as a transgression by those who either championed it or repudiated it, the subject came to be an agonistic rhetorical field of far-reaching cultural significance . . . As such, homosexuality has allowed its advocates to launch liberatory critiques of oppressive features of the family, marriage, normative education, moralistic religious doctrines, and homophobic patriotism. At the same time, the public presence of homosexuality has allowed its detractors to instigate vociferous attacks on "the homosexual lifestyle" and "the gay agenda" as emblematic of the downfall of civilization and all that is good about it. (Terry 1999, p. 4)

Put in the Foucauldian terms introduced at the beginning of this chapter, public debates about sexuality still produce powerful effects in American society. This has become even more apparent as civil rights legislation has ensured the legal (if not always actual) rights of racial and ethnic minorities. Although less directly racialized than before, the questions of citizenship and belonging raised by those with nonnormative sexualities have become even more central in recent years: Who can serve in the military? Who can get married? Who can teach in public schools? Who can parent children? Who can share health and retirement benefits? Or how to address neoliberal capitalism's remarkable ability to repurpose differences of gender and sexuality without ending the inequalities those differences produce? Despite evidence on some fronts (e.g. military service, gay marriage) of increased tolerance or the erosion of traditional family values (depending on point of view), these fundamental questions are still very much up in the air. And they are more bound up in issues of sexuality than ever before. Halfway around the world, in South Africa, sexuality has become a matter of national politics and state formation in a dramatically different way.

Constitutionalizing Nonnormative Sexuality: South Africa

The Bill of Rights from the 1996 South African constitution includes this mandate:

The state may not unfairly discriminate directly or indirectly against anyone on one or more grounds, including race, gender, sex, pregnancy, marital status, ethnic or social origin, colour, sexual orientation, age, disability, religion, conscience, belief, culture, language and birth.

The provision that immediately follows prohibits discrimination by persons on these same grounds; the next requires that national legislation "be enacted to prevent or prohibit unfair discrimination" (Republic of South Africa 1996). A hallmark of the new postapartheid democracy, South Africa's constitution was the first in the world to ban discrimination on the grounds of "sexual orientation." And, when Parliament neglected to pass a law allowing same-sex couples to marry, a Constitutional Court ruling on the 2005 *Minister of Home Affairs v. Fourie* case ordered legislators to remedy the situation (Constitutional Court of South Africa 2005). In response to the court order, Parliament passed the 2006 Civil Union Act and South Africa became the second country outside Western Europe (after Canada) to legalize same-sex marriage.

This section examines the central role of sexuality in nation-building efforts in contemporary South Africa. Although many of the links between sex and nation examined so far are evident in the South African case, it is in many ways unique. Nation building in places such as Japan, the United States, and Western Europe occurred more than a century before the movement for sexual rights, but in South Africa these two processes occurred more or less simultaneously. And both are linked in important ways to the decades-long struggle against apartheid, which remained in force until the early 1990s. Postapartheid South Africa, then, is an example of a nation imagined from the start as multicultural, multiracial, multisexual, and tolerant of difference. In this instance, the seemingly unavoidable intersection of sex and nation—so often a source of exclusions in nationalist discourse— has become a positive symbol of social progress and a proud new national identity.

Tensions between sex and nation have appeared throughout Africa in recent years, as postcolonial societies have come to grips with modern challenges to traditional gender and sex roles, challenges that have produced a variety of effects "including anxieties about pregnant schoolgirls in colonial Kenya, public discourse around homosexual rights in Uganda, and gender coalitions across race and class in South Africa" (Cole et al. 2007, p. 5). Only in South Africa, however, have public institutions responded in such a deliberately "progressive" way by granting full citizenship to all individuals irrespective of their gender and sexual identities.

This sudden embrace of progressive multiculturalism—usually associated with northern European social democracies—challenges long-standing assumptions about African societies that have changed little despite (and perhaps because of) the political decolonization movements that sprang up across the continent after World War II and lasted into the 1990s. As literary scholar Brenna Munro points out:

> Europe's "civilizing mission" constituted itself through attempts to eradicate indigenous social formations that were deemed deviant, from polygamy to

"female husbands," all while unruly new sexual cultures were being forged in the cities, industries, and institutions of a changing Africa. Ideas about what constitutes "sex," as well as the formation of sexual identities and the production of sexual taboos and desires, were thus shaped by these histories, on both sides of the colonial divide. (Munro 2012, p. xiii)

Postcolonial movements and scholarship have long questioned the sincerity of the "civilizing mission" and the validity of imperialist stereotypes, which reduced one of the most culturally diverse regions of the world to a single pan-African culture. But reductionist notions of African cultures—often grounded in anthropological (and sometimes feminist) arguments about inheritance, patriarchy, and incest taboos in "simple" societies—have continued to shape everything from domestic social policy to international foreign aid.

Preconceived notions of Africans as hypersexual and promiscuous have been especially evident in family planning and public health campaigns against sexually transmitted disease. Even though colonial regimes frequently created these public health problems in the first place, they also exaggerated and exploited them for their own political advantage. Colonial public health campaigns deployed science in ways that justified punitive, moralistic interventions that frequently worsened the sexual health conditions of Africans, not least through enforced urban racial segregation and strict control of women's mobility. Postcolonial regimes and their international allies often take similar approaches. For instance, communication scholar and LGBT activist Cindy Patton observes that 1990s international efforts to curtail the spread of HIV/AIDS in sub-Saharan Africa "invented a heterosexual 'African AIDS' that promotes a new kind of colonial domination by reconstructing Africa as an uncharted, supranational mass" (Patton 1992, p. 218). The Western invention of African AIDS, she argues, involves three misleading and ultimately dangerous "texts": "Africans won't use condoms"; "Africa has such poor medical care that they can't properly diagnose AIDS"; and "In Africa, AIDS is a disease of poverty" (Patton 1990, p. 26–7). According to Patton,

the insidious, unifying theme reiterated in texts one to three is that disease and the interruption of disease in Africa are of a different type altogether from disease in North America and Europe, and that science, a logical system requiring western "intelligence," can never be conducted by Africans. (Patton 1990, p. 28)

Moreover, Westerners construct disease in Africa as "natural," effectively invoking "an evolutionary view of geopolitics" that "enables the former colonial administrators to forget their complicity in the underdevelopment and exploitation that created the particular patterns of poverty that mark Africa today" and allows them to affirm that "Africa's problems can only be solved through civilizing forces—or, in the romantic version, through a withdrawal from civilization and a return to pristine "tribal ways" (Patton 1990, p. 28). The power of neocolonial tropes to shape public health policy in Africa has had pernicious effects because national government responses to crises such as the HIV/AIDS epidemic are almost always dependent on research models and data sets derived from international and internationally funded sources.

Western-inspired misperceptions of African sexuality (whether perpetuated by Westerners or Africans), especially the preposterous notion that it might be possible to generalize across the diversity of African societies and culture, have come under attack in recent years. With a careful eye to geographical, cultural, and historical differences, a new generation of African sexuality scholars have made us aware of everything from the subtleties of nonnormative sexual behavior in African communities to the obvious point—often missed by ethnographers—"that Africans' decision-making about sexual relationships cannot be explained simply by structures and functions but also involves such ephemeral issues as intimacy, love, spirituality, and self doubt, including masculine self doubt" (Epprecht 2009, p. 1271). In other words, African sexual practices and the social meanings they invoke are as complex, contradictory, and contested as anything in the Global North.

These scholarly critiques of the conventional wisdom on African sexualities took hold in South Africa as part of the intertwined struggles to overthrow apartheid and promote sexual rights—and helped foster a sense of solidarity between the antiapartheid and sexual rights movements. As we saw in the previous case study, the intersections between race, sexuality, and nation were strong in the United States with its long history of slavery and segregation. In South Africa, these historical links, especially between struggles for racial equality and sexual rights, were even stronger. As Munro explains:

Apartheid had been deeply entangled with histories of sexuality and stigma. It was built on an alliance between Anglo-South Africans and Afrikaners forged in part through early twentieth-century "Black Peril" panics about the sexual threat that black men supposedly posed to white women, was driven by a phobic preoccupation with sexual "mixing," and was enforced through sexual violence against black people as well as the aggressive polic-ing of interracial sex, and a strict, indeed militarized regime of heteronorma-tive whiteness. (Munro 2012, p. xii)

Moreover, apartheid as an institution "was an *antimodernist* project that explicitly set itself against most of the rest of the 'developed' world" (Epprecht 2006, p. 223).

This unique convergence of intertwined liberation movements working in opposition to an antimodern, antiprogressive, segregationist nation-state set the conditions for a more inclusive South Africa, "a celebrated new political order that imagined the postcolonial nation as belonging equally to the descendants of indigenous peoples, colonizing settlers, trans-ported slaves, indentured laborers, and immigrants—and it also specifically included gays and lesbians as citizens" (Munro 2012, p. vii). Despite powerful historical links, however, the convergence of political interests between the movements for racial equality and sexual rights was not appar-ent until the early 1990s. Before that time, South African gay rights groups such as the Gay Association of South Africa (GASA) were headed almost exclusively by white, urban, middle-class gay men; reflected their particular concerns; and embraced conventional Western constructions of homo-sexuality. Although GASA accepted black members—in part to placate gay rights allies abroad—the organization refused to oppose apartheid and even allied itself on occasion with the pro-apartheid National Party in an effort to garner support for gay rights (or at least forestall initiatives to repress the urban middle-class gay community). One of its few black members, Simon Nkoli, remembered his 1980s GASA experience this way:

The best thing about membership was that, apparently, your little pink card got you into clubs at discounted prices. I got my [card] in the mail, and it was a feast of possibility: The Dungeon, The Butterfly, Mandys. I tried Mandys and they said "no blacks." The Dungeon. "No blacks." I showed them their ad . . . "All GASA members welcome at a discount." "I'm a member of GASA," I'd say. "Yes," they'd reply, "but you're black. What if the police come?" The only place I managed to get into was somewhere in Jeppe Street. I was the only black person there and I felt so intimidated that I never went back. (Gevisser 1995, p. 52)

Routine discrimination within the organization was not the only problem. When Nkoli went to prison in the 1980s on charges of treason for his political work, GASA made no effort to have him released despite his growing international notoriety as the "gay Mandela." In response, on his 1988 release from prison, Nkoli helped found a new sexual rights organization, Gay and Lesbian Organisation of the Witwatersrand (GLOW), which called on "All South Africans who are Committed to a Non-Racist, Non-Sexist, Non-Discriminatory Democratic Future" (Gevisser 1995, p. 74).

The experiences of GLOW cofounder Linda Ngcobo highlight another failing of pre-1990s white, middle-class gay rights groups in South Africa: their inability to understand (much less acknowledge) the nonnormative sexualities that characterized same-sex behavior in black communities. For Linda and the cohort of "gay" men who grew up in the black townships in the 1970s and 1980s, the sex/gender system revolved loosely around three highly gendered identities: *skesana*, a boy who behaves like a girl and "likes to be fucked"; *injonga*, a man or boy "who makes the proposals and does the fucking"; and *pantsula*, a "tough" man or boy who penetrates *skesanas* under the assumption or pretext that they are female (McLean and Ngcobo 1995). Families treated *skesana* sons as girls, assigning them women's work around the home, and *skesanas* often "married" men. Although on occasion *skesanas* switched roles as they became older—a pattern associated with male-only migrant labor camps—those who grew up in the townships often adhered to their female gender identity into adulthood (Donham 1998).

Political mobilization, beginning with the 1976 Soweto uprising, brought some acceptance for *skesana*-identified boys and their female counterparts. Interviewed several years later, Linda remembered that:

> when the time came to go and march they wanted all the boys and girls to join in. The gays said: "We're not accepted by you, so why should we march?" But then they said they didn't mind and we would go to march in drag. Even the straight boys would wear drag. You could wear what you liked. (McLean and Ngcobo 1995, p. 180)

The timing was propitious for "gay" township participants because the Soweto uprising—initiated by black high-school students protesting the introduction of Afrikaans as a principal language of instruction—centered issues of black identity and resistance to reactionary state-imposed cultural symbols. In this context, the struggle against apartheid involved the symbolic casting off of oppressive traditions of all kinds (whether from outside or within the townships) and embracing the progressive agenda of national and international antiapartheid activists, including the African National

Congress (ANC), which used the Soweto uprising as a springboard into political prominence. Indeed, by the early 1990s, ANC's exiled leadership had incorporated sexual rights into the party platform and Linda could declare optimistically that:

> The thing that has done the most for gays in the townships are the marches we have had for gay and lesbian rights. These have been very important and I hope that we will be legalized with an ANC government. Then maybe we can even get married in Regina Mundi [Soweto's principal cathedral] and they won't be throwing in the teargas. (McLean and Ngcobo 1995, p. 181)

The ANC's support for an end to sexual discrimination coincided with major cultural events such as the 1990 inauguration of an annual gay rights parade in Johannesburg, which "began to do much, through a set of such internationally recognized gay symbols as rainbow flags and pink triangles, to create a sense of transnational connections for gay South Africans" (Donham 1998, p. 12).

The 1996 constitutional prohibition on sexual discrimination and the 2005 Constitutional Court ruling on the *Minister of Home Affairs v. Fourie* case, which compelled Parliament to legalize same-sex marriages, were the direct result of the political alliance between racial justice and sexual rights advocates at the local, national, and international levels. The shared language of human rights, especially equality and dignity, is clearly reflected in the Constitutional Court's media summary:

> The claim by the applicants in *Fourie* of the right to get married should be seen as part of a comprehensive wish to be able to live openly and freely as lesbian women emancipated from all the legal taboos that historically have kept them from enjoying life in the mainstream of society. The right to celebrate their union accordingly signified far more than a right to enter into a legal arrangement with many attendant and significant consequences, important though they may be. It represented a major symbolical milestone in their long walk to equality and dignity. The greater and more secure the institutional imprimatur for their union, the more solidly would it and other such unions be rescued from legal oblivion, and the more tranquil and enduring would such unions ultimately turn out to be. (Constitutional Court of South Africa 2005)

As this eloquent defense of Fourie and her partner's right to enjoy life "in the mainstream of society" attests, the ANC's political victory in the 1994 elections—which put a definitive end to apartheid—initiated a period of progressive nation building around multicultural, multiracial, multisexual ideals that stressed inclusion and tolerance in deliberate contrast to the exclusions and intolerance of the apartheid era.

At the same time, state endorsement of a progressive sexual rights agenda produced some dramatic changes in the sex/gender system prevalent in black communities in the previous decades, as female-identified *skesanas* like Linda began to promote Western-style same-sex identities and relationships. These ongoing changes in what it means to be gay (especially poor, black, and gay) in South Africa have involved "not so much the replacement of one cultural system by another, but the addition of a new cultural model to older ones" (Donham 1998, p. 17). Nevertheless, the centrality of universalist notions of same-sex sexuality—understood as more modern and progressive than those derived from traditional and repressive sex/gender systems—reminds us of the power of social categories to shape human subjectivity and to structure the way we perceive ourselves and the ways we are perceived by others, including the "authorities."

Despite constitutional protections, sexual rights remain highly controversial in South Africa (and throughout the continent). Prominent political leaders from Winnie Mandela to Jacob Zuma (elected president in 2008) have blamed Western imperialism for homosexuality, insisting that same-sex desire in African societies resulted from sex-segregated labor regimes and the seductive power of decadent foreigners (Gevisser 1995, pp. 69–71). Others have denounced homosexuality in Christian terms. During the constitutional convention debates, for example, delegate Kenneth Meshoe reminded his colleagues that:

> in the beginning God created Adam and Eve, not Adam and Steve. To build a family Adam needed Eve not Steve. Even today Eve needs Adam not Madam to build a family. Nation-building cannot be possible while we try to legally destroy family values and the moral fiber of our society with clauses in the Constitution that promote a lifestyle that is an embarrassment even to our ancestors. (Republic of South Africa, Parliament 1995, p. 31; cited in Botha and Cameron 1997, p. 1921)

This overdetermined argument that homosexuality is both un-African and un-Christian, "an embarrassment *even* to our ancestors," as Meshoe puts it, has considerable traction in a country where, according to anti-gay-rights groups, most citizens still oppose gay marriage and sexual rights.

Figure 2.8   Paul Botha kisses his partner Albert Morton before their 2009 wedding in Cape Town, South Africa. While South Africa's openness to same-sex marriage has benefited some middle-class (mostly white male) citizens, observers worry that those benefits have bypassed many of the country's poorer black citizens. *Source*: Pieter Bauermeister / NYT / Redux / eyevine.

A recent spate of vicious hate crimes—gruesome murders involving castration, beheading, and immolation—against gays and lesbians in South Africa suggests that constitutional mandates against sexual discrimination have failed to translate into social acceptance and may even have contributed to homophobia in the country (Davis 2012). Moreover, sex crimes in general appear to be on the rise with reported rapes at fifty thousand in 2012 (women's rights groups estimate that only one in ten rapes is reported) and extremely low rates of conviction (one in twenty-five in Johannesburg). Included in these rape statistics are "corrective" rapes in which men and boys, usually in groups, rape lesbians in order to "correct" their supposedly unnatural sexual orientation. In 2007, for example, five men gang-raped and murdered sexual rights spokesperson and former national soccer player Eudy Simelane, stabbing her twenty-five times, because she admitted publicly to being a lesbian. And a 2008 South African Human Rights Commission report on violence in schools noted a growing acceptance of

Figure 2.9   A lesbian couple takes a break during a 2006 march in Soweto, South Africa, to protest ongoing oppression and bad treatment of LGBT individuals. *Source*: © Siphiwe Sibeko / X01918 / Reuters / Corbis.

corrective rape among school-aged boys. This growing acceptance is hardly confined to schoolboys. Accused of raping a lesbian anti-AIDS activist in 2006, President Jacob Zuma argued that, because the young woman wore a miniskirt and showed him her thigh during the interview, she was asking for sex and "in the Zulu culture, you cannot just leave a woman if she is ready." The court dismissed the charges despite the protests of women's rights organizations (Hughes 2009).

As these examples make clear, the superficially idyllic relationship between sexually nonnormative individuals and the postapartheid South African state has been uneasy and complicated from the beginning. Progressive ANC activists such as revered first president Nelson Mandela came out firmly in favor of sexual rights and many have continued to offer strong support. These supporters do not include Mandela's presidential successors. Thabo Mbeki (1999–2008), for example, distressed national and international anti-AIDS organizations by publicly insisting that poverty rather than exposure to HIV virus caused AIDS, a position that delayed the distribution of antiretroviral drugs and led to hundreds of unnecessary deaths. Mbeki's successor, Jacob Zuma, has been more overtly homophobic. In addition to his "she asked for it" defense against rape charges, Zuma had to apologize for a 2006 comment to a Soweto newspaper that same-sex marriages were "a disgrace to the nation and to God" (Munro 2012, p. xvii). This last comment—which then Deputy President Zuma explained was his personal response as a man rather than his official position as a public figure—gives some sense of the mixed messages often sent by supposed supporters of sexual rights. Moreover, the admission that "as a man" he felt same-sex marriages were a "disgrace to the nation" suggests that constitutional protections have failed altogether to ease the historical tensions between sexuality and that nation-state, even at the highest levels of government.

Conclusions

As the preceding case studies of Japan, the United States, and South Africa have shown, the historical and cultural changes at the intersection of sexualities and the nation-state have been various, fractured, and incomplete. The establishment of modern sexual regimes around the world has been driven by a variety of motivations that follow distinct local logics. Nation-state formation everywhere has invariably generated a great deal of anxiety around issues of sexuality as the perceived locus of a "modern" social order. At the same time, the significance of modernity has been hotly debated, as professionals and ordinary people alike fight to tie sexuality to the state or protect it from state intrusion. They have fought, too, over what would constitute "true" sexual knowledge. Meanwhile, an ever-changing rhetorical configuration of nature, liberation, and rights contributed to the shifting *and* the solidifying of the boundaries of socially condoned sexual behavior. New theories and new cultural anxieties have emerged at particular moments in response to specific dynamics within the overlapping histories of scientific invention, medical knowledge and treatment, political discourses regarding proper citizenship, and moral discourses about what constitutes normalcy. These new "technologies of power" have provided the basis for modern notions of sexual identity and politicized the production and circulation of sexual knowledge.

It has only been in the past century that scholars have begun to center the historicity of "culture"—to understand it as something highly malleable and in constant flux rather than relatively stable and resistant to change. As this chapter has made clear, this insight applies to sexual cultures as well. An analysis of the emergence of "modern" sexualities necessarily engages differences in culture and history, nation and narration. There is no linear, uniform story of the formation of modern sexuality, just as there is no singular web of relations that connect sex and sexuality to the nation-state. The transfer and translation of sexual cultures across national boundaries and historical periods has been limited in some places, extensive in others.

Variations around the world notwithstanding, the nation-state, with its distinctive technologies of population management, has become the preferred model of social organization throughout the world. In the wake of nation building, various states and the populations governed by them have developed their own answers to questions pertaining to sex. These answers have changed as nineteenth- and twentieth-century "modernities" have played out differently in various parts of the world. Still, most modern sexual regimes share some striking characteristics. For instance, revolutionary attempts at modernization have encouraged the legal and medical professions to pursue social engineering through the use of specialized training and disciplinary expertise. In the modernizing world from Germany and Japan to the United States and South Africa, the flourishing of commercial culture and the expansion of urban life have contributed to the widening of public discourses about sex and sexuality. The highly politicized issues of culture, health, and sexuality have been debated in an increasingly diverse context as trained professionals have found themselves in conversation with a wide range of interest groups including social reformers, feminists, and political ideologues. Moreover, everyone from technocrats and policymakers to social commentators and sexual rights advocates has come to believe that our understanding of sexuality should not only be defined in medical terms but also draw from a number of emerging disciplines in the biological and social sciences. These understandings—complex, contested, and contradictory as they often are—are at the heart and soul of the modern nation-state.

Notes

1   Nation and state—while bound up together in complicated ways that are beyond the scope of this chapter—are distinct concepts. Anthropologist Benedict Anderson has famously described nations as "imagined communities"

that are "imagined as both inherently limited and sovereign" (Anderson 1983, p. 5), while states represent "a particular machinery for the exercise of 'government over a given population'" (Yuval-Davis and Anthias 1989, p. 5).

2 The term "sexual culture" includes both individual experience and collective interpretations of those experiences (Eder et al. 1999, p. 1).

3 The study of sexuality in China is a growing field. See for example Dikötter (1995), Jeffreys (2006), and Jackson et al. (2008).

4 Discovery was also invention. As Michel Foucault and others have noted, the desire to study sexual attitudes and practices was couched in the language of "seeking the truth" about sex and thus was closely intertwined with the *making* of a modern sexuality, or the transformation of sexual practice into a discourse about modernity (Foucault 1990).

5 The political slogan "Volk ohne Raum," or "people without space," was popular first in the Weimar Republic and later in Nazi Germany. The slogan was originally coined by nationalist writer Hans Grimm, whose novel *Volk ohne Raum* appeared in 1926 and sold nearly 700,000 copies. The slogan implied that the 1919 Treaty of Versailles, which ended World War I, had deprived Germany of its colonial empire and subjected its "people without space" to lives of poverty, misery, hunger, and overpopulation.

6 For decades, German scholars had come to Japan to teach at the country's most renowned universities and professional schools, while Japanese scholars and scholars in training went to Germany for study and research at some of its most reputable universities and research laboratories. Until well into the twentieth century, German prevailed in Japan as the international language of science and technology, and most Japanese scientists and medical experts learned German as their first foreign language.

7 Although Hiratsuka Raichō first made her case for forced sterilization in 1917, the Japanese state waited until 1941 to implement eugenic legislation and most sterilization occurred in the 1950s and 1960s.

8 Recent estimates put sales of the Kinsey Reports at close to 1 million copies, and they have been translated into over a dozen languages.

References

Algoso, T.A. (2011) Thoughts on hermaphroditism: Miyatake Gaikotsu and the convergence of the sexes in Taishô Japan. *Journal of Asian Studies*, 65 (3), 555–73.

Anderson, B. (1983) *Imagined Communities: Reflections on the Origin and Spread of Nationalism*. Verso, New York.

Bérubé, A. (1990) *Coming Out Under Fire: The History of Gay Men and Women in World War II*. University of North Carolina Press, Chapel Hill.

Bhabha, H.K. (1990) *Nation and Narration*. Routledge, London.

Boag, P. (2011) *Re-dressing America's Frontier Past*. University of California Press, Berkeley.

Botha, K. and Cameron, E. (1997) South Africa, in *Sociolegal Control of Homosexuality* (ed. D.J. West and R. Green). Plenum Press, New York, pp. 5–42.

Butler, J. (1990) *Gender Trouble: Feminism and the Subversion of Identity*. Routledge, New York.

Chauncey, G. (1994) *Gay New York: Gender, Urban Culture, and the Making of the Gay Male World, 1890–1940*. Basic Books, New York.

Cole, C.M., Manuh, T., and Miescher, S. (eds) (2007) *Africa after Gender?* Indiana University Press, Bloomington.

Constitutional Court of South Africa (2005) Minister of Home Affairs and Another v Fourie and Another . . . Media Summary. www.saflii.org/za/cases/ZACC/2005/19media.pdf (accessed July 30, 2013).

D'Emilio, J. and Freedman, E.B. (1988) *Intimate Matters: A History of Sexuality in America*. Harper & Row, New York.

Davis, R. (2012) Mandela Day: 67 minutes of protest. *Daily Maverick*, July 19. http://dailymaverick.co.za/article/2012-07-19-mandela-day-67-minutes-of-protest (accessed July 30, 2013).

Dikötter, F. (1995) *Sex, Culture and Modernity in China*. C. Hurst & Co., London.

Donham, D.L. (1998) Freeing South Africa: The "modernization" of male–male sexuality in Soweto. *Cultural Anthropology*, 13 (1), 3–21.

Eder, F.X., Hall, L., and Hekma, G. (1999) *Sexual Cultures in Europe, Volume 1: National Histories*. Manchester University Press, Manchester.

Epprecht, M. (2006) *Hungochani: The History of Dissident Sexuality in Southern Africa*. McGill-Queens University Press, Montreal.

Epprecht, M. (2009) Sexuality, Africa, history. *American Historical Review*, 114 (5), 1258–72.

Foucault, M. (1990) *The History of Sexuality, Volume 1: An Introduction*, 5th edn (trans. R. Hurley). Vintage, New York.

Frühstück, S. (2003) *Colonizing Sex: Sexuality and Social Control in Modern Japan*. University of California Press, Berkeley.

Gevisser, M. (1995) A different fight for freedom: A history of South African lesbian and gay organization from the 1950s to 1990s, in *Defiant Desire: Gay and Lesbian Lives in South Africa* (ed. M. Gevisser and E. Cameron). Routledge, New York, pp. 14–98.

Harris, V. (2010) *Selling Sex in the Reich: Prostitutes in German Society, 1914–1945*. Oxford University Press, Oxford.

Heap, C. (2003) The city as a sexual laboratory: The queer heritage of the Chicago School. *Qualitative Sociology*, 26 (4), 457–87.

Heap, C. (2009) *Slumming: Sexual and Racial Encounters in American Nightlife, 1885–1940*. University of Chicago Press, Chicago.

Hedgepeth, S.M. and Saidel, R.G. (2010) *Sexual Violence against Jewish Women during the Holocaust*. Brandeis University Press, Waltham.

Herzog, D. (2005) *Sex after Fascism: Memory and Morality in Twentieth-Century Germany*. Princeton University Press, Princeton.

Hirschfeld, M. (1941 [1930]) *The Sexual History of the World War*. New York Cadillac Publishing, New York.

Hirschfeld, M. (2006 [1933]) *Die Weltreise eines Sexualforschers im Jahre 1931/32* [The World Travels of a Sexologist in the Year 1931/32]. Eichborn Verlag, Frankfurt am Main.

Hughes, D. (2009) Being gay in South Africa: Lesbians fear "corrective" rape. *ABC News*, May 29. http://abcnews.go.com/International/story?id=7577169&page =1 (accessed July 30, 2013).

Jackson, S., Liu, J., and Woo, J. (eds) (2008) *East Asian Sexualities: Modernity, Gender and New Sexual Cultures*. Zed Books, New York.

Jarvis, C.S. (2010) *The Male Body at War: American Masculinity during World War II*. Northern Illinois University Press, DeKalb, IL.

Jeffreys, E. (ed.) (2006) *Sex and Sexuality in China*. Routledge, London.

Kinsey Institute (2013) Data from Alfred Kinsey's Studies. www.indiana.edu/~kinsey/ resources/ak-data.html (accessed July 30, 2013).

Kinsey, A.C., Pomeroy, W.B., and Martin, C.E. (1948) *Sexual Behavior in the Human Male*. W.B. Saunders, Philadelphia.

Kinsey, A.C., Pomeroy, W.B., Martin, C.E., and Gebhard, P.H. (1953) *Sexual Behavior in the Human Female*. W.B. Saunders, Philadelphia.

Krauss, F.S. (1911 [1907]) *Das Geschlechtsleben in Glauben, Sitte und Brauch der Japaner* [The Sex Life in Beliefs, Manners, Customs, and Common Law of the Japanese]. Deutsche Verlagsgesellschaft, Leipzig.

Laqueur, T. (1992) *Making Sex: Body and Gender from the Greeks to Freud*. Harvard University Press, Cambridge.

Laqueur, T. (2004) *Solitary Sex: A Cultural History of Masturbation*. Zone Books, New York.

McLean, H. and Ngcobo, L. (1994) Abangibhamayo bathi ngimnandi (those who fuck me say I'm tasty): Gay sexuality in Reef townships, in *Defiant Desire: Gay and Lesbian Lives in South Africa* (ed. M. Gevisser and E. Cameron). Ravan Press, Johannesburg, pp. 158–85.

Meyer, L. (1996) *Creating GI Jane: Sexuality and Power in the Women's Army Corps during World War II*. Columbia University Press, New York.

Mosse, G.L. (1982) Nationalism and respectability: normal and abnormal sexuality in the nineteenth century. *Journal of Contemporary History*, 17, 221–46.

Munro, B. (2012) *South Africa and the Dream of Love to Come: Queer Sexuality and the Struggle for Freedom*. University of Minnesota Press, Minneapolis.

Muta, K. (1996) *Senryaku toshite no kazoku: Kindai Nihon no kokumin kokka keisei to josei* [Family as Strategy: The Formation of the Japanese Modern Nation State and Women]. Shinyôsha, Tokyo.

Parker, A., Russo, M., Sommer, D., and Yaeger, P. (1992) Introduction, in *Nationalisms and Sexualities*. Routledge, New York, pp. 1–22.

Patton, C. (1990) Inventing "African AIDS." *New Formations*, 10, 25–39.

Patton, C. (1992) From nation to family: containing "African AIDS" in *Nationalisms and Sexualities* (ed. A. Parker, M. Russo, D. Sommer, and P. Yaeger). Routledge, New York, pp. 218–34.

Republic of South Africa (1996) Constitution of the Republic of South Africa, No. 108 of 1996. www.info.gov.za/documents/constitution/1996/a108-96.pdf (accessed July 30, 2013).

Republic of South Africa, Parliament (1995) *Debates of the Constitutional Assembly*. Government Printer, Pretoria.

Rocha, L.A. (2010) *Xing*: The discourse of sex and human nature in modern China. *Gender & History*, 22 (3), 603–28.

Sanger, M. (1922) Birth Control in China and Japan. Margaret Sanger Papers, Library of Congress, LCM 128:491.

Screech, T. (2009) *Sex and the Floating World: Erotic Images in Japan 1700–1820*. Reaktion Books, London.

Silverberg, M.R. (2009) *Erotic Grotesque Nonsense: The Mass Culture of Japanese Modern Times*. University of California Press, Berkley.

Smith, A. (2005) *Conquest: Sexual Violence and American Indian Genocide*. South End Press, Cambridge.

Soh, C.S. (2008) *The Comfort Women: Sexual Violence and Postcolonial Memory in Korea and Japan*. University of Chicago Press, Chicago.

Somerville, S.S. (2000) *Queering the Color Line*. Duke University Press, Durham, NC.

Stern, A.M. (2005) *Eugenic Nation: Faults and Frontiers of Better Breeding in Modern America*. University of California Press, Berkeley.

Terry, J. (1999) *An American Obsession: Science, Medicine and Homosexuality in Modern Society*. University of Chicago Press, Chicago.

Yoshimi, Y. (2000) *Comfort Women: Sexual Slavery in the Japanese Military during World War II*. Columbia University Press, New York.

Yuval-Davis, N. and Anthias, F. (1989) Introduction, in *Woman-Nation-State*. Palgrave MacMillan, London, pp. 1–15.

Suggested Reading

Butler, J. (1990) *Gender Trouble: Feminism and the Subversion of Identity*. Routledge, New York.

Foucault, M. (1990) *The History of Sexuality, Volume 1: An Introduction*, 5th edn (trans. R. Hurley). Vintage, New York.

Frühstück, S. (2003) *Colonizing Sex: Sexuality and Social Control in Modern Japan*. University of California Press, Berkeley.

Herzog, D. (2005) *Sex after Fascism: Memory and Morality in Twentieth-Century Germany*. Princeton University Press, Princeton.

Laqueur, T. (1992) *Making Sex: Body and Gender from the Greeks to Freud*. Harvard University Press, Cambridge.

Terry, J. (1999) *An American Obsession: Science, Medicine and Homosexuality in Modern Society*. University of Chicago Press, Chicago.

3

Sexuality and Modern Imperialism

Mytheli Sreenivas

Sex had an important, but often overlooked, role in building and sustaining modern imperialism. Imperial encounters always included sexual encounters, and sexual intimacies shaped relationships between colonizing and colonized populations. These sexual relationships were varied and diverse. They included heterosexual and same-sex encounters and encompassed long-term and short-term connections. Some relationships found legal recognition in marriage, but many others existed outside the boundaries of legality and gained varying degrees of social acceptance. Given the power differences that existed in many of these relationships, it is not always easy for historians to understand the extent of coercion in imperial sexual encounters. However, we do know that some relations were more coercive than others and that at least some relationships appear to have been consensual. We know, as well, that in all colonies there emerged mixed-race populations but that their numbers varied from place to place.[1] These variations were due, in part, to the timing and duration of colonization but also depended upon how mixed-race individuals were recognized, counted, or categorized—and this changed across time and place as well.

In all imperial contexts, sex played a role in shaping the distinctions between colonizer and colonized. The offspring of interracial sexual encounters could, quite literally, blur the boundaries between the colonizing power and the colonized population. Sometimes, intimate relationships between colonizing men and colonized women could buttress hierarchies. However,

A Global History of Sexuality: The Modern Era, First Edition.
Edited by Robert M. Buffington, Eithne Luibhéid, and Donna J. Guy.
© 2014 Robert M. Buffington, Eithne Luibhéid, and Donna J. Guy.
Published 2014 by Blackwell Publishing Ltd.

if the colonizer seemed to "lose" his cultural or racial identity and became too closely aligned with "native" cultural practice, these relations could also call into question the cultural supremacy of the imperial power. Homosexual encounters were seen to pose an even more dangerous threat, and by the nineteenth century became linked to fears of European racial degeneracy. Therefore, sex in the colonies was never simply a private act that was irrelevant to empire. Instead, who could legitimately engage in sexual activity with whom, alongside related questions about emotional intimacies, domestic arrangements, and raising children, all became matters of imperial consequence. Yet, although sexuality was important to all modern empires, ideas about sex differed across imperial contexts. The historical time period, specific imperial ideologies, and conditions within each colony were all important to how governments and societies understood and regulated sexual encounters. At the same time, sexual behaviors could transform imperial encounters in various ways.

In examining these connections between sexuality and modern imperialism, this chapter focuses on Western Europe and the United States as imperial powers whose empires extended across much of Africa, Asia, and the Pacific Islands.[2] By the eighteenth century, Britain, France, the Netherlands, Portugal, and Spain already had a long history of overseas empires and had established colonies in the Americas and the Caribbean, as well as smaller outposts in port cities across Africa and Asia. We are interested here in a "second wave" of European empire that, by the end of the nineteenth century, had resulted in the formal conquest of much of the African and Asian continents. The United States entered this process of overseas colonization later than the countries of Western Europe. North American involvement in a coastal African slave trade predated US independence, but for much of the nineteenth century the US government focused on a westward conquest and "settlement" that aspired to extend the nation's borders from Atlantic to Pacific. Only after the 1890s did the United States turn its attention to securing colonies overseas.

Historians who study sexuality and modern imperialism have asked several questions, each of we will discuss here: 1) What kinds of sexual relationships existed in the past between colonizing and colonized populations, and what traces have they left in historical records? In many cases, we have more evidence about how these relationships were regulated than about how they were experienced by individuals. As a result, most historical research is devoted to understanding how sex was understood, prohibited, or encouraged in various modern empires. 2) How did these regulations shape sexual ideologies and hierarchies in both colony and metropole, especially in relation to race, gender, class, and the distinctions between colonized and colonizer? 3) Were some empires more sexually "permissive" than others? Since historians have shown that ideas about sex were not static but changed over time, our inquiry will pay attention to chronology, asking how changes in the history of sexuality were intimately related to change in the history of modern empires.

We begin in the eighteenth century and proceed through the nineteenth and early twentieth centuries. Alongside this chronology, we will pay attention to several key themes: the intersection of sexuality with developing ideas about race in both colonies and metropoles; the regulation of interracial sexual contact, including prostitution, concubinage, and legal marriage; and imperial interventions in the sexualities of colonized populations. For each theme, we ask how sex played a role in shaping empire, and in turn how imperialism shaped sexual ideologies and practices.

Eighteenth-Century Encounters

Encounters between Europeans on the one hand and Asians and Africans (and to a lesser extent Native Americans) on the other typically began through trade. In some places, Europeans had maintained trading relationships for a century or more before engaging in the territorial conquests that resulted in modern imperialism. Typically, European governments granted monopolies to private companies to carry on this trade. For example, the Dutch East India Company, founded in 1602, was granted the right by the Dutch government to conduct all trade between Asia and the Netherlands. The British, French, Spanish, and Portuguese governments also chartered similar companies, each of which hired men—not women—to establish trading posts along African and Asian coastlines. So from the outset, European trading relationships depended upon the labor of single European men who were willing for reasons of profit, adventure, or lack of opportunity in Europe to leave their homes—often for many years at a time, or even for their entire lives—and live in port settlements thousands of miles away. Few European women accompanied or followed them, since dominant norms about femininity rendered these outposts unsuitable for "respectable" women. Perceptions about the brutal nature of some of this trade, especially the slave trade from West Africa to the Americas, furthered the impression that these outposts were no place for European women. In some instances, as in Canton (Guangzhou) in China in the latter half of the eighteenth century, Western merchants were forbidden by the Chinese government from bringing women into their settlement, creating a European community that was entirely male. If we pay attention to the identities of these eighteenth and early nineteenth-century merchants—not only as British, Dutch, French, etc. but also as masculine—we can begin asking how ideas about gender and sexuality shaped trading relationships and, eventually, the forms of imperial conquest and governance.

Even before Europeans conquered territories, sexualized imagery pervaded their representations of Asia, Africa, and the Americas. Romantic visions of the "virgin" land of the Americas, the hypersexual African woman, and the lush sexualities of Pacific Islanders all shaped how European traders and conquerors understood and justified their imperial ventures. This imagery could suggest to European men that empire offered a field of sexual opportunity that exceeded what was available to them in their countries of origin. Some historians, most notably Ronald Hyam, have argued that this vision of "native" sexualities was in fact fundamental to the imperialist enterprise; the promise of new and "exotic" sexual experiences helped to sustain men in otherwise difficult situations (Hyam 1991). However, many historians have critiqued Hyam's argument to show that, in fact, sexual mores were not necessarily more fluid in the colonies and that sometimes sexual prohibitions were rigorously enforced by the Europeans' trading partners and by emerging colonial regimes (Forman 2005, p. 113). Moreover, imperial "sexual opportunities" for men never existed on a blank slate but were enmeshed in systems of imperial power that depended upon racism, colonial exploitation, and patriarchal privilege.

Let us take, for example, the British conquest of India during the eighteenth and early nineteenth centuries. The British and French engaged in stiff competition for dominance in India, with the British eventually gaining the upper hand through a combination of military victories, political negotiations with local rulers, and alliances with merchant groups. These victories meant that by the mid-eighteenth century the British East India Company, which monopolized trade between Britain and Asia, had begun to transform from a corporation into a state; by the nineteenth century, the trading company had conquered an expanding subcontinental empire. Existing historical evidence suggests that, throughout this period, European men—as company employees, private traders, military officers, and mercenary soldiers—engaged in sexual relationships with Indians they encountered.

Some of these relationships developed between elite men and women. Major (later General) William Palmer, for instance, was an East India Company official. Having previously served in the Caribbean, where he contracted a relationship with a creole woman with whom he had three sons, in 1766 Palmer arrived in India. Possibly while in the city of Lucknow, Palmer met Bibi Faiz Baksh, a Muslim woman who was part of the Mughal elite. We do not know whether they ever contracted a legal marriage, but their children were accepted as legitimate. Palmer's letters reveal his anxieties about whether he would be able to secure a place for these children in British society, but his sons eventually obtained military commissions with the East India Company and also occupied prominent positions in banking and finance; his daughter married a Company military officer (Ghosh 2008, pp. 84–7).[3] Palmer, Faiz Baksh, their children, and other

Figure 3.1 Johann Zoffany, *The Palmer Family* (oil on canvas), 1785. This family portrait by one of England's most sought-after portrait painters depicts Major (later General) William Palmer with his Indian wife and mixed-race children. *Source*: British Library, London, UK / The Bridgeman Art Library.

members of the household sat for a portrait in 1786, and the resulting representation by Johannes Zoffany—one of England's most prominent portrait painters—reveals both the intimacies and the hierarchies of their interracial household.

While the Palmers occupied a prominent position in colonial society, and were somewhat unusual in finding social acceptance for their inter-racial household, the majority of liaisons between British men and Indian women occurred among less elite classes. Some observers claimed that for British soldiers, who were required to be unmarried as a condition of their service, relations with local women offered many advantages. Thomas Williamson, the author of a guide for soldiers in the East India Company published in 1810, enumerated these benefits:

> Whether married or not, each soldier is generally provided with a compan-ion, who takes care of his linen, aids in cleaning his accoutrements, dresses his hair . . . These doxies do, certainly, now and then kick up a famous row in the barracks; but on the whole, may be considered highly serviceable; especially during illness, at which time their attendance is invaluable. (Williamson 1810, p. 458)[4]

Combining the roles of domestic and personal servant, nurse, launderer, and—implicitly—sexual companion, these "highly serviceable" women allowed the East India Company's military force to be maintained with a minimum of expense. Military budgets depended upon women providing "low-cost" services, and sexual and domestic intimacies were woven into the fabric of early colonial rule. Women, while certainly not empowered within relationships that were often temporary and hinged upon racial and gendered hierarchies, were also not passive victims. On occasion, for example, women took the initiative to have their relationships with British soldiers recognized by demanding a right to receive a widow's pension if their male companion had died while in service (Ghosh 2008, pp. 212–44).

Some historians have suggested that the existence of these interracial relationships is evidence of racially harmonious empire building in the eighteenth and early nineteenth centuries, not just in India but in other parts of Asia and the Caribbean as well. Careful research by historian Durba Ghosh has shown, however, that these relationships were fraught with racial and sexual anxieties from the outset (Ghosh 2008, pp. 35–68). The British East India Company administration only selectively recognized mixed-race children, and officials disciplined European men whom they deemed too close to Indian women, or too involved in "native" affairs. In the case of British India, much of the historical record simply ignores the presence of "native" female companions of British men. This absence from the record makes it all the more difficult for historians to find evidence about these women's activities, or even about their existence.

The kinds of tensions and anxieties created by sexual relationships between British men and local women in India is not necessarily representative of all eighteenth and early nineteenth-century imperial encounters. For example, the Portuguese had a maritime empire across Asia (including in India) that predated that of the British by several centuries. By the eighteenth century, with fewer prohibitions on miscegenation, Portuguese colonies typically had large mixed-race populations. This did not mean they were necessarily less racialized or hierarchical; rather, Portuguese colonial societies tended to operate with complex, graded hierarchies based on ancestry (Forman 2005, p. 120). British and French colonies in the Caribbean were also long-standing, and during the eighteenth century were prosperous plantation economies dependent upon slave labor. The rape and sexual exploitation of enslaved women by slave owners and overseers was part of the landscape of these plantation economies. So also was a mixed-race population, which in the case of the French colony of St. Domingue (modern-day Haiti) was seen by European planters as central to the slave revolution there (1791–1804).

Sex, Race, and Empire

In much of Asia and Africa around 1800, the era of formal colonization was yet to begin. As the nineteenth century advanced, however, trading relationships along seacoasts were transformed into direct conquests extending into inland territories in Africa and Southeast Asia that had hitherto had less contact with Europeans. Earlier empires based in mercantilist trade gave way to systems of industrial capitalism, in which colonies served as sources for raw materials and markets for manufactured goods. Empires expanded, most notably in the African continent, and developed more formal, bureaucratic, and authoritarian structures of rule. In this context, European women began to arrive in significant numbers in the colonies. The expansion of settler colonies in French Algeria, British South Africa, and German Southwest Africa also drew larger European populations. Major uprisings against imperial rule, such as the Sepoy Rebellion in India in 1857–8, produced anxiety among Europeans about the future of empire and also questioned imperial ideas about "civilizing" or Christianizing native populations. The seeds of anticolonial nationalism, visible in India by the late nineteenth century, questioned imperial civilizing missions as well.

Meanwhile, economic depression and national crises in Britain, France, Germany, and the Netherlands during the late nineteenth and early twentieth centuries heightened imperial anxieties. By the 1870s, for example, Britain was losing its status as the dominant industrial power and faced growing competition from Germany and the United States; economic depression added to this sense of crisis (McClintock 1995, pp. 46–7). France's defeat in the Franco-Prussian war of 1871 fueled anxieties about French national identity; the incorporation of some hundred thousand Algerian Jews as "French" at about the same time heightened debates about the content of French nationality (Edwards 1998, pp. 111–12; Stoler 1992, pp. 517–18). Economic depression had an impact on the Netherlands as well, and exacerbated concerns about the viability of Dutch imperial control in the East Indies. Competition between these European powers, along with Germany and Belgium, in the "Scramble for Africa" in the 1880s furthered these intra-European national rivalries. In the aftermath of the Spanish–American War of 1898, the United States also began to conquer an overseas empire, thus joining the ranks of the more established imperial powers in Asia and the Caribbean. Even as empires expanded in the last decades of the nineteenth century, they were haunted by fears of their own vulnerability.

Developing ideas about race contributed to these perceived vulnerabilities. Prior to the mid-nineteenth century, some intellectuals ascribed to monogenist theories about race, which maintained that environmental conditions were responsible for racial difference; by contrast, polygenists suggested that different races were actually different species. Following the publication of Darwin's *On the Origin of Species* in 1859, polygenist theories began to recede, only to be replaced by evolutionary models of race. These models posited a racial hierarchy in which Western Europeans were situated at the top and other "races" were ranged beneath them (Forman 2005, pp. 123–5). These divisions did not always accord with how "whiteness" is typically understood today; the Irish "race," for instance, was seen to be substantially below an Anglo-Saxon one. Late nineteenth-century ethnographers actively developed this project of racial differentiation and hierarchy by producing studies purporting to connect differences in physical appearance to intellectual capacity, sexual appetites, and level of "civilization." Historians now call this way of thinking about racial difference "scientific racism," which "argues that race conforms to scientific principles and manifests itself in specific, measurable ways" (Forman 2005, p. 123).

The development of these ideas about race was deeply intertwined with ideas about sex; neither could be sustained without the other, and both came together to define European bourgeois identity in the nineteenth century. For example, European representations of "others" typically connected racial inferiority to sexual deviance, as in the case of developing ideas about same-sex sexual encounters among men. The production and stigmatization of male homosexual identity in Europe, as historian Rudi Bleys suggests, was closely intertwined with theories about racial degeneration and the supposedly perverse sexualities of non-European peoples (Bleys 1995, pp. 145–92). Representations of African female sexuality also played an important role in linking race to sex. According to scholar Sander Gilman (1985), European art, literature, and medicine in the nineteenth century were deeply interested in black female sexuality, which on the one hand came to stand in for all African sexualities and on the other represented the threatening potential of all female sexualities. This was an era when exhibiting African female bodies to European audiences helped to fix notions about the sexual pathologies of black women. The exhibition of Sara Baartman is the best-known example. Baartman, a Khoi woman who lived in what is now South Africa, was brought to Europe in 1810. She was exhibited before audiences in England and France to show her large buttocks (steatopygia), and her genitals were preserved in Paris's Musée de l'Homme after her death. Baartman's exhibition engendered some controversy, including from abolitionists who opposed the slave trade. Nevertheless, Gilman suggests that Baartman's case is one example of a much larger European discourse in which black female sexuality was marked as an antithetical "other." That is, Baartman's body served as evidence of the "primitive" and "animal-like" sexuality ascribed to black women, and to Africans as a whole. European sexuality was defined as "civilized" and "human" in contrast to these representations of African women. But, even while European discourses asserted differences between Europe and Africa, they also suggested that European sexuality had to be regulated and managed so that it did not become its African "other." The threat of sexual "deviance" was not limited to the African colonies but haunted the metropole too. In this context, Gilman concludes, the imperialist discourse

Figure 3.2 Christopher Crupper Rumford, *Sartjee the Hottentot Venus* (etching), 1811. The print shows Sarah Baartman, a South African woman known as the Hottentot Venus, mostly naked, holding a long pole and smoking a pipe. The cupid who sits on her exaggerated buttocks says: "Take care of your hearts." *Source*: Library of Congress Prints and Photographs Division, Washington, DC, LC-USZ62-137332.

of the "white man's burden" had a sexual component as well. The burden lay in the white man's "sexuality and its control, and it is this which is transferred into the need to control the sexuality of the Other," both the colonized native and the sexualized female (Gilman 1985, p. 237).

Some scholars, including Ann McClintock, turn to Freudian psychoanalytic theories to investigate these connections between race, sex, and empire. In her analysis of British imperialism, McClintock draws from Freud's analysis of abjection, in which she says the "abject is everything that the subject seeks to expunge in order to become social [but] it is also a symptom of the failure of this ambition." McClintock suggests that this paradox of abjection plays a formative role in the structures of modern imperialism. Empires expelled certain groups to the margins of modernity—to slums and ghettos in the cities of Western Europe, and segregated Bantustans in a colony such as South Africa. Yet, while rejecting the abject, modern imperialism also could not do without them—slaves, prostitutes, and the colonized were all critical to the functioning of empire. The literal and figurative places inhabited by the abject were thus policed and regulated as part of the assertion of imperial power (McClintock 1995, pp. 71-2). In this reading, Freud's claim that sexuality and its repression were at the heart of modern (European) civilization is linked to European imperialist projects. The repression of specific desires and their transference onto the abject played a central role in imperialist ideas about race on the one hand and in European sexualities on the other.

Ideas that linked racial inferiority to sexual deviance not only circulated in the European metropoles but also shaped conquest and imperial administration in the colonies. According to historian Nerissa Balce, a "foundational project of European and American imperialisms" was the production of an "archive of images of the non-Western other whose inferiority was marked by female nakedness" (Balce 2006, p. 89). The circulation of these images of naked women served to justify imperial violence because imperialists could claim that they were merely "civilizing" savage populations through conquest. During the United States's conquest of the Philippines, for instance, representations of the bare breasts of Filipina women helped to mark the Filipino population as both savage and perverse and thus in need of American imperial control. Even after conquest, norms and assumptions about race and sex continued to impact colonized populations in a variety of ways. One important example concerns rape and other forms of sexual violence. Across a number of geographic contexts, the imagined hypersexuality of the black woman rendered her supposedly "unrapeable"

Figure 3.3   Jean-Auguste-Dominique Ingres, *The Turkish Bath* (oil on canvas), 1862. This "keyhole" painting with its deliberately voyeuristic perspective exemplifies European "Orientalism," especially its tendency to eroticize the Middle East. *Source*: akg-images / Erich Lessing.

(i.e. her rape did not count as rape because of her supposed lack of sexual self-control). This was true in the slaveholding United States, where the rape of slave women by white slave owners carried neither social nor legal sanction. But it was also true in colonial South Africa, where "free" (i.e. non-slave) women found their charges of rape judged on the basis of their assigned racial identities (Scully 1995). Women identified as "colored" found it much harder to secure prosecutions for rape than women who were seen as "white."

Separating Colonizer and Colonized

These developing ideas about racial inferiority and sexual deviance recast the threat posed by interracial sex in the colonies. Racially mixed offspring threatened racial purity and came to represent racial decline and degeneracy. Consequently, as the nineteenth century advanced, European men's sexual relations with non-European women were not perceived as individual acts judged according to moral, political, or religious norms alone. Instead, this activity threatened to corrupt the entire "race" and called into question the superiority of the colonizing power. Alongside heterosexual sex, same-sex encounters—and in particular male homosexuality—also raised the specter of degeneracy. Same-sex relationships between colonizer and colonized were not always well documented in colonial archives, leading some historians to conclude that evidence of homosexual encounters exists as a palpable absence in historical records. By examining representations in art and literature, as well as evidence from individual biographies, however, historian Robert Aldrich has documented a range of activities and discourses he terms homosexual, homoerotic, and homosocial in British, Dutch, and French colonies (Aldrich 2002, pp. 6–7).[5] Yet, although some male colonizers may have found same-sex intimacies in the colonies, by the late nineteenth century, homosexual behaviors had become criminalized in new ways; for example, in Britain the Criminal Law Amendment Act (1885) introduced new prohibitions against sex between men, and British colonies including Australia enacted related, but not identical, measures (Philips 2006, pp. 165, 180–1).

Under these circumstances, male sexual continence became a hallmark virtue of white racial identity. White men, especially those of middle-class status, were perceived to have greater control over their sexual desires than both nonwhite populations and women of all races. This reputation for self-control in turn marked their racial superiority in comparison to Asians and Africans and buttressed the strength and purity of the race. Yet advocacy of white male sexual continence did not serve to allay fears about interracial and/or same-sex intimacies. Imperial administrators remained concerned that many men would be unable to conform to these norms, and they especially voiced anxieties about working-class men or "poor whites," whose lower-class status marked them as sexually suspect in the eyes of white elites. Consequently, the existence of largely male European communities in the colonies (such as the military) required imperial

administrators to weigh two perceived risks. First, they feared the consequences of heterosexual sex between colonizer and colonized. Second, they
were anxious about the effects of homosexual sex among male recruits
deprived of female sexual intimacies. How various administrators responded
to these "risks" varied across time and space, and depended both on specific
local circumstances in each colony and upon global shifts in imperial power
and governance.

All imperial administrations sought to demarcate the boundaries
between "white" and "native" in order to buttress the separation between
rulers and the ruled. However, there was no obvious way to make these
distinctions. The assumption—both then and now—is that racial differentiation between colonizer and colonized was self-evident, but, as historian
and anthropologist Ann Stoler points out, the reality was far more ambigu-
ous. We often think that imperial racial categories were based on appearance and skin color, yet Stoler claims that racism was "not really a visual
ideology at all" (Stoler 2002, p. 84). Consequently, who counted as "white"
and who did not was a question that had to be continually debated and
enforced in all European, and also American, colonies. No single measure
could ever suffice to make this determination:

> Skin shade was too ambiguous; bank accounts were mercurial; religious
> belief and education were crucial but never enough. Social and legal standing
> derived not only from color, but from the silences, acknowledgements, and
> denials of the social circumstances in which one's parents had sex. (Stoler
> 1997, p. 374)

Debates about concubinage (nonmarital sexual relationships between
Euro-American men and "native" women) offer an important example of
this process. On the one hand, since concubinage was a relationship in
which colonizing men exercised patriarchal power over Asian and African
women and displaced "native" husbands and patriarchs, it could reinforce
the hierarchy between colonizer and colonized. The man, in other words,
was structurally in a superior position to the woman in such a relationship.
And, as we have seen, this arrangement also allowed men to obtain domestic services cheaply, thus permitting imperial governments to pay lower
wages to its administrators and military personnel. But, on the other hand,
concubinage threatened to blur these racial hierarchies by producing a
mixed-race population.

Despite this perceived risk, well into the twentieth century many imperial governments and European and American-owned plantations and corporations encouraged concubinage by restricting marriage among their employees. In British Malaya through the 1920s, for example, the government and estate administrators were concerned that, with the existing wages, European men would be unable to maintain European wives in a middle-class lifestyle. The white community risked impoverishment, and the existence of a poor white population, in turn, could threaten imperial prestige. The answer to this dilemma was concubinage, since the assumption was that "native" women cost less to maintain. In Stoler's terms, in this colony, "concubinage was tolerated precisely because 'poor whites' were not" (Stoler 1997, p. 378). European poverty, in other words, was seen as the greatest threat to the boundaries marking the colonizer from colonized populations, and concubinage helped to resolve this problem. By contrast, in Java, which was part of the Dutch East Indies (modern-day Indonesia) at the turn of the twentieth century, concubinage itself was seen as a major cause of white poverty, presumably because it would create a class of poor, mixed-race individuals who, within the logic of Dutch governance, would be classified as "European." Consequently, the early 1900s witnessed a condemnation of concubinage alongside a tacit condoning of illegal brothels; the latter presumably would allow European men sexual access to women while eliminating the threat that European biological fathers would confer social parentage on their mixed-race offspring (Stoler 1997, p. 378). Therefore, the presence or absence of concubinage does not, by itself, tell us anything about racial and sexual hierarchies. Instead, we learn that both in British Malaya and in Dutch Java the core concern of government and business elites was to maintain the distinction between colonizer and colonized. In one context concubinage served these ends, and in the other it threatened them.

Sometimes, the stories of individuals can help us to understand how these broad structures of sex and empire came together in people's daily lives. Ann Stoler has unearthed just such a case in French Indochina (modern-day Vietnam), concerning a low-level French naval employee, Sieur Icard, and his nineteen-year-old son, whom the French court referred to as "Nguyen van Thinh *dit* Lucien" (Nguyen van Thinh called Lucien). In 1898, the son was prosecuted and sentenced for assaulting a German naval mechanic in the city of Haiphong. Icard appealed for a reduced prison term but was ultimately unsuccessful. As Stoler shows us, the decisions in this case hinged on race and nationality (was the son French?), and this in turn depended on the court's evaluation of Icard's relationship with Nguyen van Thinh/Lucien. Icard himself claimed that the boy, whom he called "Lucien," was his son by a Vietnamese mother. But this was a time of imperial concern in French Indochina that so-called "fraudulent recognition" of mixed-race children by European fathers was adding poor "natives" to the ranks of the French population. In this context, the court was dubious about Icard's claims. Noting that the son did not possess any of the attributes of French identity, the court condemned Icard's "dedication and love for a child who was illiterate, ignorant of the French language, and spent most of his time in a cultural milieu that was less French than Vietnamese" (Stoler 2002, p. 86). If he could not raise the boy as properly French, the court implied, it would have been better for Icard to abandon him. The judge even went so far as to suggest that Icard was not truly the boy's biological father and was perhaps instead engaged in a homosexual relationship with him. As this case suggests, there was a lot at stake in the designation of Nguyen van Thinh/Lucien as French. It depended not simply upon the boy's appearance or parentage but also upon how those facts intersected with the needs of imperial governance. The threat of "fraudulent recognition" by European men, and the increase of a poor population identified as "French," posed a threat to the boundaries of colonizer and colonized in French Indochina. To manage this threat, the court rejected Icard's claims to fatherhood.

We know less about sexual relationships, and the meanings ascribed to them, in German colonies. The historical scholarship on German imperialism is sparser than that for its British, French, or even American counterparts, due in part to political and intellectual developments in post-World War II Germany and in part to the fact that Germany's formal overseas empire was more short-lived than the imperial projects of other European powers (Friedrichsmeyer et al. 1998, pp. 3–4). Nevertheless, we do know that sexuality remained a contested field in German colonies and played a role in shaping the relationships between colonizing and colonized populations. In German Southwest Africa (modern-day Namibia), for instance, insurrections by the Herero and Nama peoples against German control (1904–7) provoked a harsh imperial military campaign that many have called genocidal. According to historian Helmut Walser Smith, this brutal suppression of the insurrection led to debates in the German Reichstag calling for a separation and hierarchical ordering of black and white races in the colony. However, such separation was rendered problematic by the fact of interracial sex, and led one conservative German parliamentarian to argue that for "the white race to consider itself everywhere to be the master race . . . every sexual relation of blacks with whites in the colonies must be put under penalty of the law" (cited in Walser Smith 1998, p. 116). In the wake of the insurrection, German settlers in the colony excluded mixed-race children from schools, and the government of German Southwest Africa outlawed interracial marriage in 1905. Similar rules were passed in German East Africa (1906) and in Samoa (1912) (Walser Smith 1998, p. 117). Drawing from Stoler's insights on French Indochina and the Dutch East Indies, we can see these German ordinances as an attempt to close ranks around a white/German identity by policing sexuality at a moment when resistance threatened imperial control. At the same time, it is significant that interracial marriage—and not interracial sex per se—was the target, suggesting that the socio-legal recognition of mixed-race relationships, and of mixed-race children, posed the real threat to German imperial control. The exclusion of mixed-race children from schools, by effectively denying access to German language and culture, served a similar purpose. Sexual relations, when they occurred, would not be accorded legal or social recognition.

Regulating Prostitution

In addition to the potential problems posed for empires by longer-term sexual relationships, such as marriage and concubinage, another major area of imperial concern and regulation was prostitution. Imperial administrators were especially concerned about the relationships between European soldiers and the colonized women who serviced them. This was a point of interracial sexual contact that, like concubinage, both reinforced and threatened imperial hierarchies between colonizer and colonized. On the one hand, many military planners assumed that prostitution was a necessity for soldiers who were unmarried and stationed for years at a time away from their homes. Brothels often developed alongside military garrisons, many times with the consent and active support of senior officers who preferred prostitution with "native" women to the supposed threat of homosexual activity among their men. On the other hand, prostitution also posed a threat to the imperial moral and social order, and potentially endangered the health of European soldiers. Although venereal disease was never the greatest public health problem in the colonies, since other diseases had higher death rates and worse symptoms, the threat of syphilis and gonorrhea provoked intense anxieties among administrators both in the colonies and in the metropolitan capitals (Levine 2003, pp. 4–5). They thus sought solutions to contain the spread of disease among soldiers while also guaranteeing these soldiers continuing sexual access to women. For some imperial administrators, the answer to this quandary was a system of registration and medical inspection of prostitutes.

First developed by the French, this system of registration and inspection circled the globe on the heels of British imperial expansion. The British first instituted these methods in Hong Kong in 1857, where Hong Kong Ordinance no. 12 required all brothels to register with medical authorities and mandated that their inmates be regularly examined. Several years later, the British government passed a domestic version of this legislation, the Contagious Diseases Act of 1864, which, unlike in the colonies, was only applicable in specific military districts. In subsequent years, similar acts were passed in other colonies; American, French, and Spanish imperial administrations all instituted some form of registration and inspection in at least some of their colonies. Although varied across time and space, all operated from the assumption that prostitutes (not their solider clients) were responsible for the spread of disease and, in response, they developed an often punitive system of "lock" hospitals where infected women were confined. In Britain, the Contagious Diseases Act provoked a vocal antagonism by a coalition of reformers who protested that the acts gave state sanction to prostitution, and the act was repealed in Britain in 1886. Repeal efforts in the colonies met with mixed results; formal repeal, as in the case of India, existed alongside modified ordinances that continued systems of regulation and inspection of prostitutes.

Under contagious diseases acts in the colonies, women suspected of venereal disease were typically subjected to humiliating, and often painful, medical inspection even while their male clients were not similarly regulated. Some of these practices existed in Britain as well, but there they were applied more narrowly—both because the law was limited to military areas and because of differences in how "prostitutes" were identified. Moreover, in British and other colonies, the acts also served as a way to monitor the activities of women to ensure that prostitutes who serviced European and American men did not also accept "native" male clients. Assumptions about racial difference often undergirded these attempts at sexual policing. According to historian Philippa Levine, some imperial administrators argued that the existence of prostitution in the colonies was a sign of sexual laxity and "racial primitivism" among colonized subjects that could justify a greater degree of intervention and regulation in the colonies (Levine 2003, p. 179). Similar assumptions and anxieties motivated the regulation of prostitution by the United States as well. For example, the United States experimented with various systems of regulation in Puerto Rico, and in 1918 began a system of incarcerating prostitutes who were identified as diseased. As historian Laura Briggs notes, this level of intrusion into the lives of women hinged on imperial ideologies about race and the American "civilizing mission" in the colony. As a result, via the regulation of prostitution, "the sexuality and reproduction of poor women would become the battleground—symbolic and real—for the meaning of the U.S. presence in Puerto Rico" (Briggs 2002, p. 51).

Although prostitution evoked racial, sexual, and imperial anxieties in many colonies, not all responded with a system of registration and medical inspection. As historian Michael Phillips points out, most of British Africa—with a few exceptions—did not adopt contagious diseases acts. Taking the British colony of Sierra Leone as an example, Phillips shows us that these measures were considered, but were never adopted for a variety of economic, political, and ideological reasons. Prostitution was still policed in Sierra Leone, and concerns about interracial sex remained. However, the means of sexual regulation varied; in Phillips's terms, "sexuality, never simply harnessed to imperial power, was an open-ended vehicle for differentiated and constantly changing systems of power" (Phillips 2005, p. 315). Imperial governance did not require a single or predetermined sexual ideology but, as the case of Sierra Leone shows us, sexuality could operate in multiple, sometimes competing, ways to uphold shifting imperial priorities.

Further signals of the racial politics involved in prostitution were the different concerns that emerged if prostitutes were perceived as "white." White prostitutes servicing "native" men triggered racial anxieties about the overturning of colonial hierarchies, since such circumstances appeared to put these men in positions of power over white women. Sexual access to white women had to be closely guarded in order to uphold imperial authority, and so the existence of white prostitutes in the colonies posed a serious challenge to this hierarchical system. Contemporaries sought to guard against this threat. According to the Attorney General of South Africa, for instance, any "Kaffir" in Cape Town could, with payment, have "illicit intercourse" with "white European women." He continued:

> This [is] a matter of the gravest importance. For once the barriers were broken down between the European and native races in this country, there

was no limit to the terrible dangers to which women would be submitted, particularly in isolated places. (cited in Briggs 2002, pp. 43–4)

White prostitution thus held the potential to upend the hierarchical separation of races in South Africa. Seeking to guard against this possibility, in Transvaal, Africans who had sex with white prostitutes were punished, and the 1920 Alien Immigration Act barred the immigration of Eastern European Jews to South Africa, which virtually ended the flow of European prostitutes to the Cape Colony (Briggs 2002, p. 44).

Colonized Sexualities

Beyond regulating interracial sex, imperial actors including governments, missionaries, and reformers of various kinds also aimed to transform the sexual behaviors of "native" populations—even when these behaviors did not directly involve European or American colonizers. Why might imperialists have been interested in the sexualities of their colonized subjects? The reasons varied, depending on the specific circumstances of the colony, the structures of imperial rule, and the broader historical context. But, in virtually all cases, imperialists justified their interventions in sexuality as part of a broader mission to "civilize" their colonized subjects by introducing them to European and Christian modes of behavior. They attacked local practices they deemed primitive, savage, or oppressive toward women. While some imperial actors may have been motivated by a humanitarian concern, one important outcome of these efforts was to allow imperialists to claim that empire was benevolent and that it improved the lives of colonized populations. In practice, however, imperialist interventions in sexuality could also enforce local patriarchies, stigmatize alternative sexualities, and serve as instruments of imperial control over colonized peoples. Many historians have thus shown that claims of imperial benevolence do not often hold up when subjected to careful scrutiny. Historical research also demonstrates that, although some changes in the sexual cultures of colonized populations were the direct result of imperial policies, others were the indirect results of other actions. For example, the inheritance laws or labor policies enforced by a colonial government could have a deep impact on the sexual, marital, and domestic arrangements of local people.

In many colonial contexts, in both Africa and Asia, European and American imperialists measured "native" sexual practices against the ideal of

In de feestdagen.

Teekening van
ALBERT HAHN

Leve de onafhankelijkheid!

Manoeuvres.

Daar gáát ons goeie geld,
Ons leger trekt naar 't veld.
Het gaat wel niet op buit,
Maar op manoeuvre uit.
Zie de heldenschaar marcheeren,
Zie de sabels en geweren;
Zie de paarden en kanonnen,
't Spul is weer begonnen!

Officieren (zonder doel)
Hebben nu de grootste ... mond.
Hoor die branies kommandeeren,
Zie die stumpers paradeeren.
O, wat heeft zoo'n ongeluk
Het toch vrees'lijk, vrees'lijk druk.
Eén illusie, één ideaal:
Wit voetje bij den generaal.

Jongens uit de groote stad,
Die men thuis hard noodig had,
Om hun ouders bij te springen,
Haten al die malle dingen ...
Loopen uren in de pas,
Met 'n ransel op d'r jas,
Wenschen 't heele zotte spel,
Zonder uitstel naar de hel.

En de oogst staat op het land,
Wachtend op de rappe hand
Van de kerels, stoer en sterk,

Die verlangen naar d'r werk.
Maar ze moeten manoeuvreeren,
Tijdig moord-en-doodslag leeren;
Heb je dáárvan geen verstand,
Waardeloos voor 't vaderland ...

Vliegers stijgen in de lucht,
Maken meen'ge stoute vlucht,
Om den vijand op te sporen ...
Oók al weten ze tevoren,
Wáár die vijand zich bevindt ...
't Is alsof een spelend kind
Deze dwaasheid had bedacht,
Waar 'n zinnig mensch om lacht.

Maar de rooien en de blauwen
Zijn nu oorlogje aan 't houën.
Hoor ze schieten, zie ze razen,
Al die hersenlooze dwazen.
Zie ze onversaagd daar komen,
Wéér een stelling ingenomen.
Wéér een fortje overmand
Voor het dierbaar vaderland.

In het holste van den nacht
Overvallen zij de wacht.
En de wacht — God zal ze straffen ! —
Ligt juist zaligjes te maffen.
En de blauwen sluipen voort,
Niemand heeft hun stap gehoord.
Overromp'ling in den nacht .. ,
Is 't geen pracht?

Twintig eeuwen Christendom,
En dit volk is nog zoo dom !
Speelt met moordtuig op Gods akker,
Menschen, maakt die kerels wakker !
Trekt ze duchtig aan d'r ooren,
Laat ze nieuwe stemmen hooren,
Want, verdomd, die malle kuren
Kunnen nu niet langer dúren.

►◄

Waarde Notenkraker,

Gij vraagt mij : Wat is een slag-
schip? Het antwoord luidt: Een klip
waarop een ministerie kan vergaan. —
Een reddingsboei voor verdrinkende
klerikalen. — De zwarte vlek in de
troonrede. — Een schip dat geen
Spaansche matten brengt, maar ze
kost. — De steen des aanstoots in
de concentratie. — Een ding dat den
reaktionairen te weinig en den vooruit-
strevenden te veel is. — De vrees
van groote zeevarende mogendheden.
— De vermoedelijke doodkist van
den minister.

►◄

Overpeinzing.

— Wat een geluk dat Nederland
maar eens om de honderd jaren
onafhankelijk is. Als het elke week
gebeurde, schoot ik er een derde van
mijn loon bij in.

6

C6./41

THE CUBAN MELODRAMA.

The Noble Hero *(to the* Heavy Villain*).*— Stand back, there, gol darn ye !— If you force this thing to a fifth act, remember that 's where I git in *my* work !

Figure 3.5   C. Jay Taylor, *The Cuban Melodrama* (political cartoon), 1896. This American political cartoon from just before the Spanish–American War (1898) casts Uncle Sam as the hero, Spain as the villain, and Cuba as the damsel in distress. *Source*: The Granger Collection / TopFoto.

heterosexual, monogamous marriage, and its attendant practices of domesticity and a gendered division of labor. Missionaries and imperial administrators alike held up a form of marriage in which wives were primarily responsible for a domestic sphere, husbands entered the world of economic activity, and couples were companionate. They believed that this form of monogamous marriage represented the epitome of civilization. This marital form, however, was a relatively recent development in Western Europe and the United States. Over the course of the eighteenth and nineteenth centuries, the rise of industrial capitalism had prompted changes in marital and domestic arrangements in the West; among the bourgeois middle classes, work became physically separated from the home, and middle-class women were increasingly defined as consumers, not producers. The Victorian image of women as the "angel of the home" thus became a defining norm of middle-class marriage and domesticity at roughly the same time that the United States and Western European countries became imperial powers.

In the colonies, missionaries were at the forefront of bringing this model to colonized populations, sometimes with considerable force. In colonial south India, for instance, missionaries were deeply critical of all nonmonogamous sexual arrangements, ranging from serial monogamy to polygyny and polyandry. They also criticized the so-called "Hindu joint family," which privileged the connections between fathers, sons, and brothers, arguing that joint families prevented the development of intimacy between husband and wife. When proselytizing or guiding their congregants, missionaries placed "at the pinnacle of development the nuclear family with an intimate heterosexual couple at its center" and challenged all sexual practices that did not conform to this model (Kent 2004, p. 165). Similarly, in colonial Lagos (capital of modern-day Nigeria), missionaries aimed to replace existing forms of Yoruban marriage, which could be polygynous, with monogamous Christian marriage. In Yoruban marriage wives were expected to be economic producers, but missionary ideals maintained that wives should remain within a domestic sphere that was separated from economic activity (Mann 1985, pp. 35–53). Missionaries sought to spread these ideals in a variety of ways, ranging from persuasion to formal sanctions for congregants who would not transform their marital, sexual, and domestic arrangements. Even practices that we may think of as mundane, such as styles of clothing or domestic architecture, played an important role in effecting these transformations (Comaroff and Comaroff 1991).

Colonized populations could be deeply influenced by missionary ideals, although local circumstances always shaped how individuals and communities adopted forms of Christian marriage and domesticity. Consider, for example, the south Indian Christians who entered into a missionary-inspired monogamous marriage. On the one hand, they may have followed the teachings of their pastors or church-based schools. Yet, on the other hand, in south Indian society in the nineteenth and early twentieth centuries, monogamy was increasingly associated with a higher social status. Monogamous marriage allowed these men and women a way both to proclaim their adherence to the Christian faith and to assert their "respectability" vis-à-vis other Indians. This leads historian Eliza Kent to conclude that, for some south Indian Christians, missionary desires to "civilize" colonized populations via monogamy coincided with these groups' own attempts to elevate their social standing (Kent 2004, p. 127). Returning to colonial Lagos, we find an analogous process at work. Christian marriage could be a way for Africans to lay claim to, or reinforce, their elite status. At the same time, monogamous marriage—in contrast to Yoruban polygyny—helped to concentrate economic resources within a small number of elites by changing the norms of inheritance and family property. In Lagos, then, Christian marriage both marked elite status and helped to maintain it. But even the adoption of Christian marriage—and its related sexual and domestic norms—did not mean that other sexual arrangements disappeared. As historian Kristin Mann has documented, many elite men in Lagos contracted only one Christian marriage but married other women through Yoruban forms (Mann 1985, pp. 120–3). As in the case of south India, missionary norms were not simply imposed but adapted and modified by local populations.

While missionaries were most directly involved with regulating the intimate practices of colonized populations, colonial governments also intervened in important ways. These governments instituted laws and policies that impacted the sexual practices of colonized people. Reactions to these efforts varied greatly. Since colonized populations were not homogenous, their responses to colonial polices depended upon whether and how they were affected by the changes. As in the case of missionary efforts, government interventions were motivated by many factors specific to their time and place. However, historians have demonstrated that, across these differences, many colonial laws and policies were based on a shared assumption about patriarchal authority that was held in common both by colonizers and by indigenous male elites. In these patriarchal bargains, colonial regimes helped to shore up elite men's power over "their" women and, in exchange, these male elites offered the colonial government their support. Feminist historians, in particular, have demonstrated that even legislation that claimed to benefit women often resulted in increased patriarchal control over female sexualities and over nonnormative sexualities among both men and women.

Legislation about the age of consent offers a useful example of the complex relationship between government intervention and colonized sexualities. In late nineteenth-century Britain and its empire, debate flourished about the age at which a girl or woman could give consent to heterosexual sexual relations. In 1885, Britain's Criminal Law Amendment Act raised the female age of consent to thirteen years; in the following years, a number of British colonies also passed age-of-consent legislation. These efforts concentrated in the 1890s, but different colonies produced significantly different pieces of legislation about female sexual consent that were linked to British perceptions about race, climate, and sexual maturity as well as distinct local circumstances in specific colonies. Debates about the age of sexual consent raised multiple questions about the nature of imperial and national sovereignty and about the relationship between the imperial state and its colonized subjects (Levine 2007, pp. 17–18).

Legislating female sexual consent was perhaps most controversial in British India. Marriage among Hindus in India was nearly universal; among some Hindu upper castes, marriage occurred early for women, sometimes before puberty. A few highly publicized controversies, alongside the campaigning of Indian reformers, brought the question of women's age of consent to the forefront of public debate, and in 1891 the colonial government passed legislation instituting twelve as the age of consent for girls. This sparked massive controversy. Hindus opposed to legislation alleged that the British government had interfered with their religious practice; in their view, the Hindu religion required the marriage of upper-caste girls before puberty, with consummation to occur soon after menstruation. By instituting the age of twelve, the new law would make these practices illegal for girls who menstruated before that age. This argument was opposed by Indian reformers including Hindus and members of other faiths who wanted to raise the age of consent. They insisted that prepuberty marriage was not required by Hinduism and pointed to the dangers of early marriage and motherhood. Despite their significant differences, however, all sides tacitly agreed that female consent was primarily a function of biology; the question was not about a girl or woman's choice in marriage or sexual relations but instead her physiological readiness for sexual penetration, pregnancy, and maternity.

In the ensuing debate, indigenous sexual practices became critical to assertions of both imperial authority and Indian national identity. British imperial administrators linked their legislation to a civilizing mission; early marriage supposedly represented the backwardness of Hindu–Indian civilization, and legislation marked British modernizing progress. Conservative Hindus, by contrast, insisted that marital sex soon after puberty was central to a Hindu–Indian national tradition. Legislation on this subject, they argued, represented an imperial encroachment on national sovereignty. As a result, the age-of-consent debates of the 1890s helped to produce a religiously inspired Indian nationalism that offered a forceful critique of colonial rule (Sarkar 2010, pp. 23–52).[6] Although the colonial government implemented age-of-consent legislation in the face of this nationalist opposition, the new law was largely of symbolic importance and its provisions were almost never enforced. A tacit patriarchal understanding between the British regime and Indian male elites ultimately agreed that indigenous men would have control over the sexuality of "their" women.

A second example, this one from British East Africa, can help us to better understand how indigenous sexual practices could become a site of imperial intervention and nationalist resistance. In 1926, governors of the East African dependencies issued new guidelines about female genital cutting, seeking to reduce the extent of cutting to "simple clitoridectomy" and opposing the practice of removing the entire external genitalia. The 1926 law, however, remained a dead letter until 1929, when some Christian missions sought to enforce it by refusing communion to all Christians unwilling to forswear the practice. The missions' decision provoked the largest protest among the Kikuyu people that the British government had yet seen. In her analysis of these protests, historian Susan Pederson argues that the so-called "female circumcision controversy" illuminates the "usefulness of sexual politics to the formation of African nationalism" (Pederson 1991, p. 648). Clitoridectomy had been an important public ritual among the Kikuyu; as a rite of passage from childhood to adulthood, it marked women's full entry into their community and also helped to form age groups, which were a basic unit of social organization. However, this tradition was not unchanging but was powerfully shaped by the intervention of the Kikuyu Central Association (KCA). According to Pederson, the KCA endowed clitoridectomy practices with new political meanings. The organization's defense of the practice "became entangled with long-standing Kikuyu grievances about mission influence and access to land, [and] clitoridectomy, always the sign of the 'true Kikuyu,' also came to be seen as a mark of loyalty to the incipient, as yet imaginary, nation" (Pederson 1991, p. 651). Just as prepuberty marriage became essential to a Hindu–Indian cultural nationalism in the wake of colonial interventions in the practice, so also the defense of clitoridectomy was, for the KCA, a defense of a Kikuyu nationalism. Ultimately, the colonial government was forced to give up its efforts to regulate the practice.

Conclusion

Returning to the point that began this chapter, we can see that sex played an important role in all modern empires, yet the meanings assigned to "sex" were not fixed and unchanging. Sexual encounters sometimes enforced, and sometimes transgressed, the boundaries between colonizer and colonized. Virtually all imperial governments instituted laws, policies, or more informal norms to regulate under what circumstances interracial sexual contact could occur, how such sexual relationships would be recognized in law or social practice, and whether any children born of such relationships would be accorded status as European. The nature of these regulations not only shaped colonial sexual encounters but also molded the contours of imperial governance itself. In the colonies, a woman's right to her sexual companion's property, a child's access to formal education, an adult's ability to enter specific professions, and a family's authority to control economic resources all depended upon how sexual behaviors were recognized, managed, and regulated. These interventions in sexuality developed in concert with imperial understandings of racial difference; at the same time, race itself was perceived in sexualized terms. European observers suggested that the so-called "primitive races" engaged in a "primitive" sexuality—and, when Sara Baartman and other Africans' bodies were put on sexualized display in Europe, they underlined a racial hierarchy through reference to sex.

The regulations governing interracial sex provoked much interest and anxiety in the colonies, where a relatively smaller number of Europeans exercised authority over larger African and Asian populations. The impact of imperial sexualities, however, was not limited only to colonial contexts but also shaped sexual ideologies and hierarchies in the metropole. The interconnection between race and sexuality—and the corollary emphasis on sexual continence as a hallmark of white, middle-class identity—shaped culture and society in Western Europe and the United States. Normative heterosexuality came to be enforced as a guard against sexual and racial "depravity." On the level of policy, laws such as the Contagious Diseases Act circulated across empires, and in the British case moved from Hong

Kong to Britain and then to other colonies in Asia. Movements to repeal these laws, and to rewrite the sexual policies of empire, also moved across boundaries, and activists who began their campaign in Britain then turned their attention to the colonies, where their sexual politics addressed new contexts of sexual practice and regulation. The ideas, anxieties, and relationships of power that underpinned imperial regulations of sexuality thus impacted both colony and metropole.

The fact that sexual regulation occurred across empires did not mean that it was homogenous. Colonial administrators encountered diverse sexual cultures, and the sexual ideologies and practices of colonized populations varied across time; sometimes, these changes were provoked by the colonial encounter itself. Thus, while Christian missionaries and colonial governments held up a model of middle-class domesticity and monogamy for their colonized subjects to emulate, individuals and communities adapted this model to suit their own needs. On some occasions, as in the case of clitoridectomy among the Kikuyu or the age of consent in colonial India, colonial interventions sparked fierce resistance. Such resistance was cast in the language of anticolonial nationalism, with the result that sexual politics and practices came to define national identities not only during the colonial period but also in the aftermath of decolonization.

The intertwined histories of sexuality and modern imperialism also left important legacies that help us understand sexual ideologies and politics today. In postcolonial societies, sexuality is intimately linked to the experience of colonization. The social, economic, cultural, and political changes brought about by colonial rule reshaped sexualities in many former colonies. At the same time, as we have seen, resistance to colonial rule was sometimes conceptualized in sexual terms, such that particular sexual forms and practices became associated with an assertion of national identity. Women, in particular, have often had to bear the burden of representing "national" sexual tradition as a site of resistance to imperial rule. In the former metropoles of Western Europe and the United States, the links between sex, race, and empire have been equally durable. The notion that sexual practices measure levels of civilization resonates across contemporary discourses about the "non-West" or "Third World." The racialization of sexuality, and the sexualization of racial ideologies, did not begin or end with empire; decolonization of territories in Africa and Asia has perhaps not yet decolonized sexual ideologies and hierarchies. Recognizing these connections, however, may be an important way to begin thinking differently about both sex and empire.

Acknowledgments

For their very helpful comments on earlier versions of this essay, I would like to thank Robert Buffington, Donna Guy, and Eithne Luibhéid.

Notes

1 References to "race" or "mixed race" in this chapter do not refer to an essentialist biological category. Instead, I analyze "race" as a social construct whose meanings change over time. As we shall see, imperialism and sexuality both played important roles in defining racial identities and categories from the eighteenth through the twentieth centuries.

2 I use the term "imperialism" to refer to a nation's assertion of dominance and authority over another region, territory, or people. "Colonialism" refers more specifically to the conquest and administration of territory by the imperial power. In the period we consider here, the US and Western European powers established many formal colonies, but they also exerted less formal modes of imperial control in places that were not directly colonized.

3 Palmer's sons who settled in India included both the children of Bibi Faiz Baksh and his sons from his prior relationship with a creole woman in the Caribbean (Dalrymple 2004).

4 Thomas Williamson's *Vade Mecum* was republished in 1825, when its editor, J.B. Gilchrist, deleted some of the passages concerning "native" female companions. The 1825 text, along with the sections deleted from the 1810 edition, is available at: www.columbia.edu/itc/mealac/pritchett/00generallinks/gilchrist/index.html (accessed August 1, 2013).

5 Aldrich focuses on male homosexuality; to my knowledge, there is as yet no extensive historical study of sexual intimacies among women. Policy and legal regulation also appear to have focused on men, perhaps reflecting dominant constructions of female sexuality as passive.

6 In this context, Indian reformers negotiated a complex position, rejecting the arguments of the Hindu orthodoxy but also distancing themselves from the civilizing claims of the British administration.

References

Aldrich, R. (2002) *Colonialism and Homosexuality*. Routledge, New York.

Balce, N.S. (2006) The Filipina's breast: Savagery, docility, and the erotics of the American empire. *Social Text*, 87, 89–110.

Bleys, R.C. (1995) *The Geography of Perversion: Male-to-Male Sexual Behavior Outside the West and the Ethnographic Imagination, 1750–1918*. New York University Press, New York.

Briggs, L. (2002) *Reproducing Empire: Race, Sex, Science, and U.S. Imperialism in Puerto Rico*. University of California Press, Berkeley.

Comaroff, J. and Comaroff, J.L. (1991) *Of Revelation and Revolution, Volume 1: Christianity, Colonialism, and Consciousness in South Africa*. University of Chicago Press, Chicago.

Dalrymple, W. (2004) *White Mughals: Love and Betrayal in Eighteenth-Century India*. Penguin, New York.

Edwards, P. (1998) Womanizing Indochina: Fiction, nation, and cohabitation in colonial Cambodia, 1890–1930, in *Domesticating the Empire: Race, Gender and Family Life in French and Dutch Colonialism* (ed. J. Clancy-Smith and F. Gouda). University Press of Virginia, Charlottesville, pp. 108–30.

Forman, R. (2005) Race and empire, in *Palgrave Advances in the Modern History of Sexuality* (ed. M. Houlbrook and H. Cocks). Palgrave Macmillan, London, pp. 109–32.

Friedrichsmeyer, S., Lennox, S., and Zantop, S. (1998) Introduction, in *The Imperialist Imagination: German Colonialism and Its Legacy*. University of Michigan Press, Ann Arbor, MI, pp. 33–50.

Ghosh, D. (2008) *Sex and the Family in Colonial India: The Making of Empire*. Cambridge University Press, Cambridge.

Gilman, S.L. (1985) Black bodies, white bodies: Toward an iconography of female sexuality in late nineteenth-century art, medicine, and literature. *Critical Inquiry*, 12 (1), 204–42.

Hyam, R. (1991) *Empire and Sexuality*. Manchester University Press, Manchester.

Kent, E.F. (2004) *Converting Women: Gender and Protestant Christianity in Colonial South India*. Oxford University Press, Oxford.

Levine, P. (2003) *Prostitution, Race, and Politics: Policing Venereal Disease in the British Empire*. Routledge, New York.

Levine, P. (2007) Sovereignty and sexuality: Transnational perspectives on colonial age of consent legislation, in *Beyond Sovereignty: Britain, Empire and Transnationalism, c. 1880–1950* (ed. K. Grant, P. Levine, and F. Trentmann). Palgrave MacMillan, New York, pp. 16–33.

Mann, K. (1985) *Marrying Well: Marriage, Status and Social Change among the Educated Elite in Colonial Lagos*. Cambridge University Press, Cambridge.

McClintock, A. (1995) *Imperial Leather: Race, Gender, and Sexuality in the Colonial Contest*. Routledge, New York.

Pederson, S. (1991) National bodies, unspeakable acts: The sexual politics of colonial policy-making. *Journal of Modern History*, 63 (4), 647–80.

Phillips, R. (2005) Heterogeneous imperialism and the regulation of sexuality in British West Africa. *Journal of the History of Sexuality*, 14 (3), 291–315.

Phillips, R. (2006) *Sex, Politics and Empire: A Postcolonial Geography*. Manchester University Press, Manchester.

Sarkar, T. (2010) *Hindu Wife, Hindu Nation: Community, Religion, and Cultural Nationalism*. Indiana University Press, Bloomington.

Scully, P. (1995) Rape, race, and colonial culture: The sexual politics of identity in the nineteenth-century Cape Colony, South Africa. *American Historical Review*, 100 (2), 335–59.

Stoler, A.L. (1992) Sexual affronts and racial frontiers: European identities and the cultural politics of exclusion in colonial Southeast Asia. *Comparative Studies in Society and History*, 34 (3), 514–51.

Stoler, A.L. (1997) Making empire respectable: The politics of race and sexual morality in twentieth-century colonial cultures, in *Situated Lives: Gender and Culture in Everyday Life* (ed. L. Lamphere, H. Ragoné, and P. Zavella). Routledge, New York, pp. 373–99.

Stoler, A.L. (2002) *Carnal Knowledge and Imperial Power: Race and the Intimate in Colonial Rule*. University of California Press, Berkeley.

Walser Smith, H. (1998) The talk of genocide, the rhetoric of miscegenation: Notes on debates in the German Reichstag concerning Southwest Africa, 1904–1914, in *The Imperialist Imagination: German Colonialism and Its Legacy* (ed. S. Friedrichsmeyer, S. Lennox, and S. Zantop). University of Michigan Press, Ann Arbor, MI, pp. 107–24.

Williamson, T. (1810) *East India Vade Mecum; or, Complete Guide to Gentlemen Intended for the Civil, Military, or Naval Service of the Honourable East India Company*. Black, Parry & Kingsbury, London.

Suggested Reading

Ballantyne, T. and Burton, A. (eds) (2008) *Moving Subjects: Gender, Mobility, and Intimacy in an Age of Global Empire*. University of Illinois Press, Urbana-Champaign.

Briggs, L. (2002) *Reproducing Empire: Race, Sex, Science, and U.S. Imperialism in Puerto Rico*. University of California Press, Berkeley.

Clancy-Smith, J. and Gouda, F. (eds) (1998) *Domesticating the Empire: Race, Gender and Family Life in French and Dutch Colonialism*. University Press of Virginia, Charlottesville.

Ghosh, D. (2008) *Sex and the Family in Colonial India: The Making of Empire*. Cambridge University Press, Cambridge.

Hyam, R. (1991) *Empire and Sexuality*. Manchester University Press, Manchester.

Levine, P. (2003) *Prostitution, Race, and Politics: Policing Venereal Disease in the British Empire*. Routledge, New York.

McClintock, A. (1995) *Imperial Leather: Race, Gender, and Sexuality in the Colonial Contest.* Routledge, New York.

Phillips, R. (2006) *Sex, Politics and Empire: A Postcolonial Geography.* Manchester University Press, Manchester.

Stoler, A.L. (2002) *Carnal Knowledge and Imperial Power: Race and the Intimate in Colonial Rule.* University of California Press, Berkeley.

4

Sex and Disease from Syphilis to AIDS

Laura J. McGough and Katherine E. Bliss

O my dear Candide! You knew Paquette, that pretty lady's maid to our noble Baroness. In her arms I tasted the delights of paradise, and in turn they have led me to these torments of hell by which you now see me devoured. She had the disease, and may have died of it by now. Paquette was made a present of it by a very knowledgeable Franciscan who had traced it back to its source. For he had got it from an old countess, who had contracted it from a captain in the cavalry, who owed it to a marchioness, who had it from a page, who had caught it from a Jesuit, who, during his noviciate, had inherited it in a direct line from one of Christopher Columbus's shipmates. (Voltaire)

Sex and disease: as this quotation from the eighteenth-century French writer Voltaire suggests, the association between sex and disease forms part of our history and our cultural imagination. In this description from his famous satire *Candide*, a sexually transmitted disease (in this case, probably syphilis) is passed person-to-person—from man to woman, woman to man, and man to man—in a long chain of infection that reveals all the hypocrisy and decadence of eighteenth-century European society. Since antiquity, human beings have recognized that sexual relations can result in disease, but they have not always agreed on the actual mechanism underlying illness. Does disease arise from sexual acts that particular societies

A Global History of Sexuality: The Modern Era, First Edition.
Edited by Robert M. Buffington, Eithne Luibhéid, and Donna J. Guy.
© 2014 Robert M. Buffington, Eithne Luibhéid, and Donna J. Guy.
Published 2014 by Blackwell Publishing Ltd.

perceive to be immoral? Does disease develop from faulty processes within the body during sexual activity, such as an imbalance in bodily fluids such as semen? Does disease occur through contagion from one person to another? Or is it through some combination of the three? Voltaire's understanding is distinctively modern and Western, with its emphasis on contagion and moral hypocrisy. But other societies have also emphasized the pathologies of individual bodies and the moral transgressions of particular groups, especially marginalized groups such as prostitutes or ethnic, racial, and religious minorities. As this chapter will show, the history of sexuality and disease, particularly social commentary or debate about sexually transmitted infections, is always about much more than biology, sex, and disease: it is about deeply rooted social anxieties and fear, about the political, economic, and military security of different countries, and about how societies manage these anxieties and fears by projecting them onto others.

Methodological Issues: Problems in the Identification of Diseases

Sexually transmitted diseases or infections (STDs) are a broad modern category referring to a variety of pathogens, including viruses, bacteria, fungi, and protozoa, that manifest themselves through an equally wide variety of clinical symptoms. The common factor is the mode of transmission and acquisition: sexual relations between human beings. Many of these pathogens, such as chlamydia and human papillomavirus, have only been recently identified as part of the late twentieth-century expansion of biomedical research, which makes the historical study of these pathogens challenging. We may know STDs by their common rather than scientific names: the clap (gonorrhea), the pox (syphilis), the slim disease (HIV/ AIDS), and the hurps (herpes). Some are feared, especially HIV/AIDS, while others are regarded as less serious, even as jokes (e.g. "What's the difference between love and herpes?" "Herpes lasts forever."). Most important from a historian's perspective: STDs vary widely in how long they have been part of human history. Gonorrhea has been recognized since antiquity, while HIV/AIDS was identified only during the 1980s.

It is difficult to identify modern diseases based on the written historical record and on human remains. Descriptions of symptoms are often vague, referring to pustules or sores, or deeply influenced by changing cultural and social perceptions of disease. For example, late fifteenth- and early sixteenth-century Europeans emphasized the religious and moral dimensions of disease, often describing it as God's punishment for sin. When an epidemic of a new disease—probably syphilis—was first described in Italy in 1496 after the French troops invaded Italy, the disease was symbolically associated with the biblical figure of Job, who suffered from ugly, incurable skin sores that covered his body from head to toe. And because fifteenth-century observers perceived the new disease in this way, they recorded symptoms that conformed to their understanding of Job's illness (Arrizabalaga et al. 1997). Very few scientific accounts of disease exist for centuries of human history, which severely limits historians' ability to identify with precision whether or not a certain illness was really an STD.

Physical evidence produces equal challenges. Since blood and tissue do not survive for long after death, in nearly all cases researchers have only skeletal remains to evaluate. The problem with relying on skeletal remains is that the impact of a sexually transmitted disease such as syphilis on the human body can be similar to that of other non-sexually-transmitted diseases, such as yaws. For example, both syphilis and yaws are caused by the same species (*Treponema pallidum*), which makes precise identification difficult. In the case of diseases identified during recent times, notably HIV/AIDS, historians are much luckier. Scientists identified the retrovirus responsible for HIV/AIDS only in 1983, but, when researchers tested blood samples preserved from a mid-twentieth-century study of malaria in equatorial Africa, they encountered the earliest known case of HIV/AIDS in a man living in Leopoldville (now Kinshasa, Democratic Republic of the Congo) in 1959 (Iliffe 2006, p. 3). Although this direct evidence shows that HIV/AIDS existed as early as the 1950s in equatorial Africa, it was rare at that time and had probably existed since the late nineteenth or early twentieth century (Worobey et al. 2008).

Stigma and Shame: Enduring Themes

The stigma and shame associated with sexually transmitted disease constitute one of the most enduring themes in its global history. Stigma has made it difficult to discuss the historical origins of STDs such as syphilis and HIV/AIDS in neutral terms. HIV/AIDS was initially described during the 1980s as a gay or Haitian disease, while the origins of syphilis—possibly in the area now known as the Dominican Republic—remain a contested and heated topic. No region of the world wants its image tarnished as the originator of an STD and, since the etiology of most diseases is impossible to determine with any degree of certainty, STDs have proven especially effective at stigmatizing enemies or marginalized regions and groups. Moreover, stigma has devastating practical consequences on patients' access to care. The stigma associated with HIV/AIDS infection has been identified as one of the principal obstacles to testing and treatment worldwide. In addition, stigma keeps some patients from seeking treatment until they have reached an advanced stage of disease, when their chances of survival are less likely (Parker and Aggleton 2003).

Stigma and shame are embedded in wider social processes of power, domination, and social inequality. For this reason, they are more often directed at less powerful groups, reinforcing their marginal status. In particular, gender, race, and class prejudices are reinforced through stigma. Around the world, the stigma and shame associated with STDs have historically fallen more heavily on ethnic and racial minorities, on women rather than men, and on working classes rather than elites, serving in most cases to reproduce power structures in any given society (McGough 2011). For example, after 1800 or so, Western Europe's industrial revolution began to produce a new class of factory workers and urban dwellers, who over the course of the nineteenth century would increasingly and sometimes violently demand their political rights. The upper classes reacted to this threat by asserting class-based differences in intellectual and moral capacity, arguing among other things that their social "inferiors" were akin to animals, unable to control their sexual impulses. Thus, as European society became more hierarchical, class prejudices intersected with gender inequalities to shape attitudes toward sexuality and "venereal" diseases (named after Venus, the Roman goddess of love). Throughout Europe, efforts to control STDs by regulating sexual commerce gave widespread authority to police officers to arrest women they suspected of prostitution. And since authorities considered prostitution a prime indicator of the degeneracy of all working-class women—perhaps even a hereditary vice transmitted from mothers to daughters—any working-class woman appearing in public alone was suspect and could be forcibly detained, subjected to medical inspection, and humiliated in front of her neighbors.

The nineteenth century also witnessed the expansion of European power in Asia and Africa, as well as the development of systematic racist ideologies. In South Africa, for example, white medical officers regarded Africans as incapable of controlling their sexual impulses and therefore unfit for health education about STDs or preventive measures (Jochelson 2001).

European scientific approaches were also influential in Latin America. In Mexico, public officials began to regulate prostitution beginning in the 1860s, during the French occupation, copying the rules developed by Alexandre Parent-Duchâtelet for sexual commerce in Paris. They justified the move as intended to protect French troops from being infected by "loose" Mexican women (Bliss 2001). Other countries in the region that adopted regulatory frameworks, such as Argentina and Guatemala, viewed the rules as both essential public health measures and indicators of modernity and sophistication (McCreery 1986; Guy 1991).

Historical patterns of domination influence perceptions of who is at risk of disease and therefore which groups and geographic areas need to be "contained" as potential contagious agents. In recent years, for example, the dominant Han ethnic group in China has focused on members of the minority ethnic group Tai Lue as dangerous vectors of disease, citing their alleged lack of sexual inhibitions as a risk factor for HIV/AIDS. Because of widespread misperceptions about Tai Lue sexual mores, prostitutes of various ethnic groups, including Han, sometimes dress in traditional Tai Lue costumes to attract customers, an appropriation and commodification of Tai Lue sexuality that works to reinforce misperceptions about the alleged threat the group poses to Chinese society. Contemporary Han preoccupations with the Tai Lue as a diseased group come out of a long history of marginalization. In 1838, an American Protestant missionary described the Tai Lue region of Sipsongpanna as a country of "darkness" due to ignorance, superstition, and sin; and, during the 1950s, Communist Party ethnographers described the area as plagued by malaria and leprosy (Hyde 2007).

Domination can also influence who is actually vulnerable to disease. A vicious cycle can quickly develop in which political and economic domination of a marginalized group constrains economic options, resulting in higher rates of migration, family instability, drug and alcohol abuse, and prostitution. And these factors, in turn, make individuals more vulnerable to STD acquisition. Subsequent higher rates of disease in minority groups then confirm the misperception that their cultural practices, rather than their political and economic domination, are the underlying problem. In late 1970s West Africa, for example, the minority Krobo ethnic group of Ghana suffered disproportionately from declining world cocoa prices, which led to high rates of migration to cities and participation in prostitution. Reinforced by more than 150 years of Christian missionary criticism of the Krobo's "heathen" religious and cultural practices, the dominant

Akan ethnic majority blamed Krobo culture for higher rates of HIV rather than acknowledging underlying economic problems and restricted opportunities for ethnic Krobo people (Steegstra 2006).

Even when treatment is available, it may be provided in ways that reproduce the stigmatizing links between an STD and a marginalized group. For example, in eighteenth-century England, a middle-class patient suffering from the "foul disease," syphilis, could pay for confidential treatment from private physicians, while the poor had to make a public declaration of their disease in order to qualify for charitable treatment (Siena 2004). In early twentieth-century Uganda, colonial authorities carried out compulsory mass treatments with mercury injections of entire villages; and, during the same period, public health officials in Southern Rhodesia (now Zimbabwe) sometimes destroyed Africans' homes as a disease-prevention measure, while whites enjoyed voluntary treatment without punitive measures (Lyons 1999; McCulloch 1999). As these examples suggest, the powerful symbols that link STDs and social stigmatization of marginalized groups make it difficult for historians to see past the distortions that link produces.

Control of Prostitution: A Key Theme in STD Control

The regulation of prostitution is one of the most controversial aspects of STD control efforts—efforts that range from sixteenth-century Italian authorities' failed attempts to curb syphilis by encouraging prostitutes to repent and become nuns to the late twentieth-century Thai government's successful program to control HIV/AIDS by requiring all brothel-based prostitutes to use condoms. Efforts to control STDs have typically shifted between regulation of legalized prostitution, usually at the municipal level, by requiring registration cards and regular medical checkups to inspect for signs of sexually transmitted infection, and efforts to abolish prostitution through the criminalization and prosecution of women practicing sexual commerce. Control of STDs has been virtually synonymous with the problem of prostitution, especially from the perspective of the governments of Europe and the United States, although approaches to the problem have differed. Regardless of approach, the behavior that mattered most to public health officials was whether or not prostitutes regularly sought medical treatment and thereby avoided spreading infection to their male clients. Moreover, because authorities regarded prostitutes as a marginal class that was unlikely to seek medical care, they focused on controlling their behavior through legal regulation and police enforcement.

Regulation of prostitution reinforced class, race, and ethnic prejudices, since lower-class women or nonwhite women were regarded as potential prostitutes simply because of their marginalized status. Laws that allowed for the detention of suspect women provided police in Europe with considerable power, which they often abused through arbitrary arrest and detention. This period also witnessed considerable expansion of European power into Asia and Africa, including the colonization of non-European territories, and Europeans brought their preoccupations about STDs and prostitution to the territories that they ruled. In parts of Asia and Africa, the first large-scale efforts to control STDs occurred during the colonial period. Europeans were primarily concerned with protecting European soldiers from being infected by native prostitutes but regulation of prostitution included the segregation of commercial sex workers by race and class to ensure a "European" environment for the wealthiest and most discerning customers, while it was expected that laborers, drivers, porters, and other men of lesser means would visit the lowest-class brothels. With few if any exceptions, colonized peoples understood that STD prevention and control efforts were for the benefit of the rulers, not the ruled, and that "behavioral interventions" were directed at the colonized population, not the colonizers and their military personnel, who were also responsible for the spread of STDs.

The French took the lead in advocating the legalization and regulation of prostitution rather than its prohibition. Regarding prostitution as a necessary but unpleasant reality, much like the need for sewer systems in modern cities, French authorities favored lifelong surveillance and regular medical inspection of prostitutes as a means of reducing the dangers of extramarital activity, especially for bourgeois families. Other countries, such as Italy and Russia, emulated the French system. Unfortunately, because nineteenth-century medical therapies were of limited efficacy, the medical inspection of prostitutes was often as dangerous to their health as it was beneficial. Russian women were routinely rounded up and subjected to forced medical examinations in which the same speculum was used on successive women without cleaning the instrument, thereby making iatrogenic transmission a strong possibility (Corbin 1990; Bernstein 1995).

Britain briefly experimented with the legalization and regulation of prostitution because of demands made by the British Army to provide a "sexual outlet" for enlisted men who were not allowed to marry. The 1860s Contagious Diseases Acts granted a wide range of regulatory powers to the police, including the right to detain any woman suspected of venereal infection pending medical inspection. Because nineteenth-century medical authorities had limited ability to detect syphilis or gonorrhea through physical examinations, this approach was doomed to failure. The negative social consequences, however, were dramatic since many police and public health officials suspected virtually any working-class woman of involvement in prostitution. Although prostitution was not confined to the ranks of working-class women—men, boys, and women of considerably higher social standing also worked as prostitutes—it was working-class women who bore the brunt of police harassment. Soldiers, for example, were not subject to medical inspection. This pervasive sexual double standard provoked political protests from an alliance of working-class and middle-class women, and led to the eventual repeal of the Contagious Diseases Acts in 1886 (Walkowitz 1980).

The British brought this system of STD regulation to India. In 1886, the military authorities pushed to make attractive local women available to British troops. Although the British Army focused on Indian women as a potential source of disease for its soldiers, it is likely that the reverse was as much of a problem. In fact, hospital admission rates for STDs in the Native Army (composed of Indian soldiers) was one-tenth that of the British Army (Kaminsky 1979). From the perspective of many Indian observers, it was the behavior of white troops, not Indian women, that was causing disease transmission. For Indian nationalists, venereal disease and prostitution became symbols of the abuses of colonialism, and the eighth Indian National Congress went so far as to publicly decry state regulation of prostitution in 1892 (Levine 1996). Similarly, in Shanghai, China, where the French, British, and Americans exercised considerable political influence, the regulation of Chinese prostitutes led to tensions between whites and Chinese authorities. From the European perspectives, STDs were a local problem, spread from Chinese prostitutes to European soldiers; the Chinese perspective unsurprisingly was the opposite, especially in the case of syphilis, which Chinese physicians argued had not existed in China prior to European military domination (Hershatter 1997).

The nineteenth-century experiment in the regulation of prostitution as the key to STD control illustrates some of the problems with this strategy. Because the lower classes, racial and ethnic minorities, and women were virtually always overrepresented among the population of sex workers, efforts to regulate sex workers often exacerbated existing social and economic inequalities and increased their vulnerability to disease and exploitation. Regulatory efforts typically devolved into punitive approaches that targeted one group, sex workers, while neglecting the wider dynamics of disease transmission throughout the population. These punitive approaches also undermined disease-control efforts because many patients, fearing punishment, avoided medical treatment and care.

The Military and STD Control

As the above examples suggest, military policy toward STDs was closely allied to the control of prostitution in the civilian population. One major reason for the nineteenth-century legalization of prostitution was to provide access to sexual relationships for military personnel, especially those stationed abroad in European-dominated parts of Asia and Africa. On both the literal and symbolic levels, militaries enforce national boundaries, which makes sexual relationships with "native" women—who are typically nonwhite—a troubling issue for both colonial powers and colonized nations. Fear of biological, political, and racial contamination resulted in military policies to regulate and control relations between soldiers and prostitutes, while colonized nations resented what they perceived as an affront to their collective morality. Military prostitution policies thus provoked anticolonial sentiments at home and abroad at the same time that colonial occupations put pressure on public health authorities to come up with new means of preventing and controlling STDs, whether through new policies or new medical research.

Wartime often intensified military concerns about the spread of STDs. During World War I, military officials in the United States tried to control STDs through criminalization. Not only did military officials discourage soldiers and sailors from patronizing prostitutes but also the acquisition of an STD became a crime, subject to loss of pay. At the same time, many medical officers argued that this policy only worsened the health problems of the military forces, since soldiers and sailors avoided treatment as a means of escaping punishment (Brandt 1987). Political pressure by leading military commanders brought a change in American policy for World War II. Infected military personnel were no longer punished, and prevention and treatment were encouraged. Before the advent of penicillin, wartime brought significant government attention, as well as increased resources, to STD control. Because STDs affected precisely the demographic group (young men aged between eighteen and twenty-five) needed to fight wars and caused significant loss of fighting days due to illness, governments

Figure 4.1 World War I venereal disease prevention poster aimed at French military conscripts. The text reads: "Soldier, the country is counting on you, reserve all your strength . . . Resist the seductions of the street where you might contract the disease more dangerous than war . . . It leads its victims into decay and a useless, unhappy death."

Figure 4.2   World War II venereal disease prevention poster aimed at US servicemen, "She May Look Clean—But . . ."

changed their policies from peacetime neglect to active, comprehensive STD control.

In the United States, Surgeon General Thomas Parran, already interested in reducing syphilis prevalence, seized on World War II as an opportunity to expand both civilian and military disease-control efforts. For civilians, residential Rapid Treatment Centers were opened all across the country. These centers provided free treatment, in addition to counseling, job training for wartime industries, and job placement following treatment. For military personnel, American wartime STD control focused on a simple dichotomy: women as vectors of disease, male soldiers as victims. Racy posters of voluptuous, scantily clad women with slogans such as "Booby Trap" disseminated fear-based messages about the dangers of women (Brandt 1987). The implementation of wartime STD control programs also revealed a complex interplay of race, class, and gender that influenced who was perceived as "innocent" and hence eligible for treatment and who was seen as "guilty" and hence subject to detention. In practice, some women— especially African American and working-class women—were subject to arbitrary arrest, inspection, and detention, simply for being suspected of being prostitutes (McGough and Handsfield 2007; McGough 2008). And, it was during this period that African American men were denied treatment for syphilis during the infamous Tuskegee experiment on the assumption that theirs was a "syphilis-soaked race"—a case that will be discussed later in this chapter.

Penicillin versus Prevention: The End of STDs?

World War II biomedical research also yielded one of the major triumphs of STD control: the 1943 discovery of penicillin as an effective therapy for the treatment of syphilis and gonorrhea. Although the discovery of penicillin was a major therapeutic breakthrough that saved lives, public health officials quickly came to regard it as a "magic bullet" that effectively ended the need for STD control (Brandt 1987). One unfortunate, unintended consequence of penicillin was a neglect of STD prevention and control efforts during the postwar era, making the world less prepared for and arguably more vulnerable to the eventual HIV/AIDS epidemic. Public health efforts to control STDs during peacetime were not a big priority; the availability of penicillin further accelerated this trend, with commercial sales of condoms being one of the few methods of STD prevention.

Condoms became widely available in the United States after a 1918 Supreme Court ruling established a solid legal basis for their sale. During the 1920s, condom sales moved from the "shameful" secrecy of mail-order purchases and the sanitized space of the pharmacy to the street as street peddlers, elevator operators, waiters, and bartenders were among the many who hawked condoms to ordinary men from every walk of life (Tone 2001). Meanwhile, other types of prevention, especially public education, were either completely ignored or poorly implemented. In the United States, for example, prevention efforts were undermined by the content of the messages themselves. Adolescent American boys, white and black, viewed educational posters about white men's responsibility to "lift up" inferior races by acting as role models of moral behavior and physical fitness (Lord 2003). After the advent of penicillin, colonial public health authorities in Africa and Asia lost interest in STD control and made no effort to initiate prevention and education activities since the "inferior races" were incapable of sexual control (Lyons 1999; Jochelson 2001).

Some have argued that the availability of penicillin increased sexual promiscuity, since people no longer feared STDs. Evidence for that hypothesis, however, is not persuasive. In fact, STD rates increased in Europe, the United States, and Australia between 1945 and 1948. Moreover, it is difficult to disaggregate the psychological effects of penicillin on sexual behavior from other factors during this same period. Most importantly, the end of war brought an end to the heavy fighting that characterized the final years of World War II, a period when few military personnel had the time or opportunity for sexual relations. During the postwar occupation, however, overseas military personnel had plenty of leisure time and disposable income. In occupied postwar Germany, for example, despite an American official ban on fraternization with German citizens, 25 percent of American GIs spent at least ten hours "talking" with German women every week (Willoughby 1998). And economic hardships, especially in occupied countries, made casual prostitution or relationships with soldiers one of the few economic opportunities for young women and men. Moreover, penicillin was unavailable for civilian populations in occupied countries for several years after the war. In 1948, when civilians gained access to penicillin in Germany, rates of STDs began to decline (Freund 2001). In short, penicillin was introduced at a time of massive social upheaval, increased mobility of displaced populations and military personnel, and unequal power relations between occupying armies and occupied countries. The combined effect of these factors (exacerbated by long-standing inequalities around race, ethnicity, class, and gender) on sexual behavior make it difficult to blame penicillin for increased STD rates in the years immediately following the war.

As previously noted, one major effect of the introduction of penicillin was a loss of interest in STD control. The public health and the medical fields alike regarded the threat of STDs as a thing of the past, a belief that would come back to haunt them in the era of AIDS. One significant exception to this trend was China. Partly because the Chinese had blamed STDs on foreign occupation and foreign cultural decadence, the Communist government adopted STD control as one of its major policy initiatives immediately after its 1949 political victory. In a campaign that included widespread public relations efforts through plays, radio programs, and small discussion groups, the government undertook a massive screening and treatment program, including vocational rehabilitation for former female sex workers (Dikötter 1997).

Controversies in STD History: Research Ethics and Surveillance

The history of STDs has generated its fair share of controversies, especially for violations of research ethics and personal privacy. The most notorious example of a breach in research ethics is the infamous Tuskegee syphilis study, described below. Controversies about the importance of patient confidentiality versus the protection of public health, which emerged as major issues in the postwar United States and Europe, still continue in the era of HIV/AIDS.

In 1972, when a journalist exposed the ongoing forty-year study of untreated syphilis in African Americans in Macon County, Alabama, the public reacted with shock and outrage. Because many African Americans still cite this study as one of the reasons for their mistrust of the public health system in general and AIDS prevention and treatment programs in particular, it is worth describing the study's historical origins as well as its legacy (Bogart and Thorburn 2005). Throughout the study's forty-year history, the United States Public Health Service (USPHS) misled the study subjects, 399 poor, rural African American men, who thought that they were receiving treatment for a serious disease when in fact treatment was withheld. Given the current importance of establishing and maintaining ethical research studies in developing countries, the lessons of Tuskegee have relevance to a wider audience than just the American public.

Prior to and during World War II, standards for experimental research differed significantly from what they are today. Although most researchers insisted that research subjects agree voluntarily to their roles, abuses occurred, especially in experiments on soldiers, who could be forced to participate by their superiors. Regardless, the concept of "voluntary consent" was interpreted much more broadly than today, with fewer protections of subjects' health and safety. A 1915 study on the causes of pellagra, for example, placed healthy male prisoners on a poor diet to determine whether they would develop the disease (and some did). The prisoners consented because they were offered pardons if they followed the diet for six months. Although a few critics argued that prisoners were in an inherently coercive situation in which they could not make independent decisions about participating in research, most people who knew about the study thought the conditions were fair or even generous. By today's standards, other research studies exploited the economic vulnerability of the poor, especially in the Depression years, when participation in research studies constituted the only available form of employment for some destitute subjects (Lederer 1995). These studies would not meet today's standards of voluntary, informed consent and freedom from coercion.

Even for its time, the Tuskegee study pushed the boundaries of acceptable research ethics. From the beginning, the research subjects were under the impression that they were receiving treatment for "bad blood," a vernacular term that covered a variety of conditions; they were never told that they had syphilis and were not receiving treatment for this disease. Consent was impossible because the subjects were never fully informed of what was happening (Jones 1993).

How did this situation arise? Part of the answer lies in the fact that the study was originally conceived in 1929 as a treatment program to show that syphilis could be controlled in rural parts of the South, where high disease burden, poverty, and the lack of roads and clinics made public health efforts particularly challenging. If public health officials could conquer syphilis in the rural South, then they thought they could provide convincing evidence of their ability to control syphilis throughout the country. Treatment at the time consisted of a series of painful intravenous injections of arsphenamine. With a charitable foundation on board to finance this massive treatment program, the initial work of testing blood began in 1930 in five counties in the rural South. By 1932, however, the Great Depression had wiped out the financial reserves of many foundations, making this ambitious treatment program unaffordable. In order to "salvage" the efforts that the USPHS had already directed toward blood testing and developing relationships with black churches and institutions, the USPHS leadership decided to convert the treatment program into a one-county research study, originally conceived as a project lasting between six months and a year (Jones 1993).

Race and class inequalities played a central role in the development of the study, since the researchers failed to treat their subjects as capable and competent adults. Furthermore, the subjects' inadequate access to health care provided a further justification for research since at the beginning of the trial medical facilities were so limited that none of the subjects would have been able to obtain treatment. The researchers thought that their study offered an improvement over existing conditions, since they provided hot meals, routine tonics and pain relievers such as aspirin, and $50 toward burial costs. The subjects' poverty thus served as a partial justification for the study (Brandt 2000). And, in a period of particularly brutal race relations characterized by public lynching and a resurgence of Ku Klux Klan activities, the researchers' milder, paternalistic (but nonetheless insidious) form of racial prejudice no doubt seemed less "racist" than the openly genocidal fantasies of some of their contemporaries.

The injustices of the original study were compounded and prolonged as the study continued. After penicillin became available in 1943, it was never offered to study subjects. Worse yet, those who would have received penicillin because of their military service were denied treatment. Only after a journalist reported the story in 1972 was the study halted (Jones 1993). The factors that made the Tuskegee experiment so controversial—racialized beliefs about disease vulnerability and the use of vulnerable populations as research subjects—also characterized medical research in other countries within the United States' sphere of influence. In Guatemala from 1946 to 1948, USPHS officials developed a study of the effects of syphilis infection on prison inmates, children living in orphanages, soldiers living in barracks, and mental asylum patients that involved deliberately infecting research subjects with syphilis and then treating them with penicillin. The abuses of the Guatemala studies far exceeded those of the Tuskegee experiment, because African American subjects were never deliberately infected with syphilis as happened with the Guatemalan subjects. These overseas ethical violations were not reported until a few decades after the story broke about Tuskegee, and elicited a 2010 public apology from President Barack Obama to President Álvaro Colom of Guatemala (Reverby 2011). Apologies aside, the Guatemala example underscores the ease with which questionable research experiments carried out on marginalized and often racialized populations traveled across national borders.

But the Tuskegee study's ethical violations were troubling enough in their own right. The Tuskegee study quickly became a powerful symbol of the systemic racial injustice that African Americans had endured for more than a century after Emancipation. But it came as no surprise to an African American community whose mistrust of the medical profession and the "good intentions" of white society preceded the 1972 exposure of

Tuskegee. It is therefore important to understand African Americans' reaction to Tuskegee not in terms of a single, isolated event but in terms of its power to evoke their long historical experience of injustice and abuse (Gamble 1997).

While the Tuskegee research project involved the exploitation of a group of men because of their race and class, routine STD control efforts by public health agencies have sometimes exposed individuals to invasions of privacy, harassment, and loss of jobs because of their alleged deviation from societal norms regarding gender and sexuality. In postwar America, gay men were especially vulnerable to invasions of their privacy and, consequently, mistrustful of public health efforts to control STDs, which included keeping records on infected individuals. Among other things, the availability of penicillin had made public health officials less concerned with shielding patients' privacy and more concerned with tracking down as many carriers as possible to eliminate the disease before they infected others. Before the discovery of penicillin, most states had protected STD patients' confidentiality, treating them differently from people with diseases such as measles and smallpox. Because of the social stigma attached to STDs, most states allowed cases to be reported by a patient's initials or a serial number rather than by full name in order to protect their privacy. This "shielded" reporting became standard public health practice until 1946, when public health officials launched efforts to find the "missing million" patients with syphilis and later when laboratory-based reporting became widespread in the 1960s. Before 1946, public health officials had not known the names of patients. Afterwards, in order to contact STD patients identified in laboratory reports and interview them for names of sexual contacts, public health officials recorded their names and other identifying information. Although public health officials did not release the name of the original patient to the contacts they later interviewed, the definition of confidentiality and privacy had changed dramatically, and after the 1960s public health officials had access to information about patients that they had not previously possessed (Fairchild et al. 2003).

The fact that government employees (i.e., public health officials) had access to patients' names likely undermined efforts to build trust, especially with groups already suffering from government persecution. In 1947, for example, the US Park Police launched its "Pervert Elimination Campaign" to find and arrest gay men. Following this campaign, the McCarthy-inspired Federal Loyalty Program began, in which several thousand men and women lost their jobs because of allegations of homosexuality. To gather information about alleged traitors, vice squad officers frequented gay bars and clubs, interviewed suspects' coworkers, and compiled lists of "known" homosexuals (Johnson 2004). Public health officials frequently complained about homosexual men's unwillingness to cooperate during interviews but never connected their mistrust to the real risks homosexual men faced from local and federal government officials during the 1950s and 1960s. Trust between gay men and the public health system was already strained when gay American men began dying of a mysterious illness during the late 1970s and 1980s.

HIV/AIDS: From Panic to Activism

As happened with earlier STDs, the HIV/AIDS epidemic that began in the 1980s and continues to this day produced familiar tropes of stigma and shame directed at marginalized groups, first in the United States and later in other parts of the world, especially Africa. In June 1981 the US Centers for Disease Control and Prevention (CDC) released a brief study noting the appearance of unusual clusters of disease among young, otherwise healthy, gay men in New York and San Francisco. Over the next four years, scientists in the United States, Canada, and Europe rushed to study what appeared to be a previously unknown sexually transmitted infection believed to be associated with homosexual men and Haitians. When 2000 scientists from around the world met in Atlanta at the first International AIDS Conference to compare notes on the outbreak and to consider its implications for public health, many sharply criticized the Ronald Reagan administration's slow response to what was clearly becoming an epidemic. Critics charged that the administration was failing to prioritize research on AIDS or to adequately fund the CDC, National Institutes of Health, and federal agencies carrying out research on AIDS, because most AIDS victims at the time were homosexuals, immigrants, commercial sex workers, or Haitians—groups viewed with great suspicion by most Republican Party politicians and constituents. Two years later, in his first public address on the AIDS crisis, Reagan proposed mandatory testing for all prison inmates, immigrants, and those seeking a marriage license, a prevention strategy that human rights groups and others argued would lead to discrimination against people infected with HIV. By this point advocacy organizations, including Gay Men's Health Crisis and ACT UP (AIDS Coalition to Unleash Power), had formed to fight the homophobia in the public debate about AIDS and to urge a greater political response to the epidemic. In June 1987, activists mounted a vociferous protest against the administration including a march to the White House, where they confronted police wearing rubber gloves and protective personal gear.

By the late 1980s, limited successes in developing treatments and a sense that governments were not prioritizing research on HIV/AIDS because of its apparent concentration among stigmatized populations led advocates to adopt more dramatic tactics to ensure that their concerns were heard. In Montreal in 1989, during a speech by Prime Minister Brian Mulroney at the opening session of the International AIDS Conference, a coalition of advocates took advantage of media attention generated by the event to take the stage and make known their concerns about funding for research and the need for greater attention to stigma and discrimination. During this period it also became clear that HIV/AIDS was becoming more of a challenge in sub-Saharan Africa, with African governments reaching out to aid agencies in developed countries for help in dealing with an apparent AIDS epidemic concentrated for the most part within the heterosexual population. Some African leaders even broke their silence on HIV/AIDS in an effort to lessen the stigma associated with the disease. Taking the stage in Montreal, Zambian president Kenneth D. Kaunda apologized to the gathered crowd for his earlier indifference to HIV/AIDS, confessing that he had lost a son to the disease just three years earlier.

The dramatic upsurge in activism directed at a global media audience reached a peak at the 1990 International AIDS Conference in San Francisco. At the height of public debate over 1987 congressional legislation that barred HIV-infected people from immigrating or traveling to the United States, the Seattle chapter of ACT UP staged an "invasion" of San Francisco's Nordstrom department store to protest alleged discrimination against an HIV-infected employee, and during the closing session of the conference shouting protesters drowned out the closing speech of the US Secretary of Health and Human Services, Louis Sullivan. As advocacy for funding and research for HIV/AIDS continued to escalate, activist pressure and a growing awareness that the epidemic was increasingly international lent greater urgency to scientific efforts to identify potential treatments, vaccines, and cures for HIV/AIDS (Bliss 2012).

HIV/AIDS in Africa

Although HIV/AIDS was first identified in North America, the virus itself probably originated in equatorial Africa. Claims about the African origins of HIV/AIDS are controversial, because, as already discussed, theories about the origins of STDs are often deployed to stigmatize marginalized populations, countries, and even continents. It is not the intention of this chapter to contribute to this problem. Every part of the world, after all, has contributed its share of infectious diseases to the human population: according to the best evidence available, tuberculosis and smallpox originated in Europe, avian influenza in Asia, the 1918 influenza pandemic in North America, and syphilis in the Caribbean. And, wherever their origins, each disease was quickly caught up in transnational circuits of conquest, commercial exchange, and migration that spread far beyond its point of origin. But, if the HIV virus did indeed originate in Africa, this might explain why Africa has been hit the hardest by the epidemic and might dispel suggestions—derived most likely from missionary accounts and colonial racist ideologies—that African sexual behavior differs significantly from that anywhere else in the world.

The theory that HIV/AIDS originated in equatorial Africa rests on analyses of the DNA of various strains of HIV. According to this theory, HIV is an adaptation of Simian Immunodeficiency Virus (SIV), which transferred from animals to human somewhere in western equatorial Africa, the broad area spanning Cameroon to the Democratic Republic of the Congo. There are two major types of HIV, known as HIV-1 and HIV-2, but HIV-1 is the one responsible for the pandemic. In addition, HIV-1 has a multitude of subvarieties. Western equatorial Africa harbored all three groups of HIV-1 (M, N, and O) and all subgroups of the dominant group M. By contrast, all other regions of the world have just one or two dominant subgroups. The great diversity of strains of HIV-1 in western equatorial Africa suggests that it originated and had time to evolve various strains there (Iliffe 2006).

If HIV/AIDS originated in Africa, why was it not first detected there? First, western equatorial Africa lacked the public health infrastructure to detect new diseases that existed in the United States in the 1980s. Second, the biology of the disease—the slow progress from infection to the actual onset of symptoms, often as long as nine years—meant the virus could spread widely before it caused illness and came to the attention of health workers. Third, in Africa, HIV coexisted with an already entrenched tuberculosis epidemic. Those dying of tuberculosis may have been coinfected with HIV, but no one thought to investigate because their symptoms were attributed to tuberculosis (Iliffe 2006). By contrast, the Americans who were dying of HIV/AIDS in the 1970s and 1980s were, by and large, young and otherwise healthy. Medical knowledge of the time could not account for their deaths, which sparked further inquiry by a medical community with the resources to research the cause. Finally, twentieth-century Africa has experienced the dislocations of colonial rule, apartheid, independence struggles, civil wars, economic hardships, and large-scale migration. These dislocations have made African populations more vulnerable to infectious diseases.

It is nearly impossible to exaggerate the impact that the HIV/AIDS epidemic has had on certain regions of Africa, especially in the south. With over 30 percent of pregnant women in South Africa living with HIV in 2010, the epidemic has far-reaching consequences for households, the economy, and governance (AVERT 2011). Because AIDS deaths occur primarily among adults of reproductive age, their deaths impact household income, agricultural productivity, and care of children and the elderly. HIV/AIDS creates long-term changes in farming practices and agricultural productivity, as households reduce their involvement in labor-intensive practices, slowly allowing farmland to return to bush with subsequent environmental changes. Because of illness and mortality from HIV/AIDS, households have dissolved, family members dispersed, with orphans in particular less likely to attend school or get adequate nutrition and health care. In addition, the children of families who accept orphans into their households also suffer because of increased demands on scarce resources. Parts of sub-Saharan Africa remain severely stressed due to the impact of the epidemic.

HIV/AIDS: The Fight against the Disease Goes Global

By the late 1980s it had become clear to policymakers and AIDS researchers alike that the epidemic presented a special challenge in sub-Saharan Africa, with heterosexual transmission and mother-to-child transmission in particular requiring concerted action and intervention. As the epidemic continued to develop in North America and Europe primarily among groups considered to be at "high risk" and in Africa within a largely heterosexual population, scientific efforts focused on developing and perfecting pharmaceutical treatments that could alleviate the symptoms of HIV/AIDS and prolong the lives of patients living with the disease. At the 1996 International AIDS Conference in Vancouver, researchers announced the success of clinical trials of a combination of drugs known as antiretrovirals (ARVs).

Scientists noted that these "drug cocktails" appeared to reduce the presence of the virus in the blood and could extend life expectancy for people living with HIV/AIDS. But treatment was slow to reach the majority of those in need since most people with access to ARVs lived in developed countries whereas most of those infected resided in the developing world. As people began talking hopefully about "living with HIV" in developed countries, the majority was still dying of HIV globally.

This inequality began to change in the aftermath of the 2000 International AIDS Conference in Durban. The first meeting in a developing country, the Durban conference was significant because it took place against the backdrop of South African president Thabo Mbeki's continued refusal to recognize the links between HIV and AIDS. At the same time, its location in southern Africa, the epicenter of the global pandemic, enabled thousands of people living with HIV/AIDS to participate. Civil society organizations demanded that donor governments and aid agencies do more to ensure drug access for the neediest and most vulnerable populations, which prompted greater international collaboration on the issues. Following the Durban conference, the United Nations General Assembly held a special session on AIDS, the Group of Eight (G8) countries convened to discuss ways to scale up treatment options, and a combination of private donors and public agencies came together to form the Global Fund to Fight HIV/AIDS, Tuberculosis and Malaria. In the United States, efforts to support global AIDS programs finally accelerated with the announcement of the 2003 President's Emergency Plan for AIDS Relief (or PEPFAR). Some observers credit the influence of evangelical Christian groups, with their focus on "innocent" women and children victims of AIDS in Africa, as inspiring the George W. Bush administration to scale up the US response to the global crisis, including the implementation of controversial abstinence and monogamy campaigns (Burkhalter 2004).

HIV/AIDS: Effective Prevention and Control in Brazil, Thailand, and Uganda

Since the 1990s, three countries have emerged as global leaders in efforts to reverse the course of AIDS epidemics in their countries: Brazil, Uganda, and Thailand. A combination of treatment delivery and prevention efforts that emphasized changing risky sexual behaviors accounts for these successes. In Brazil, a condom distribution campaign, along with an emphasis on providing access to ARVs for all who need them, explain the country's successful response to HIV/AIDS, while in Uganda and Thailand partner reduction campaigns, along with condom distribution (in Thailand) in the early 1990s, led to apparent reductions in the number of HIV/AIDS cases (Wilson 2004). In all three cases, authorities made a conscious effort to avoid stigmatizing or shaming their target populations.

Following the Vancouver conference announcement that researchers had succeeded in developing drug "cocktail" therapies to arrest the course of AIDS in HIV-infected patients, the Brazilian government determined that it would make the ARVs available to all Brazilians who required access to them, free of charge (Biehl 2007). This decision was the result of at least two processes. First, in the early 1990s Brazilian officials had been dismayed to discover that the country was projected to have a potential 1.2 million AIDS cases by 2005 if aggressive action were not taken (Smallman 2007). Second, the health system established in Brazil following the 1985 transition to democracy from military dictatorship had a focus on the provision of universal care, with health declared a human right in Article 196 of the 1988 Constitution. Following the 1996 announcements, Brazilian officials worked quickly to negotiate advantageous prices for the purchase of mass quantities of combination drugs with pharmaceutical companies, threatening to issue compulsory licenses and to reverse engineer some of the most expensive drugs in order to produce generics directly for the national population if companies refused to lower prices.

Beyond providing treatment for those who needed it, Brazilian officials sought to address HIV/AIDS prevention, realizing that the sex trade among men and women was a prominent source of disease transmission. From the mid to late 1990s, the country benefited from a series of World Bank loans to carry out prevention campaigns emphasizing testing, condom use (particularly with multiple sex partners), and reaching out to vulnerable populations such as drug users, male and female sex workers, and men who have sex with men but do not consider themselves to be homosexual (Biehl 2007). Devising distinct safe-sex messages to reach these disparate groups, rather than focusing on a one-size-fits-all message, was key to Brazil's success (Smallman 2007). But Brazil's focus on prevention and treatment for sex workers, as well as its effort to uphold the constitutional promise of universal access to health care, presented problems in the international arena. In a highly publicized case that drew international attention, Brazil rejected $40 million in funding from the US PEPFAR and the US Agency for International Development in 2005 because of PEPFAR's "prostitution clause," which prohibited assisting sex workers. In their rejection of PEP-FAR's moralistic agenda, Brazilian officials explained that sexual commerce was not illegal in Brazil and that to refrain from funding organizations that provide assistance to sex workers would contradict its policy of universal access to health as a human right (Bliss 2010).

In Uganda, strong political leadership combined with a sustained campaign to change risky sexual behaviors led to early successes in reversing the country's HIV/AIDS epidemic. In the 1980s, Uganda faced one of the heaviest HIV burdens in sub-Saharan Africa. Starting in the 1990s, well before the infusion of massive overseas development dollars, political leadership promoted changes in sexual behavior and public health response to HIV/AIDS. The Ministry of Health initiated regular surveillance and monitoring in order to have an accurate assessment of the HIV/AIDS situation, while the creation of the multisectoral Ugandan AIDS Commission, involving not just the Ministry of Health but also the labor and defense ministries, moved HIV prevention and treatment efforts outside clinics and hospitals and into the mainstream of society. At the same time, Uganda's President Yoweri Museveni openly discussed HIV and promoted initiatives to reduce stigma (Parkhurst 2001). Uganda is perhaps best known for its programs aimed at changing sexual behavior, including "love carefully," "love faithfully," and "zero grazing," all of which emphasized the importance of reducing the number of sex partners and delaying the onset of sexual relations. These programs involved some tradeoffs. Ugandan officials were discreet about distributing condoms so as not to offend the Catholic Church, which was a powerful force in the country. For its part, the Catholic Church became active in spreading AIDS-prevention messages, with priests reading testimonies by prominent citizens with AIDS exhorting the population not to follow their examples of sexual promiscuity (Allen and Heald 2004).

Thailand's successes at HIV/AIDS prevention have also rested on open policies toward sexual behavior, with condom distribution and surveillance of commercial sex establishments being a key element of the country's 1990s campaign to reverse the course of the HIV/AIDS epidemic. Just a few years earlier, in 1988, Thai authorities had noted the relatively higher prevalence of HIV among sex workers in the country. Thai public health experts were also aware that for some time most men seeking treatment in the country's network of STD clinics had indicated that they had become ill after visiting a prostitute. Indeed, by the early 1990s they had observed a sharp uptick in the number of HIV/AIDS cases, particularly notable among military recruits and commercial sex workers in the northern part of the country. Over the next few years, the Ministry of Public Health, in cooperation with the national HIV/AIDS Prevention and Control Programme, instituted the 100% Condoms program, which was focused exclusively on promoting the use of condoms to prevent the spread of HIV within commercial sex establishments, including brothels, tea houses, bars, and massage parlors where prostitutes were believed to offer direct and indirect services. By December 1994 surveys showed that nearly 90 percent of sex acts within commercial establishments involved condom use (Rojanapithayakorn and Hanenberg 1996, p. 6).

Several factors account for the decline in the number of HIV/AIDS diagnoses after the institution of the 100% Condom campaign, particularly once condom use in brothels became mandatory after 1992. First, the number of commercial sex workers declined, as did the number of clients, perhaps in response to the perceived dangers of being infected with HIV through sex work. Second, the public sector provided condoms free of charge to sex workers who reported to STD clinics for weekly checkups. Prostitution has been illegal in Thailand since 1960, but the government's relatively tolerant policy toward sexual commerce enabled frequent contact between public health authorities and prostitutes as well as brothel operators in order to enforce the condom use requirements. Third, the 100% Condom program took place at the same time as a relatively explicit mass marketing campaign on the radio, television, and print media that promoted condom use with sex workers (Rojanapithayakorn and Hanenberg 1996). In all three cases, then, governments' willingness to engage with the realities of HIV/AIDS transmission and downplay the stigmatizing effects of STDs on marginalized groups produced impressive results.

Global Response and Continued Challenges

On World AIDS Day, December 1, 2011, the joint United Nations program on HIV/AIDS (UNAIDS) estimated that there were then 34 million people living with the disease. The news is not all bad. The availability of ARVs extends the lives of those who formerly would have died, therefore increasing the overall numbers of people living with HIV/AIDS. Treatment is reaching 6.6 million people in middle- and low-income countries, which represents significant progress in a decade but still means that less than half of those who need treatment are receiving it (UNAIDS 2011, p. 6). The examples of Brazil, Thailand, and Uganda show that countries can make a difference in controlling their epidemics and reducing new infections, if they have the political will and take a realistic (rather than moralistic) approach to the problem. Since 2008 and the onset of the global economic crisis, HIV/AIDS has been retreating from the global agenda, threatening to leave millions untreated. In a time of cutbacks in government spending, a new era of activism may be required to sustain prevention and treatment programs. As the historical example of penicillin shows, new drugs represent a major breakthrough, but if public health efforts to prevent and control STDs wane, the disease can stage a comeback.

As the global HIV/AIDS pandemic continues to unfold, STDs persist in many populations worldwide. In the United States, the CDC reported there was an upward trend in diagnosed syphilis cases between 2000 and 2006, especially among men, with most reported cases occurring among men who have sex with men (CDC 2009). While syphilis remains susceptible to control by antibiotics, several strains of gonorrhea have become antibiotic resistant, creating challenges for public health authorities in regions as diverse as North America, East Asia, and Australia (Blue 2011). Recent controversies over administering vaccines to young women to prevent human papillomavirus infection, and thus cervical cancer, signal that public debates over sex, disease, and morality continue to proliferate (Goldstein 2011).

Disentangling and analyzing the complex relationships between sexuality, morality, and disease remains an essential part of the struggle to control STDs. The social and legal discrimination against those infected with STDs—partly stemming from the conflation of morality and disease—remains among the greatest hindrances to public health efforts to mitigate the death and suffering that STDs cause. In recent years, groups ranging from sex worker networks to advocates for the decriminalization of drug use have advanced the concept of human rights as a way of addressing social and cultural obstacles that stand in the way of enhanced response to STDs and especially the global HIV/AIDS pandemic. Participants at the 2008 International AIDS Conference in Mexico City staged the first International March against Stigma, Discrimination, and Homophobia, perhaps initiating the new era of activism. If so, activists will need to keep in mind the historical lessons of centuries of human response to STDs. Stigma and discrimination are enmeshed in wider relations of power and inequality: geopolitical inequalities between and within nations, and the complex interplay of race, ethnicity, gender, and class. To tackle STDs and the HIV/AIDS epidemic, activists will need to confront the legacy of stigma and discrimination that is enmeshed with and implicated in these multiple inequalities.

References

Allen, T. and Heald S. (2004) HIV/AIDS policy in Africa: What has worked in Uganda and what has failed in Botswana? *Journal of International Development*, 16, 1141–54.

Arrizabalaga, J., Henderson, J., and French, R. (1997) *The Great Pox: The French Disease in Renaissance Europe*. Yale University Press, New Haven.

AVERT (2011) South Africa HIV and AIDS Statistics. www.avert.org/south-africa -hiv-aids-statistics.htm (accessed July 30, 2013).

Bernstein, L. (1995) *Sonia's Daughters: Prostitutes and Their Regulation in Imperial Russia*. University of California Press, Berkeley.

Biehl, J. (2007) *Will to Live: AIDS Therapies and the Politics of Survival*. Princeton University Press, Princeton.

Bliss, K.E. (2001) *Compromised Positions: Prostitution, Public Health and Gender Politics in Revolutionary Mexico City*. Penn State University Press, University Park, PA.

Bliss, K.E. (2010) Health in all policies: Brazil's approach to global health within foreign policy and development cooperation initiatives, in *Key Players in Global Health: How Brazil, China, India, Russia and South Africa Are Influencing the Game* (ed. K.E. Bliss). Center for Strategic and International Studies, Washington, DC, p. 7.

Bliss, K.E. (2012) The International AIDS Conference Returns to the United States: Lessons from the Past and Opportunities for July 2012. A Report of the CSIS Global Health Policy Center. Center for Strategic and International Studies, Washington, DC.

Blue, L. (2011) Scientists discover drug-resistant gonorrhea "superbug." *Time*, July 11. http://healthland.time.com/2011/07/11/scientists-discover-drug-resistant -gonorrhea-superbug (accessed July 30, 2013).

Bogart, L.M. and Thorburn, S. (2005) Are HIV/AIDS conspiracy beliefs a barrier to HIV prevention among African Americans? *JAIDS*, 38, 213.

Brandt, A.M. (1987) *No Magic Bullet: A Social History of Venereal Disease in the United States Since 1880*. Oxford University Press, New York.

Brandt, A.M. (2000) Racism and research: The case of the Tuskegee syphilis experiment, in *Tuskegee's Truths: Rethinking the Tuskegee Syphilis Study* (ed. S.M. Reverby). University of North Carolina Press, Chapel Hill, pp. 15–33.

Burkhalter, H. (2004) The politics of AIDS: Engaging conservative activists. *Foreign Affairs*, January/February. www.foreignaffairs.com/articles/59526/

holly-burkhalter/the-politics-of-aids-engaging-conservative-activists (accessed July 30, 2013).

Centers for Disease Control and Prevention (CDC) (2009) Syphilis & MSM (Men Who Have Sex with Men)—CDC Fact Sheet. www.cdc.gov/std/syphilis/STDFact-MSM-Syphilis.htm (accessed August 8, 2013).

Corbin, A. (1990) *Women for Hire: Prostitution and Sexuality in France after 1850* (trans. A. Sheridan). Harvard University Press, Cambridge, MA.

Dikötter, F. (1997) A history of sexually transmitted diseases in China, in *Sex, Disease, and Society: A Comparative History of Sexually Transmitted Diseases and HIV/AIDS in Asia and the Pacific* (ed. M. Lewis, S. Bamber, and M. Waugh). Greenwood Press, Westport, CT, pp. 67–83.

Fairchild, A.L., Colgrove, J., and Bayer, R. (2003) The myth of exceptionalism: The history of venereal disease reporting in the twentieth century. *Journal of Law, Medicine & Ethics*, 31, 624–37.

Freund, M. (2001) Women, venereal disease and the control of female sexuality in post-war Hamburg, in *Sex, Sin and Suffering: Venereal Disease and European Society since 1870* (ed. R. Davidson and L.A. Hall). Routledge, New York, pp. 205–19.

Gamble, V.N. (1997) Under the shadow of Tuskegee: African Americans and health care. *American Journal of Public Health*, 87 (11), 1773–8.

Goldstein, D. (2011) Untangling the HPV vaccine debate. *The Nation*, September 14. www.thenation.com/blog/163378/untangling-hpv-vaccine-debate#axzz2a Wk7MHXY (accessed July 30, 2013).

Guy, D.J. (1991) *Sex and Danger in Buenos Aires: Prostitution, Family and Nation in Argentina*. University of Nebraska Press, Lincoln.

Hershatter, G. (1997) *Dangerous Pleasures: Prostitution and Modernity in Twentieth-Century Shanghai*. University of California Press, Berkeley.

Hyde, S.T. (2007) *Eating Spring Rice: The Cultural Politics of AIDS in Southwest China*. University of California Press, Berkeley.

Iliffe, J. (2006) *The African AIDS Epidemic: A History*. James Currey, Oxford.

Jochelson, K. (2001) *The Colour of Disease: Syphilis and Racism in South Africa, 1880–1950*. Palgrave, New York.

Johnson, D.K. (2004) *The Lavender Scare: The Cold War Persecution of Gays and Lesbians in the Federal Government*. University of Chicago Press, Chicago.

Jones, J.H. (1993) *Bad Blood: The Tuskegee Syphilis Experiment*, 2nd edn. Free Press, New York.

Kaminsky, A.P. (1979) Morality legislation and British troops in late nineteenth-century India. *Military Affairs*, 43 (2), 78–84.

Lederer, S.E. (1995) *Subjected to Science: Human Experimentation in America before the Second World War*. Johns Hopkins University Press, Baltimore.

Levine, P. (1996) Rereading the 1890s: Venereal disease as "constitutional crisis" in Britain and British India. *Journal of Asian Studies*, 55 (3), 585–612.

Lord, A. (2003) Models of masculinity: Sex education, the United States public health service, and the YMCA, 1919–1924. *Journal of the History of Medicine*, 58, 123–52.

Lyons, M. (1999) Medicine and morality: A review of responses to sexually transmitted diseases in Uganda in the twentieth century, in *Histories of Sexually Transmitted Diseases and HIV/AIDS in Sub-Saharan Africa* (ed. P.W. Setel, M. Lewis, and M. Lyons). Greenwood Press, Westport, CT, pp. 97–117.

McCreery, D. (1986) This life of misery and shame: Female prostitution in Guatemala City, 1880–1920. *Journal of Latin American Studies*, 18, 333–53.

McCulloch, J. (1999) The management of venereal disease in a settler society: Colonial Zimbabwe, 1900–1930, in *Histories of Sexually Transmitted Diseases and HIV/AIDS in Sub-Saharan Africa* (ed. P.W. Setel, M. Lewis, and M. Lyons). Greenwood Press, Westport, CT, pp. 195–216.

McGough, L.J. (2008) Historical perspectives on sexually transmitted diseases: Challenges for prevention and control, in *Sexually Transmitted Diseases*, 4th edn (ed. K.K. Holmes and P. Piot). McGraw-Hill, New York, pp. 3–12.

McGough, L.J. (2011) *Gender, Sexuality and Syphilis in Early Modern Venice: The Disease that Came to Stay*. Palgrave Macmillan, Basingstoke.

McGough, L.J. and Handsfield, H. (2007). History of behavioral interventions for STDs, in *Behavioral Interventions for Prevention and Control of STDs, including HIV* (ed. S. Aral and J. Douglas). Springer SBM, New York, pp. 3–22.

Parker, R. and Aggleton, P. (2003) HIV and AIDS-related stigma and discrimination. *Social Science and Medicine*, 57 (1), 13–24.

Parkhurst, J.O. (2001) The crisis of AIDS and the politics of response: The case of Uganda. *International Relations*, 15 (6), 69–87.

Reverby, S.M. (2011) "Normal exposure" and inoculation syphilis: A PHS Tuskegee doctor in Guatemala, 1946–1948. *Journal of Policy History*, 23 (1), 6–28.

Rojanapithayakorn, W. and Hanenberg, R. (1996) The 100% condom program in Thailand. *AIDS*, 10, 1–7.

Siena, K.P. (2004) *Venereal Disease, Hospitals and the Urban Poor: London's "Foul Wards," 1600–1800*. University of Rochester Press, Rochester.

Smallman, S. (2007) *The AIDS Pandemic in Latin America*. University of North Carolina Press, Chapel Hill.

Steegstra, M. (2006) A "license to indulge in premature sexual activities"? Dipo and the image of Krobo women, in *Sex and Gender in an Era of AIDS: Ghana at the Turn of the Millenium* (ed. C. Oppong, I. Odotei, and P.A. Oppong). Sub-Saharan Publishers, Legon, Ghana, pp. 59–90.

Tone, A. (2001) *Devices and Desires: A History of Contraceptives in America*. Hill & Wang, New York.

UNAIDS (2011) *How to Get to Zero Faster, Smarter, Better*. Geneva, UNAIDS.

Walkowitz, J. (1980) *Prostitution and Victorian Society: Women, Class and the State*. Cambridge University Press, New York.

Willoughby, J. (1998) The sexual behavior of American GIs during the early years of the occupation of Germany. *Journal of Military History*, 62, 155.

Wilson, D. (2004) Partner reduction and the prevention of HIV/AIDS: The most effective strategies come from communities. *British Medical Journal*, 328 (7444), 848–9.

Worobey, M., Gemmel, M., Tuewen, D.E., et al. (2008) Direct evidence of extensive diversity of HIV-1 in Kinshasa by 1960. *Nature*, 455, 661–4.

Suggested Reading

Brandt, A.M. (1987) *No Magic Bullet: A Social History of Venereal Disease in the United States Since 1880*. Oxford University Press, New York.

Iliffe, J. (2006) *The African AIDS Epidemic: A History*. James Currey, Oxford.

Lewis, M., Bamber, S., and Waugh, M. (eds.) (1997) *Sex, Disease, and Society: A Comparative History of Sexually Transmitted Diseases and HIV/AIDS in Asia and the Pacific*. Greenwood Press, Westport, CT.

McGough, L.J. (2011) *Gender, Sexuality and Syphilis in Early Modern Venice: The Disease that Came to Stay*. Palgrave Macmillan, Basingstoke.

Setel, P.W., Lewis, M., and Lyons, M. (eds.) (1999) *Histories of Sexually Transmitted Diseases and HIV/AIDS in Sub-Saharan Africa*. Greenwood Press, Westport, CT.

Smallman, S. (2007) *The AIDS Pandemic in Latin America*. University of North Carolina Press, Chapel Hill, NC.

5

Sexuality and International Migration

Eithne Luibhéid

Political controversies reveal some of the dense connections between sexual regimes and international migration movements. Consider the heated debates about these questions: How to address sexual trafficking across borders? Should same-sex couples be recognized under immigration or asylum law? Is it acceptable to use images of same-sex couples kissing to assess the "citizenship readiness" of migrants in the Netherlands? Should migrants' children automatically receive citizenship at birth? On what grounds may government officials, employees, or private citizens who rape, sexually abuse, or sexually exploit migrants be prosecuted? Is it acceptable to send gay men and lesbians who sought asylum back to countries that prescribe the death penalty for homosexuality? When and how may immigration policy be used as a tool to fight the spread of HIV/AIDS? Do immigrants have fertility rates that differ from those of citizens, and, if they do, does this matter? These and other controversies reveal the myriad ways that sexual and immigration politics connect.

This chapter explores the historical connections between sexuality and international migration. It particularly focuses on migration since the late nineteenth century, when nation-states began to monopolize control over migration across international borders and increasingly justified such control as a matter of exercising "national sovereignty." Nation-state migration control systems grew from histories and practices associated with capitalism, colonialism, imperialism, slavery, the forced transportation of prisoners overseas, the expulsion of minorities and conquered peoples, and

A Global History of Sexuality: The Modern Era, First Edition.
Edited by Robert M. Buffington, Eithne Luibhéid, and Donna J. Guy.
© 2014 Robert M. Buffington, Eithne Luibhéid, and Donna J. Guy.
Published 2014 by Blackwell Publishing Ltd.

control over the movement of the poor. Over the course of the nineteenth and twentieth centuries, an international system of nation-states emerged from these processes and, although in theory each nation-state was equal, in practice, the international system continued to be dominated by certain nation-states at the expense of others. Nation-state strategies for controlling migration across borders became an important means to perpetuate these inequalities, although nation-states have rarely described immigration control in these ways.

The chapter first addresses the dynamics that have driven international migration. The second section explores the role of sexuality in these dynamics, a role that was largely overlooked or framed within other rubrics until the 1990s, when scholars began to challenge its erasure. The third section reviews key questions through which the interconnections between sexuality and migration have been researched and debated: 1) how do sexual norms, ideologies, and expectations shape and become reshaped by migration? and 2) how do receiving nation-states select and govern migrants through sexual regimes—and how do migrants respond? The conclusion draws the three sections together.

Rather than making distinctions between categories such as immigrant, emigrant, refugee, asylum seeker, undocumented immigrant, or temporary worker, this chapter uses the term "migrant" to refer to anyone who has crossed an international border. Further distinctions do not necessarily reflect empirical differences between migrants, who often shift from one status to another; rather, nation-states variously construct these categorical distinctions in order to constrain migrants' rights and legitimate their surveillance, discipline, and regulation.

Dynamics of Migration

Establishing control over migration was part of the more general rise of the centralized bureaucratic state and the "identification revolution" in the late nineteenth and early twentieth centuries that included the creation of the census, individual identity documents, and passports. It is important to understand that these documents did not codify identities that people already "had" but, rather, were tools through which people became classified, grouped, and managed in new ways that served nation- and state-building processes (Torpey 2000). The documents drew on technologies such as photography and fingerprinting that developed in the context of empire, policing, and transformations in the human sciences, and thus deployed and further entrenched long-standing racist, sexist, and colonial forms of knowledge. Identity cards and passports in particular tied individuals to bureaucratic identities and state-making projects that enabled their monitoring and governance.

Since the late nineteenth century, nation-states have often attempted to control migration across their borders, but achieving this goal was challenging in large part because control efforts rarely addressed the larger dynamics that drive migration in the first place. Yet, we need to understand these dynamics if we are to understand how sexuality interconnects with migration processes. The dynamics that drive migration are usually understood within one of three frameworks: push–pull, world systems, or transnationalism. In the United States, the push–pull framework dominates in policy-making and media coverage. This framework conceives migration as a rational act that is undertaken by a sovereign, implicitly male, individual who has calculated that the benefits outweigh the costs of crossing borders. The factors beyond individual decision-making that drive migration—and the role of powerful nation-states in creating and sustaining these factors—are largely ignored by the push–pull model. Also ignored is that, while people may wish to migrate, they often lack the necessary resources to do so (indeed, the poorest can rarely afford to migrate); the nation-states to which they want to migrate may not permit their entry (many countries are erecting more and more barriers); and processes that encourage or discourage migration are embedded in social and cultural networks that are larger than any individual.

A world-systems framework theorizes migration very differently from the push–pull model. Rather than focusing on sovereign individuals who make supposedly rational economic decisions, world-systems analysis links migration to the changing structures and demands of the global economy. According to world-systems analysis, migration across borders is driven by global economic dynamics. For example, "owners and managers of large firms in developed nations enter poor countries on the periphery of the world economy in search of land, raw material, labor, and markets. Migration is a natural outgrowth of the disruptions that occur" (Massey et al. 2002, p. 13), because these processes uproot people *and* create "bridges for migration" (Sassen 1992, pp. 14–15) between nation-states. The transportation and communication links that are formed under these conditions "not only facilitate the movement of goods, commodities, information, and capital but promote an opposing flow of people" (Massey et al. 2002,

p. 14). In many instances, such migration follows paths carved by prior colonial relationships, as when Jamaicans migrate to London, Indonesians to Amsterdam, and Algerians to France, while in other instances, new paths are emerging, such as the migration of Eastern European women to South Korea.

A world-systems approach thus stresses the importance of analyzing migration as a process that is rooted in the histories and dynamics of global capitalism over the past five centuries or more. This is a valuable corrective to the push–pull model, which focuses on individual decision-making at the expense of the larger context. Nonetheless, world-systems analysis has been criticized for suggesting that migrants are primarily victims of capitalism without any capacity for exercising agency. Partly in response, a range of migration theories explore the importance of households, social networks, and migration intermediaries including recruiters, brokers, lawyers, and smugglers in shaping migration dynamics. These theories connect different levels of analysis, showing how individual, social, and global forces interact within migration movements.

Generally, migration has been

> analyzed mainly in *bipolar* terms . . . as a move between essentially autonomous communities and, within this framework, settlement has been treated as a process in which people steadily shift their focus of attention and the locus of their principal social ties from one community to another. (Rouse 1992, pp. 25–6)

In recent years, however, a transnational framework has transformed our understanding of international migration. This framework conceives communities of origin and settlement as linked; migrants as actively engaged in "build[ing] social fields that link together their country of origin and their country of settlement"; and settlement as a process that may entail continually moving between two often contradictory worlds, rather than erasing the cultural values and material ties associated with communities of origin (Glick Schiller et al. 1992, p. 1). As we will see, a transnational framework has been especially useful for theorizing the connections between migration and sexuality.

Factoring Sexuality into Migration Histories and Theories

Sexuality has always shaped and been reshaped by migration processes. But, historically, sexuality was either ignored in migration scholarship or else subsumed under rubrics such as gender, deviance, or morality (Manalansan 2006, p. 224). After queer theory entered academic and activist circles in the late 1980s and early 1990s, some scholars began to insist that sexuality be acknowledged as an important factor that thoroughly informs migration processes. Groundbreaking scholarship about the experiences of migrant gay and bisexual men and sometimes lesbians, as well as about those with HIV/AIDS, highlighted the connections between sexuality and migration.[1] That scholarship achieved two important outcomes: it challenged the ways that lesbian and gay experiences remained shrouded in silence within mainstream migration scholarship, and it provided a basis for scholars to argue that sexual-minority experiences should not just be "added on" to existing scholarship but rather that scholarship as a whole needed to be reframed to address how sexuality shapes migration experiences for *everyone*. Moreover, since international migration is an important mechanism for and measure of globalization processes, exploring the intersections between sexuality and migration provides valuable information about the nature and complexities of globalization.

Queer theory, which foregrounds sexuality as an axis of analysis that should not be subsumed under other rubrics, has proven particularly useful in this regard. Queer theory moves away from essentialist approaches to sexuality and instead analyzes and historicizes sexuality as a basis of power, governance, normalization, and struggle that changes over time and involves multiple actors and institutions (Somerville 2007). Queer theory makes clear that sexual identities and categories (including English-language categories such as lesbian, gay, bi, trans, heterosexual) are not timeless, unchanging, or equivalent across cultures; rather, all sexual categories emerge from specific histories and struggles and are constantly recreated and transformed. Thus, the categories used throughout this chapter should be understood as contingent and reflecting histories of power. Moreover, theorists use "queer" not just as a synonym for LGBT but also as an analytic strategy that calls into question taken-for-granted norms and assumptions. Most importantly, queer scholarship underscores that sexual norms and struggles always articulate hierarchies of gender, race, class, and geopolitics, which must be addressed together including when analyzing migration.

Several key questions have organized much of the research on sexuality and international migration: How does sexuality shape migration? How does sexuality shape the governance and incorporation of migrants? How do migrants inhabit, conform to, or transform sexual norms under these circumstances? The next sections provide an overview of some of the findings about these questions. The findings illuminate how large-scale political, economic, and social processes interact with migrants' experiences and actions in regard to sexuality.

How do Sexual Norms, Ideologies and Expectations Shape Migration across Borders?

Male–female marriages have been promoted as the desired sexual norm in virtually all societies, although the forms assumed by marriages, and their associated ideologies and practices, vary considerably across time and location, and continue to rapidly change in the present. Marriages have both institutionalized and naturalized hierarchies of gender, sexual practice, age, and race/ethnicity and have also ensured that property transmission occurs along particular lines. Given the importance of marriage, it is not surprising that nation-states, employers, churches, and families have long sought to control the ways that marriage and international migration are linked.

During the centuries of European colonialism, for example, "whom bedded and wedded whom in the colonies . . . was never left to chance" (Stoler 2002, p. 47). The Dutch East India Company operated from 1602 until 1796, after which it was nationalized and its possessions became part of the Dutch colonial empire that lasted into the twentieth century. It generally sent young unmarried men to the colonies; there, authorities often promoted concubinage rather than prostitution, since concubines were seen as stabilizing the political order by providing sexual services, local knowledge, intimate care, and household labor for colonial men, whereas prostitutes did not offer the same services and were often viewed as spreading diseases that weakened European men. Concubines, however, were not partners whom European men could ever expect to wed, because this would disrupt the expected transmission of property as well as challenge the racial and cultural hierarchies on which colonial identities and arrangements depended. These arrangements, combined with restrictions on colonial men's marriages, lasted into the twentieth century. Sexual and marital arrangements worked somewhat differently in colonial Latin America and Africa, but there, too, they reflected the importance of control over sexuality (whether inside or outside marriage) to colonial and eventually national authorities.

After immigration control passed largely into the hands of nation-states, many governments prioritized the admission of workers who filled important occupational niches. Quickly, however, governments began to differentiate between migrants who were designated as temporary labor and migrants who were permitted to settle and form families. Explicit racial, gendered, geopolitical, and economic hierarchies strongly shaped these differentiations. For example, beginning in the late nineteenth century, Asian and Mexican workers were designated by the United States as temporary laborers who were to be prevented from settling and either forming or reunifying with their families; laws against interracial marriages reinforced these migrants' temporariness, and the policies only began shifting after World War II. Similarly, the Australian government implemented a "White Australia" policy that was only fully removed from the law in the

Figure 5.1 "Caution: Immigrants Crossing" sign on California Interstate 5 north of the Mexican border crossing at San Ysidro/San Diego. The image was designed in 1990 by graphic artist John Hood, a Navajo Vietnam veteran who drew on images of fleeing families from his war experience and stories from his parents about Navajo families escaping from US soldiers. Although intended to cut down on pedestrian highway deaths on a busy interstate, the sign has attracted the attention of antiimmigrant groups such as the Minutemen, who interpret the family group as a symbol of illegal immigration and uncontrolled reproduction. *Source*: Photographers Direct / James Kirkikis Photography.

1970s. Most nation-states still differentiate between migrants who are admitted for short-term labor contracts and then expected to leave and migrants who are permitted to settle and form or reunify with families. Explicit racism is no longer written into most countries' immigration laws, but racial, ethnic, geopolitical, economic, and gendered considerations nonetheless continue to structure these distinctions. For instance, low-wage migrant workers who fill crucial labor niches in Singapore are not permitted to marry a Singaporean or a permanent resident without the approval of the controller of work permits, and instead are mandated to leave at the end of two years. Labor, population, social welfare, and citizenship policies interact with immigration laws to reinforce these differentiations.

Even as receiving countries have attempted to regulate migrants' possibilities for settlement and family formation, marriage has been important to migrants and sending countries in other ways. Frequently, marriage has impelled and legitimized migration. Married men have migrated overseas to earn money to support their families and, increasingly, married women are doing the same. For instance, since the Philippine government introduced its policy of labor export in 1974, significant numbers of married Filipina women have left husbands, children, and extended families to earn money overseas in jobs including nursing, domestic work, caregiving, entertainment, and teaching. Their migration is the latest chapter in a long history of Filipino migration rooted in experiences of colonization, the country's peripheral position in the world economy, and long-standing global racial and gender hierarchies. A vast scholarship has explored the impact on families of being spread across borders and the extent to which sexual "infidelity" occurs in these contexts. Although the scholarship has historically focused on men, more recent work has also explored women's sexual agency and subjectivity under circumstances of separation, and has analyzed what changing sexual arrangements reveal about the shifting forms, functions, and ideologies of marriage, family, property, employment, and subjectivity.[2] To further complicate matters, migrants have become paradigmatic figures through which governments and researchers have tracked the flow of sexually transmitted diseases, often using racist, sexist, and colonialist models in their analysis while envisioning normative marriage as a "solution."

It is not only the responsibilities associated with marriage and familial support that sometimes impel migration; marriage may also make migration acceptable and feasible, particularly for women. Families, communities, and government officials in both sending and receiving countries often express deep anxiety about unmarried women's migration, including concern that they will "deviate" from sexual norms as a result of bad judgment or being lured, tricked, or forced into "improper" sexual behavior. Deviation from sexual norms is seen as reflecting poorly on women's families, communities, and countries of origin. At the same time, officials and publics in receiving countries often worry that unattached migrant women may contribute to disease, immorality, crime, or social disorder through their sexual behaviors. By supposedly placing women's sexualities under the control of husbands, marriage alleviates these fears, making women's migration more acceptable—and revealing the patriarchal logic that underpins the familial, community, national, and transnational arrangements in which migration is embedded.

There have been exceptions to these patterns; for instance, single women migrated in great numbers from Ireland in the late nineteenth and early twentieth centuries. But, given the continuing importance attached to marriage, women have sometimes had to strategically seek out male marriage partners who would make their migration acceptable—and, in some cases, literally feasible in the face of otherwise restrictive immigration laws. For instance, since the Japanese government does not currently issue visas for migrant domestic or care workers, Chinese, Filipina, and Korean women sometimes use marriage as a means to legally enter Japan for employment. Similarly, resorting to marriage generally offers working-class women from the Dominican Republic their best (and often only) opportunity to legally migrate for employment in Europe, the United States, or Canada, given immigration barriers in those countries and the Dominican Republic's relative lack of power in the international order (Brennan 2004).

Some migrants' reliance on marriage as a means to legally migrate generates periodic panics that they are undermining the laws of receiving nations as well as subverting the institution of marriage itself, which remains central to state and nation building. Yet Gracia Liu-Farrar rightly notes, "instrumental marriages were common in history. Men and women married to bring peace to two countries, to serve the economic interests of two families, to lift up their social status or for allowing survival of their family" (Liu-Farrar 2010, p. 110). Instrumental marriages for purposes of migration also have a long history globally, for the reasons described by Liu-Farrar and also because sending and receiving states often require marriage as a condition for women's migration in the first place, or because marriage has become the only available route for legal migration.

Just because a marriage involves instrumental considerations does not mean that it lacks feelings, hopes, and dreams. As Lucy Williams argues, "marriage choices have always been strategic and based on compromises of ideals, aspirations, and practicalities" (2012, p. 30). Indeed, the combination of strategy, affect, and aspiration characterizes both immigrant and

Figure 5.2 Members of the Falash Mura—Ethiopians who returned to Judaism after their ancestors converted to Christianity to escape persecution at the end of the nineteenth century—arrive at Ben Gurion Airport in Tel Aviv, Israel, in 2010. The image of immigrant mothers and children with Israeli flags represents Israel as a racial democracy at a time when the country has come under increased international criticism for religious discrimination, especially against its Muslim minority. *Source*: Bernat Armangue / AP / Press Association Images.

citizen marriages. Williams suggests that the persistent association of cultural and ethnic "others" with purely instrumental marriages that supposedly reflect either timeless "tradition" or else immigration fraud reveals the harsh double standard by which immigrants are often judged. At the same time, the association of global northern citizens with romantic love ignores the fact that their marriages also entail calculation. The unnecessary binary between instrumental and romantic marriage contributes to racializing and colonialist discourses that not only position global northern marriages as markers of modernity, progress, and superiority (Povinelli 2006) but also shape immigration control strategies in ways that greatly impact migration possibilities.[3]

Even as officials seek to regulate marriage migration through simplifying binary frameworks, employers, too, often have clear preferences for married or unmarried migrant employees, depending on the nature of the work, the historical period, and the ways that marriage obligations are expected to affect the workers' pliability as well as social mores. In the southwestern United States in the early twentieth century, for instance, some employers preferred to recruit married migrant men as fieldworkers because they believed that family obligations made men less likely to resist terrible working conditions or chase women. In other cases, single male workers were preferred because they were seen as mobile, cheap, and disposable. In still other cases, marital status per se has not been decisive; migrant domestic workers in Singapore, for example, regardless of their marital status, are subjected to regular medical checkups, and women who are found to be pregnant are summarily returned to their home countries. Transportation and communication technologies, including most recently the Internet, cellphones, and video cameras, have had huge roles in shaping the interplay between marriage and migration. Commercial brokers, matchmakers, immigration agents, recruiters, and travel providers also shape migration (Yang and Lu 2010).

As the form, function, and meaning of marriage have changed, so too have the connections between marriage and migration. For example, in recent decades, some women and men have sought out overseas marriage partners not only as a means to migrate and as a strategy for economic or social survival or advancement but also because doing so allows migrants to construct themselves in new ways, including as "modern" subjects who are capable of desiring and choosing a partner without family intervention (Hirsh 2003). Yet, given that sexual desires have been deeply formed by histories of colonial, racialized, and gendered encounters and inequalities, these productions of the self remain entangled in complex relations of power. Moreover, significant inequalities still shape who may or may not legally migrate across international borders in response to desire: authorized migration is far easier for those holding passports from global northern states than for anyone else. As the editors of *Love and Globalization* describe, we need to track the continual interactions between "large scale structures at the level of nations or global systems . . . and the personal and emotional experiences of real people . . . who struggle within constraints to establish emotional connections and intimacy with others" (Padilla et al. 2007, p. xxii). Sexuality remains a crucial site where the interplay between agency, subjectivity, and structural hierarchies of power get contested and remade through struggles over migration possibilities.

Marriages implicate not just couples but also children and other relatives. Scholars have explored the historical experiences of families that became divided by national borders as a result of racist immigration laws. In these split families, wage and reproductive labor were negotiated at the interface of global, national, and local scales and hierarchies. The acceleration of migration in recent decades, in the context of a rapidly changing global economy and new communication and transportation technologies, has inspired many studies of contemporary transnational families that remain divided across national borders. Scholars suggest that, for poor and working-class families, transnationalism is often a survival strategy that is rooted in global economic inequalities, whereas for middle- and upper-middle-class families, transnationalism may provide a means to enhance family members' social, economic, and cultural capital. In either case, gender, sexual, generational, racial, and geopolitical hierarchies become reformulated, but not abolished, by transnationalism. Nation-states often facilitate transnationalism among the middle and upper classes while keeping poor and working-class families separated or excluded.

Martin F. Manalansan IV suggests that using queer theory to critically reexamine common assumptions about sexuality within migrant heterosexual marriages and families will enable us to better understand all of these dynamics. He focuses on married women from the Global South who have migrated in recent decades to work as domestics and caregivers in the Global North while leaving children and other family members behind, in a process that is commonly described as a "global care chain" that reproduces colonial, racial, and gender hierarchies. In order to critically rethink these migration dynamics, Manalansan suggests that we need to conceive of the chain of care not as a set of discreet relationships between worlds and bodies strung up in a teleological manner, but rather as a series of conflicting and diverse bonds between labor, emotions and corporeality that do not line up neatly in terms of gender binaries and normative familial arrangements. (Manalansan 2008)

He applies the model to rethink the experiences of migrant Filipina and Filipino domestics and careworkers worldwide (Manalansan 2008).

Liu-Farrar's research into extramarital sexual activities among Chinese migrants in Japan also beautifully illustrates strategies for, and some of the benefits of, using queer and critical sexuality scholarship to rethink migration dynamics. Liu-Farrar describes the experiences of Jie, a woman from Fujian, China, who entered Japan through a fake marriage but became undocumented after a year. While in Japan, Jie met an undocumented Chinese man whom she came to consider her husband, although they did not have an official marriage ceremony, register the marriage, or involve their families. Jie and the man had a baby together, but after he became addicted to pinball she paid someone to bring the child back to China. She confided her worries to a Japanese store manager with whom she worked and to whom she had grown close. He offered to help by "faking a marriage" with her and promised not to take sexual advantage, so she married him and moved in to allay any suspicion on the part of the immigration authorities. At the same time:

> She only spent one day a week with her "real husband" whom she had lots of complaints about. "The store manager says if I want the marriage to be real, he is willing to take care of me and my son. But I don't want it to be real. After all, my husband is the father of my son." But what pained her even more was that the "husband" suspected she was having a sexual relationship with the manager. (Liu-Farrer 2010, p. 108)

Jie's experiences force us to rethink common understandings about the interconnections between marriage, sexuality, intimacy, affect, and obligations, especially when individuals' experiences and interpretations of these matters significantly differ from official or legal constructions.

Analyzing the experiences of those who are unable or unwilling to match up to dominant sexual norms also offers opportunities to ask new questions about the ways that sexuality and migration interact. These interactions include shoring up the sexual norms of sending countries. For instance, many countries have informal traditions of ensuring that pregnant but unmarried women are sent overseas, so that families' shame may be lessened and women may partially avoid the discrimination and stigma attached to pregnancy outside marriage. This reflects the way that norms concerning female gender, sexuality, and class intertwine in migration processes.

Gay men and lesbians, too, are popularly thought to migrate as a means to escape sexually based stigma and discrimination. Certainly, in the twentieth and twenty-first centuries, many nation-states have constructed homosexuality as antithetical to valued forms of nationalism and citizenship, symptomatic of corruption by "alien" forces, and a betrayal of one's country and culture. These harsh messages are reinforced through laws and practices that marginalize, exclude, stigmatize, and discriminate, sometimes to the point of imprisonment or death. At the same time, the post-1970s global flow of gay and lesbian cultural products, information, and ideologies often contribute to the association with gay and lesbian life as possible—but only when lived abroad. Gay men and lesbians often internalize these messages and face these risks, which suggest that their futures are bleak and they should either change or leave.

Yet, gay and lesbian experiences are more complex than simply that of making the choice to move from "repression" to "freedom." For one thing, vast numbers of gay men and lesbians do not migrate across international borders but instead relocate within their own countries, or never move at all. Their actions challenge images of particular nation-states as being monolithically homophobic or not, and show the need for more nuanced analysis. For those who do migrate across borders, studies show that gender, class, and cultural factors play decisive roles in shaping migration possibilities and desires. For example, Lionel Cantú's research (1995–1998) found that well-to-do Mexican men who could maintain a gay or bisexual lifestyle with minimal costs were less likely to migrate, while at the other end of the spectrum some gay or bisexual men wanted to migrate but lacked the economic resources and social networks to make this possible (Cantú 2009, p. 165). This finding makes clear that sexuality intertwines with other factors including political economy in shaping gay, lesbian, and bisexual migration (as is also the case with heterosexual marriage migration).

Social networks, which provide access to vital information and material resources, greatly facilitate migration across borders. While research has typically focused on household and sex worker networks, recent studies suggest that gay, lesbian, and transgender social networks similarly enable migration. A study of twenty-four self-identified gay migrant Mexican men in Los Angeles showed that "immigrant-based gay transnational social networks have played central roles in the immigration, settlement, and identity formation processes" of the men, by providing incentives and resources for migration, housing opportunities, access to jobs, and social spaces (Thing 2010, p. 821). Transgender migrants often rely on similar networks.[4] Global forces also structure gay, lesbian, and transgender migration, including as expanded travel and tourism circuits (and Internet dating sites) generate relationships between citizens from different countries that may result in migration.

Gay migrants in studies like these generally expected to experience new opportunities for self-expression and self-fashioning in the country to which they migrated, but instead often found themselves negotiating racism, heterosexism, cultural and language barriers, limited work opportunities, and (in some cases) anxieties around their undocumented status. Changes in the men's sexual, ethnic, racial, gender, and class identities, practices, and ways of living resulted from negotiating these challenges, often with the help of networks—rather than from "exposure" to dominant culture, which is the usual mainstream explanation for change, but one that ignores structural inequalities within receiving countries as well as the frequently segregated lives that migrants face. Changes resulting from migration were complex; as one Mexican gay interviewee discovered, "it wasn't true that homosexuals are free, that they can hold hands or that Americans like Mexicans" (Cantú 2009, pp. 138–9). Effectively, their sexualities "became only one layer of identity" among Mexican gay and bisexual migrants; "in Los Angeles, it is the intersection of their social class, ethnic, immigrant and sexual identities" that shaped their lives and experiences (Thing 2010, p. 826).

Manalansan's research on gay Filipino men in New York City (1990–1995) further expands our understanding of gay migration specifically, and sexuality and migration in general, by insisting on the importance of a transnational framework. Given the complex, historically long-standing, and frequently unequal ties between nation-states as a result of colonialism, capitalism, warfare, and asymmetrical cultural exchange, Manalansan argues that migrants often arrive not to begin a process of assimilation but rather to continue their engagement with economic, social, cultural, and political systems that have already profoundly affected their lives (Manalansan 2003). Thus, rather than experiencing "assimilation," they create "multiple hybrid cultures and . . . spaces for community activities and new cultural 'traditions' that depart from both their own migrant communities and from mainstream 'straight' and 'gay and lesbian' cultures" (Manalansan 2006, p. 236). Moreover, their negotiations between local and global draw on and further contribute to gay cultural formations in the Philippines. Manalansan illustrates these arguments through his analysis of how Filipino gay men in New York City create homes and families, negotiate gay clubs and AIDS service provision, and engage in cross-dressing performances. Comparable detailed research on lesbian migration has yet to be produced.

The demand for sex workers has also generated a continuing flow of migrants across borders. Donna Guy illustrates some of the connections between sex work, social hierarchies, and international migration within the context of nineteenth-century capitalist expansion:

> European prostitutes in Buenos Aires, for the most part, came from poverty-stricken families and worked out of desperation. Marginalized by the industrial revolution, driven from their homelands by hunger or by family, political, or religious persecution, they saw immigration to a new land or even a new continent as the key to survival. Cheap steamship fares and imbalanced sex ratios in the rapidly growing port cities made it easier and more attractive for them to emigrate. Under these conditions, prostitution was more typically a self-conscious response to poverty than the result of trickery by an evil procurer. When deception led women into prostitution, family members often played key roles. (Guy 1991, p. 7)

Contemporary sex work takes place in a vastly restructured sex industry. The drive to increase profits has "led to a proliferation of new products, goods, and services, and the cultivation of new desires and needs" (Kempadoo 1998, p. 16). This includes short-term migration by men for sex tourism, which is further entrenched by many states' dependence on tourism in general as an economic survival strategy. Some women also engage in sex tourism. Vast numbers of women—and trans people, biological males, and children—work in various sectors of the sex industry under conditions ranging from coercion to consent. In countries where sex work is criminalized, migrants are barred from legal admission, and any migrant caught selling sex after admission risks deportation. Rather than preventing migration for sex work, however, these laws work mainly to increase the exploitability of migrant sex workers.

In recent years, many nation-states have enacted antitrafficking laws. Unfortunately, the laws often rely on anticrime rather than human rights frameworks, and frequently confuse trafficking, smuggling, and undocumented migration. As a result, antitrafficking laws often strengthen the hand of criminal traffickers and employers over migrants, without appreciably addressing the conditions that give rise to their migration in the first place. Moreover, the laws often create problematic distinctions between migrants who are trafficked for sex work and migrants who are trafficked for other kinds of labor. (For further discussion of the connections between sex work and migration, see Chapter 7.)

Overall, sexuality shapes (and is reshaped by) migration across borders in multifaceted ways. Studies of marriage migration, LGBT migration, migrant sex work, and other labor migrations illuminate these interconnections. At the same time, migrants often move between and blur categorical distinctions. LGBT people sometimes cross borders as heterosexual marriage migrants, sex workers, or other types of labor migrants; women use heterosexual marriage to legally migrate for paid domestic work; migrant domestic or sex work sometimes becomes a route to heterosexual marriage; Internet dating and marriage is popularly conflated with sex trafficking; and so on. The fact that migrants move between these categorical distinctions underlines the complexity of migration processes—but confounds nation-states that seek to manage migration through simplified, stable categories that can be used to tie migrants to normative nationalist sexual orders. It also contributes to the stereotyping of migrants by mainstream media and the public.

How Do Receiving Nation-States Select and Govern Migrants through Sexual Regimes—and How Do Migrants Respond?

Nation-state immigration and asylum laws determine which migrants are legally admitted or excluded. Preference for admission is often given to migrants with work skills that are in demand, but the selection of these migrants is frequently tied to explicit or implicit sexual norms. For example, some employers prefer to hire migrants without marital ties; others force women who migrate to work in low-wage jobs to undergo pregnancy testing before admission and expel them if they become pregnant. Admission preferences are also commonly based on family ties to citizens or legal residents. Yet, states rather than migrants get to decide who counts as "family" for purposes of immigration. In many receiving states, "family" is "limited to spouses and dependent children within the nuclear family," which is a definition that fails to accord with the varied kinds of families in which many people are embedded, including same-sex families, unmarried male–female couples, extended families, families with fictive kin, and arranged marriages (Kofman 2004, p. 244).[5]

Some countries selectively recognize same-sex relationships as a basis for legal admission. Yet, such recognition generally occurs only when the couple can show that their relationship is similar to heterosexual marriage, which is understood as involving cohabitation, financial interdependency, privacy, domesticity, monogamy, and depoliticized identities (Simmons 2008). The idealized heterosexual marriage norm, moreover, is crosscut by racial, cultural, class, and gender hierarchies. For example, requirements concerning "minimum income and accommodation are common in Europe, creating socio-economic differentials in access to spousal reunification" that often translate into distinct racial, national, and ethnic patterns (Charsley 2012, p. 8). Unknown numbers of same-sex couples—and other kinds of couples—remain shut out from legal admission to Australia, Britain, Canada, and elsewhere because they cannot or will not conform to these standards. The continuing preference for racially and ethnically desirable middle- and upper-middle-class married heterosexual couples is usually matched by the exclusion of migrants who are deemed to threaten that norm (sex worker exclusion is a classic example; same-sex couples are often excluded on this basis, too). Moreover, migrants who cannot directly match legal preferences often cannot gain entry, even when they are not explicitly excluded. In these and other ways, sexual regimes directly and indirectly shape who acquires legal status and who does not.

Beginning in the 1990s, asylum laws in some countries created possibilities for the admission of migrants who are persecuted either because they do not adhere to dominant sexual norms or because their persecution has taken a sexualized form (e.g. rape). Historically, the Geneva Convention has restricted refugee status to those who establish a well-founded fear of persecution on account of their race, religion, nationality, political opinion, or membership in a particular social group. In the 1990s, some countries began to recognize that sexual minorities constitute a "particular social group" and may experience persecution on that basis. At the same time, feminist advocates successfully challenged models of rape as a private act driven by individual desire, showing instead that it is an act of violence with political significance that may provide a basis for asylum (Luibhéid 2002). These developments had an important impact on refugee and asylum laws in some countries, including South Africa, which was the first global southern country to incorporate such concerns into its refugee legislation (Middleton 2008, p. 8). Nonetheless, asylum claims involving sexuality are rarely successful.

Difficulties occur because people often do not even know that asylum is an option; they face barriers to leaving their countries because of lack of funds, documents, or legal permission, and women face additional gendered restrictions on travel; global northern states are continually erecting barriers and often incarcerating asylum seekers; and language skills, cultural knowledge, and possession of sufficient finances to hire legal assistance significantly determine success in the asylum system.[6] Moreover, those who have been persecuted in sexualized ways, or because of their sexual identities, are often frightened or ashamed to describe their experiences to government officials, whom they associate with persecution. Migrants must also establish that persecution occurred because of one of the grounds listed in the Geneva Convention, which is generally very difficult. Officials and courts are often uninformed about how to handle cases where persecution took sexualized form or sexual identity was a basis for persecution.

Those seeking asylum because of persecution for their sexual identities must prove they are "really" gay or lesbian, often according to ethnocentric and stereotypical standards. For example, courts are most likely to award asylum to gay men who present themselves as very effeminate and to deny asylum to gay men who do not match up to mainstream gender (crosscut by racial and class) stereotypes about homosexuality. Proving one's lesbianism to the satisfaction of a judge is equally difficult; for example, lesbian women may be forced into heterosexual marriages as an element of their persecution, yet judges generally understand forced marriage as "proof" that the women are not really lesbians. Gay and lesbian applicants are frequently denied asylum because the judge believes that, if they would just hide their sexuality or "tone down" their self-presentation and public behavior, they would not risk persecution. Yet, no other categories of applicant are denied asylum on the basis that they should hide or lie about their identities to avoid persecution.[7] Gay men, lesbians, and transgender people (as well as women and men who have experienced sexualized persecution) are often told that they should have relocated within their countries rather than fleeing across borders. These kinds of barriers to protection are widespread, as shown by Jansen and Spijkerboer's 2011 study of LGBTI asylum seekers in Europe as well as studies about asylum in the United States and elsewhere. Overall, asylum cases involve transnational looking and

judging processes that are fraught with power (Miller 2005). The cases
remake sexual norms and ideologies at scales ranging from the local to
the global, and among diverse constituencies including asylum seekers
themselves, LGBT and immigrant communities, nongovernmental organizations, national governments, and transnational bodies.

In addition to jurisprudence concerning lesbians, gay men, and sexualized persecution, cases have addressed asylum based on fear of female
genital cutting, forced abortion, forced sterilization, forced marriage,
and HIV status, among other sexuality issues. The growing case law on
transgender asylum applicants shows that gender and sexuality considerations are often complexly woven together. Overall, asylum provides only a
narrow door of opportunity for legal admission to a select few. This has
generated considerable debate about the extent to which human rights
discourses and practices may work to reinforce rather than transform
existing inequalities.

The sexual norms underpinning immigration and asylum laws not only
directly shape who is likely to be legally admitted or not; they also affect
how legally admitted migrants are governed *after* their admission. As
Helena Wray describes, "crossing the border has become an indefinite
process. . . . The border has moved well beyond the entry clearance process
and embedded itself into the daily lives of . . . migrants long after they enter"
(Wray 2012, pp. 56–7). Even after legally entering, migrants may lose their
legal status if their visas expire, if they fail to follow bureaucratic rules, if
they are accused of a crime or misdemeanor, or if they transgress in other
ways. Yet, sexual norms affect migrants' efforts to maintain their legal
status, as illustrated by the experiences of immigrant spouses who gain
legal admission on the basis of their heterosexual marriage to citizens. In
the United States, since 1986, migrant spouses have been given two years'
conditional residency, after which the migrant and the citizen must petition
the immigration service together, seeking permanent legal residency for the
migrant. However, the majority of US migrant spouses are foreign-born
women joining citizen husbands. And these requirements have tied some
migrant women into abusive relationships that include sexual and other
forms of violence, which women endure because they need their husbands
to file paperwork for them. Husbands sometimes use this need to further
coerce and abuse their wives. Yet, at the end of the two years, if abusive
husbands fail to file the necessary paperwork for their migrant wives,
nothing happens to them, but the wives often become undocumented.[8] The
issue is by no means unique to the United States, either; rather, women who

migrate through heterosexual marriage face similar difficulties in numerous countries including South Korea and Taiwan.

Laws and rules concerning finances deepen the knot. For instance, increasing numbers of countries require that those who sponsor a relative for immigration must first achieve a certain income level—which effectively reserves "family" status as a privilege for the better off. The United States has gone a step further, requiring sponsors to sign a legally binding affidavit of financial support that remains in effect until the migrant has worked for ten years, died, or permanently left the country. The affidavit is not voided by divorce. Effectively, financial sponsorship laws in numerous countries mandate long-term enforced dependency within heterosexual families as a precondition for legally immigrating. This shifts responsibility for migrants during times of unemployment or illness away from states and employers and onto privatized families, even while the demand for migrants' labor persists. The effects of the affidavit system on battered women have been severe. In countries that do not recognize same-sex couples, the system also creates particular hardships for lesbian, gay, and transgender migrants because only heterosexual families can sponsor them, yet some families are hostile to queer relatives. This is not to suggest that migrants are unusually homophobic compared to citizens, but rather to highlight that immigration laws often force LGBT migrants into dependency on heterosexual relatives.

Sexuality shapes the incorporation of migrants who are admitted under worker preferences, too. The experiences of domestic workers illustrate some of these complexities. Globally, enormous numbers of workers cross borders to perform domestic and care work in private homes. Even when they are supposed to be covered by labor laws or work contracts, in practice, migrant domestics generally have few rights or protections because their work is considered menial and their workplaces are the private homes of people who are usually wealthier and more privileged. This shields employers from scrutiny while isolating workers from information and support. Under these circumstances, the abuse of migrant domestic workers is not uncommon, and includes beating, kicking, slapping, burning, withholding of food, psychological abuse, threats, nonpayment of wages, extremely long work hours, no days off—and sexual abuse and rape. The difficulty of challenging these conditions means that physical, psychological, and sexual vulnerability and suffering are defining conditions of work for significant numbers of migrant domestic workers. High-profile cases, such as that of Filipina Sarah Balabagan, a sixteen-year-old domestic worker in the United

Arab Emirates who was arrested after killing her employer and who claimed she acted in self-defense because he tried to rape her, have drawn attention to the issue, but without resulting in significant changes.

Employers' concerns about the sexualities of domestic workers structure their work experiences in other ways. For instance, Pei-Chia Lan found that female employers of migrant domestic workers in Taiwan were often deeply concerned that workers might establish romantic/sexual relationships on their days off. Therefore, they took steps to ensure that either workers had no days off or else their whereabouts were constantly monitored. "These employers consider dating a migrant boyfriend to be a sign of moral degradation in migrant women, which may lead to pregnancy or 'running away' . . . some employers worry about a connection between dating and kidnapping or burglary" being committed against the employer's household (Lan 2006, pp. 165–6). Wives also worried that their husbands might find the live-in domestic worker sexually attractive. Cognizant of the concerns, Lan argues, "migrant women . . . try to minimize contacts with male employers to ease the wife's anxiety and to lower the risk of sexual harassment" (Lan 2006, p. 112). At the same time, migrant workers often use their days off to engage in shopping, dressing in the latest and sexiest fashions and meeting others including sexual or romantic partners, while keeping their activities invisible to employers. Cell phones provide further opportunities to establish and maintain sexual/romantic ties—that are not only cross-gender but also same-gender.

In any nation-state, migrants include not just those who are admitted under work, family preference, and refugee/asylum regulations but also undocumented migrants who are unable to gain legal admission or whose legal status has expired. Undocumented status makes migrants vulnerable to exploitation and abuse, including sexually. For instance, women migrating without authorization from Central America through Mexico to the United States routinely take birth control pills, knowing that they are at great risk of being raped by smugglers, bandits, other migrants, and officials including police and immigration control agents, none of whom are likely to be held accountable for their actions. Officials and employers also routinely engage in sexual coercion of undocumented women and sometimes men in workplaces, public places, and elsewhere. Migrants incarcerated in detention centers are regularly subjected to sexual harassment and abuse. Women and children who are trafficked for sexual exploitation find that their undocumented status generally precludes any possibilities for assistance or protection; indeed, although global northern states routinely decry trafficking, trafficking tends to be handled within a law-and-order rather than human rights framework, which results in migrants' deportation back to the very same conditions that generated their predicament in the first place.

Sexual logics are used to channel certain migrants or their children into undocumented status, too. This is vividly illustrated by recent conflicts in numerous countries including Ireland, the Dominican Republic, and New Zealand about whether children born there to migrants should automatically acquire citizenship at birth. In 2005, the Irish constitution was amended to ensure that children who were born to migrants were eligible for citizenship only when at least one parent had resided legally in Ireland for a requisite number of years (time spent as an asylum seeker or international student did not count). As a result, some children born in Ireland now are not citizens—which means they are subject to immigration law and could potentially become illegal and deportable. In 2010, the Dominican Republic made a similar change to its constitution. Officials implemented the change in ways that effectively made it retroactive, and particularly targeted people of Haitian ancestry, with devastating results. Thousands have been denied birth certificates, national identity cards, and other documents that are critical for enrolling in a university, getting married, getting a passport, and other life functions. They include not just the children but also the grandchildren of Haitian workers, who often entered the Dominican Republic at the request or with the approval of the Dominican government yet whose citizenship status is now in doubt.

Even under the most challenging conditions, however, migrants are never just victims; for instance, Xóchitl Castañeda and Patricia Zavella (2007) show how migrant women farmworkers in California, many of whom are undocumented and subjected to continual sexual harassment and surveillance in the fields—as well as very low wages, limited or nonexistent healthcare, and very poor living conditions—nonetheless protect themselves as best they can and create opportunities for adventure, romance, and sexual experiences when possible. Castañeda and Zavella's research underscores the necessity of working to change conditions that place migrants' lives and wellbeing at considerable risk while acknowledging migrants' agency, complex lives, and situated perspectives. Unfortunately, when migrants' lives do not match up to official sexual norms or fit into the victim–criminal binary, this often provides an excuse to castigate migrants and abandon efforts to challenge the exploitative conditions under which they live.

This difficulty raises more general issues concerning images and discourses about migrants' sexualities—what those images and discourses are, how they circulate, the work they do, and the complex mandates they create. A thorough review is beyond the scope of this chapter, but we have already seen that sexual imagery shapes migration flows. In destination countries, images and discourses of migrants as sexual threats, sexual deviants, carriers of sexually transmitted diseases, hyperfertile, hypersexy, dangerously homosocial, and/or purveyors of vice are widespread. These images continually affect the admission, incorporation, sense of self, and material life possibilities of migrants. For example, in 2010, in an appearance on the CNN news channel, US Congressman Louis Gohmert suggested that terrorists were sending pregnant women to the United States to give birth to children. Because the children were born in the US, they acquired citizenship at birth. According to Gohmert, the women then returned home with their babies and "raised and coddled [them] as terrorists" who, when they reached adulthood, would be sent back to the United States to "destroy our way of life" (Kleefeld 2010). Gohmert's claims were quickly debunked and widely ridiculed. But they represented the latest escalation in a war over immigration that significantly works through images and discourses about race, class, and geopolitics that intersect with gender and sexual hierarchies. Through outrageous claims about migrant women's pregnancies, Gohmert invoked racist tropes about the alleged hyperfertility of certain migrants as evidence of "backwardness" and a civilizational threat. He also invoked security discourses that buttress imperialist agendas and actions, and anxieties about immigrants as excessive welfare-users that have legitimized the widespread rollback of vital social supports. Migrant women living, working, and raising children in the United States are materially and psychologically affected by these discourses, which shape how others view them; how they view themselves; their ability to access resources; their encounters on the street, in schools, in workplaces, and in hospitals; their hopes for their children; and their futures. Citizens associated with migrants are also affected. These discourses also inform research agendas and policy-making in very troubling ways; for instance, images and discourses about migrant women as either complete victims or else cynical exploiters continue to saturate research and policy-making.

Migrant communities also deploy discourses about sexuality for various ends. For instance, heterosexual Mexican migrants in the United States may claim "modern bodies, modern loves, and modern sex" in order to chal-

Figure 5.3 Two participants kiss on a boat as 350,000 people line Amsterdam's Prinsengracht canal to watch the tenth annual Gay Canal Parade in 2005. The photograph accompanied an Associated Press article titled "Film Exposes Immigrants to Dutch Liberalism." The article references a film that the Dutch immigration services requires prospective immigrants to view to test their tolerance for Dutch culture. The film includes two controversial scenes: one of two men kissing and another of a nude beach. The actual film scene depicts two nicely dressed men kissing affectionately in a public park; the photograph shown here suggests something quite different. *Source*: Bas Czerwinski / AP / Press Association Images.

lenge racist and colonialist stereotypes; reposition themselves spatially and temporally relative to family, friends, and coworkers left behind and in the United States; and as a strategy of mobility, self-protection, and ongoing negotiation of transnational identities (Hirsh 2003, pp. 280, 255). Racialized and gendered constructs of tradition and modernity shape some transnational communities' patterns of seeking wives from the homeland, who become imagined as uncorrupted bearers of tradition; in other cases, "the gendered associations of modernity are reversed" (Charsley 2012, pp. 6–7). Racialized immigrant communities may claim worthiness by asserting the morality and virtue of "their" women when compared to majority-group women. But, although this strategy challenges racism, it comes at the price of enforcing patriarchy and compulsory heterosexuality within migrant communities and abandoning or disavowing those who do adhere to these standards (Espiritu 1999). Equally, migrant communities may police other migrant communities through racialized discourses of sexuality that they adopt from the mainstream, employers, mass media, and other sources. In New York City, Latin American migrants sometimes stigmatize one another through claims about which ethnic group's women are more sexually "free," aggressive, or uncontrolled; among migrant domestics in Taiwan, some "Indonesians . . . criticize Filipina migrants for their alleged engagement in drinking, smoking and having sex out of wedlock" (Decena et al. 2006, p. 50; Lan 2006, p. 91). In making these claims, migrants "view and treat their own bodies as an extension of national territories" and "project national-ethnic differences onto the bodies of other groups of migrant women" (Lan 2006, p. 90).

In short, nation-states and employers govern migrants' incorporation into society and their everyday lives through sexual norms. At the same time, migrants continually remake their identities, cultures and communities including through challenging—or hewing to—sexual norms in their own and other communities. Their efforts have transnational dimensions, drawing from histories and cultures in other locations and affecting those who not have migrated across borders at all.

Conclusion

Sexuality is "a dense transfer point for relations of power" (Foucault 1990, p. 103). Certainly sexuality provides a rich lens through which to explore the complex relations of power that are involved in migration across international borders. Until the 1990s, though, scholars rarely explored the connections between sexuality and international migration. Instead, sexuality remained camouflaged within rubrics such as gender, deviance, and morality, or else treated as the property of those who did not match up to dominant norms. Queer theory, however, helped to show that sexuality encompasses *everybody* within dense relations of power.[9] Specifically, sexual norms distribute people in terms of their proximity to or distance from social ideals, and reward or punish them accordingly. This approach suggests that sexual identities are always relational, always formed through their contrast with other categories of identity, rather than being essential or timeless.

A relational model opens the door to understanding how gender, race, class, culture, religion, and geopolitics, among other factors, shape sexual identities, experiences, and histories—and how failure to address these crosscutting factors reinscribes an invisible norm of sexuality as white, middle-class, global northern, and heterosexual. A relational model of sexuality is also helpful for identifying myths, fallacies, and dead ends that have affected research about sexuality and migration. These include myths that migrants simply flee sexual repression in their home countries for "liberation" elsewhere and that migrants undergo processes of sexual acculturation in which they jettison their "old" sexual ways and adopt to mainstream global northern norms that are supposedly superior, more modern, and at the apex of development. Yet, as this chapter has described, sexuality shapes and is reshaped by migration processes in very complex ways, along routes that are far more circuitous than the trajectory of "from the west to the rest." Migration research that is informed by queer theory and attentive to positionality, relations of power, and questions about who represents whom—and that challenge usual assumptions—help us to understand these complexities. Such research underlines the importance of not just "adding on" sexual minorities to existing histories but instead reframing all analyses to address how sexuality and migration are mutually interconnected in every migrant's life—and how hierarchies of power involving sexuality become reworked, but not abolished, across transnational fields. Moreover, even those who "stay put" are affected by transnational flows involving sexuality and migration.

Philosophers suggest that we can discern the whole world in a grain of sand. This chapter suggests that, through analysis of everyday encounters and experiences involving sexuality, we can discern how micro- and macro-level forces interlink to shape international migration. It especially addresses how migration shaped and is reshaped by sexual norms, ideologies, and expectations; how nation-states use sexuality and intimacy to govern and police migrants; and how migrants negotiate constraints and possibilities in creative ways that link the local, national, and transnational. In the process, the chapter highlights the value of scholarship that links larger political and economic structures with subjective experiences, practices, and performances of love, sexuality, and intimacy across multiple boundaries.

Sexuality and international migration interact and continually transform one another in dense, multiple ways that this chapter has only begun to sketch. Readers are warmly invited to become contributors to knowledge about these important processes.

Acknowledgments

Warmest thanks to participants in the UA First Friday History Workshop on December 2, 2011, and the editors, who provided invaluable feedback. All errors are mine.

Notes

1 A review of the vast scholarship on HIV/AIDS and migration is beyond the scope of this chapter. For information, see Thomas et al. (2009). For a more general review of transformations in sexuality research, see Parker (2009). For an overview of sexuality and migration scholarship, see Luibhéid (2008).

2 By "subjectivity," I am referring to a sense of self that both stems from and acts on social relations of power.

3 Anxieties about the strategic use of marriage as an avenue for legal immigration reflect larger social anxieties about how intimacies and sexualities have become commodified. For a review see Constable (2009).

4 Transgender is a contested, historically contingent term that is generally used to describe people whose gender identity or expression does not neatly match up with the gender that was assigned to them at birth.

5 See also Simmons (2008), who suggests that UK immigration policies "place heterosexual marriage at the centre of the discourse of entitlement and rights of entry for 'spouses'" (p. 218). In response, some migrants strategically deploy and cultivate sexualities, intimacies, and family ties that enable them to navigate immigration rules.

6 The growing restriction on refugees and asylum seekers in global northern states contrasts greatly with the more generous regimes that have been evident in many African and Asian countries.

7 In 2010, the UK Supreme Court invalidated the "be discreet" argument as a ground for denying asylum to lesbians and gay men, but other countries continue to use it.

8 Wives may avoid becoming undocumented through seeking a "battered spouse waiver," a "VAWA [Violence Against Women Act] self-petition," or a "VAWA Cancellation of Removal," none of which are easy to obtain.

9 Just as majority-group people have a race/ethnicity and men have a gender, those who follow the dominant sexual norm have sexuality.

References

Brennan, D. (2004) *What's Love Got to Do With It? Transnational Desires and Sex Tourism in the Dominican Republic.* Duke University Press, Durham, NC.

Cantú, L. (2009) *The Sexuality of Migration* (ed. N. Naples and S. Vidal-Ortiz). New York University Press, New York.

Castañeda, X. and Zavella, P. (2007) Changing constructions of sexuality and risk: Migrant Mexican farmworkers in California, in *Women and Migration in the U.S.–Mexico Borderlands: A Reader* (ed. D. Segura and P. Zavella). Duke University Press, Durham, NC, pp. 249–68.

Charsley, K. (2012) Transnational marriage, in *Transnational Marriage: New Perspectives from Europe and Beyond* (ed. K. Charsley). Routledge, New York, pp. 3–22.

Constable, N. (2009) The commodification of intimacy: Marriage, sex, and reproductive labor. *Annual Review of Anthropology*, 38, 49–64.

Decena, C.U., Shedlin, M.S., and Martínez, A. (2006) "Los hombres no mandan aqui": Narrating immigrant genders and sexualities in New York. *Social Text*, 24 (3 88), 35–54.

Espiritu, Y.L. (1999) "We don't sleep around like white girls do": Family, culture and gender in Filipina American lives, in *Gender and U.S. Immigration: Contemporary Trends* (ed. P. Hongadneu-Sotelo). University of California Press, Berkeley, pp. 263–84.

Foucault, M. (1990) *The History of Sexuality, Volume 1: An Introduction*, 5th edn (trans. R. Hurley). Vintage, New York.

Glick Schiller, N., Basch, L., and Blanc-Szanton, C. (1992) Transnationalism: A new analytic framework for understanding migration, in *Towards a Transnational Perspective on Migration: Race, Class, Ethnicity, and Nationalism Reconsidered* (ed. N. Glick-Schiller, L. Basch, and C. Blanc-Szanton). New York Academy of Sciences, New York, pp. 1–24.

Guy, D. (1991) *Sex and Danger in Buenos Aires: Prostitution, Family and Nation in Argentina.* University of Nebraska Press, Lincoln.

Hirsh, J. (2003) *A Courtship after Marriage: Sexuality and Love in Mexican Transnational Families.* University of California Press, Berkeley.

Jansen, S. and Spijkerboer, T. (2011) *Fleeing Homophobia: Asylum Claims Related to Sexual Orientation and Gender Identity in Europe.* COC Nederland and Vrije Universiteit, Amsterdam.

Kempadoo, K. (1998) Introduction: Globalizing sex workers' rights, in *Global Sex Workers: Rights, Resistance, and Redefinition* (ed. K. Kempadoo and J. Doezma). Routledge, New York, pp. 1–28.

Kleefeld, E. (2010) Gohmert: There's a diabolical 30-year plot to have terrorist babies born in U.S.! (video) *TPM Muckraker*, June 25. tpmdc.talkingpointsmemo

.com/2010/06/gohmert-theres-a-diabolical-30-year-plot-to-have-terrorist
-babies-born-in-us-video.php (accessed July 30, 2013).

Kofman, E. (2004) Family-related migration: A critical review of European studies. *Journal of Ethnic and Migration Studies*, 30 (2), 243–62.

Lan, P.-C. (2006) *Global Cinderellas: Migrant Domestics and Newly Rich Employers in Taiwan*. Duke University Press, Durham, NC.

Liu-Farrar, G. (2010) The absent spouses: Gender, sex, race and extramarital sexuality among Chinese migrants in Japan. *Sexualities*, 13 (1), 97–121.

Luibhéid, E. (2002) *Entry Denied: Controlling Sexuality at the Border*. University of Minnesota Press, Minneapolis.

Luibhéid, E. (ed.) (2008) *Queer/Migration: A Special Issue of GLQ: A Journal of Lesbian and Gay Studies*, 14 (2–3).

Manalansan, M.F. (2003) *Global Divas: Filipino Gay Men in the Diaspora*. Duke University Press, Durham, NC.

Manalansan, M.F. (2006) Queer intersections: Sexuality and gender in migration studies. *International Migration Review*, 40 (1), 224–49.

Manalansan, M.F. (2008) Queering the chain of care paradigm. *The Scholar and Feminist Online*, 6 (3). http://sfonline.barnard.edu/immigration/manalansan_01.htm (accessed July 30, 2013).

Massey, D., Durand, J., and Malone, N.J. (2002) *Beyond Smoke and Mirrors: Mexican Immigration in an Era of Economic Integration*. Russell Sage Foundation, New York.

Middleton, J. (2008) Gender Based Persecution in the South African Asylum System. Migrant Rights Monitoring Project Special Report No. 3, Witwatersrand.

Miller, A. (2005) Gay enough? Some tensions in seeking the grant of asylum and protecting global sexual diversity, in *Passing Lines: Sexuality and Immigration* (ed. B. Epps, K. Valens, and B. Johnson-González). Harvard University Press, Cambridge, MA, pp. 137–87.

Padilla, M., Hirsch, J., Muñoz-Laboy, M., et al. (2007) Introduction, in *Love and Globalization: Transformations of Intimacy in the Contemporary World*. Vanderbilt University Press, Nashville, pp. ix–xxxi.

Parker, R. (2009) Sexuality, culture and society: Shifting paradigms in sexuality research. *Culture, Health & Sexuality*, 11 (3), 251–66.

Povinelli, E. (2006) *The Empire of Love: Toward a Theory of Intimacy, Genealogy and Carnality*. Duke University Press, Durham, NC.

Rouse, R. (1992) Making sense of settlement: Class transformation, cultural struggle, and transnationalism among Mexican migrants in the United States, in *Towards a Transnational Perspective on Migration: Race, Class, Ethnicity, and Nationalism Reconsidered* (ed. N. Glick-Schiller, L. Basch, and C. Blanc-Szanton). New York Academy of Sciences, New York, pp. 25–52.

Sassen, S. (1992) Why migration? *NACLA Report on the Americas*, 26 (1), 14–9.

Simmons, T. (2008) Sexuality and immigration: UK family reunification policy and the regulation of sexual citizens in the European Union. *Political Geography*, 27 (2), 213–30.

Somerville, S. (2007) Queer, in *Keywords in American Cultural Studies* (ed. B. Burgett and G. Hendler). New York University Press, New York, pp. 187–91.

Stoler, A.L. (2002) *Carnal Knowledge and Imperial Power*. University of California Press, Berkeley.

Thing, J. (2010) Gay, Mexican and immigrant: Intersecting identities among gay men in Los Angeles. *Social Identities*, 16 (6), 809–31.

Thomas, F., Haour-Knipe, M., and Aggleton, P. (eds) (2009) *Mobility, Sexuality, and AIDS*. Routledge, New York.

Torpey, J. (2000) *The Invention of the Passport*. Cambridge University Press, Cambridge.

Williams, L. (2012) Transnational marriage migration and marriage migration: An overview, in *Transnational Marriage: New Perspectives from Europe and Beyond* (ed. K. Charsley). Routledge, New York, pp. 23–37.

Wray, H. (2012) Any time, any place, anywhere: Entry clearance, marriage migration and the border, in *Transnational Marriage: New Perspectives from Europe and Beyond* (ed. K. Charsley). Routledge, New York, pp. 41–59.

Yang, W.-S. and Lu, M.C.-W. (eds) (2010) *Asian Cross-Border Marriage Migration: Demographic Patterns and Social Issues*. Amsterdam University Press, Amsterdam.

Suggested Reading

Decena, C. (2011) *Tacit Subjects: Belonging and Same-Sex Desire among Dominican Immigrant Men*. Duke University Press, Durham, NC.

Epps, B., Valens, K., and Johnson González, B. (eds) (2005) *Passing Lines: Sexuality and Immigration*. David Rockefeller Center for Latin American Studies, Harvard University, Cambridge, MA.

Kempadoo, K. and Doezma, J. (eds) (1998) *Global Sex Workers: Rights, Resistance, and Redefinition*. Routledge, New York.

Luibhéid, E. (2002) *Entry Denied: Controlling Sexuality at the Border*. University of Minnesota Press, Minneapolis.

Luibhéid, E. (ed.) (2008) *Queer/Migration: A Special Issue of GLQ: A Journal of Lesbian and Gay Studies*, 14 (2–3).

Manalansan, M.F. (2003) *Global Divas: Filipino Gay Men in the Diaspora*. Duke University Press, Durham, NC.

Padilla, M., Hirsch, J., Muñoz-Laboy, M., et al. (eds) (2007) *Love and Globalization: Transformations of Intimacy in the Contemporary World.* Vanderbilt University Press, Nashville, TN.

Segura, D. and Zavella, P. (eds) (2007) *Women and Migration in the U.S.–Mexico Borderlands: A Reader.* Duke University Press, Durham, NC.

Shah, N. (2011) *Stranger Intimacy: Contesting Race, Sexuality, and the Law in North America.* University of California Press, Berkeley.

6

Sex Trafficking

Robert M. Buffington and Donna J. Guy

If we take contemporary media reports and political pronouncements at their word, sex trafficking is nothing less than a form of "modern-day slavery," an unconscionable violation of human rights that, like its repugnant predecessor, must be abolished once and for all. For example, investigative journalist and professional screenwriter Peter Landesman began his influential 2004 *New York Times* exposé, "The Girls Next Door," with a police raid on a New Jersey stash house in a "leafy, middle-class Anytown" that rescued four undocumented Mexican girls aged fourteen to seventeen (Landesman 2004). The house, Landesman informed readers, was the "squalid, land-based equivalent of a 19th-century slave ship, with rancid, doorless bathrooms; bare, putrid mattresses; and a stash of penicillin, 'morning after' pills and misoprostol, an antiulcer medication that can induce abortion." In the report that followed, he told a tragic (and lurid) tale of abducted girls, depraved clients, menacing foreign traffickers, corrupt foreign officials, and overwhelmed law-enforcement agencies. Landesman's riveting story garnered immediate international attention: the piece was included in the 2005 edition of *The Best American Crime Writing* (which called it "the most requested and widely read *New York Times* story of the year"), and inspired a Canadian–US television miniseries, *Human Trafficking*, and a feature film, *Trade*, which premiered at United Nations Headquarters in New York under the auspices of the UN Office on Drugs and Crime and the international human rights organization Equality Now.

A Global History of Sexuality: The Modern Era, First Edition.
Edited by Robert M. Buffington, Eithne Luibhéid, and Donna J. Guy.
© 2014 Robert M. Buffington, Eithne Luibhéid, and Donna J. Guy.
Published 2014 by Blackwell Publishing Ltd.

Another prominent *New York Times* journalist, Nicolas Kristof, has kept the theme alive with an ongoing series of books, articles, and blogs about sex trafficking around the world. A 2009 column, "If This Isn't Slavery, What Is?," put a human face to the cruelest aspects of sex trafficking with a wrenching tale of a Cambodian girl, Pross, kidnapped by a young woman and sold into sexual slavery at age thirteen:

> She was kept locked deep inside the brothel, her hands tied behind her back . . . painfully stitched up so she could be resold as a virgin . . . beaten every day, sometimes two or three times a day . . . subjected to electric shocks. . . . Twice she became pregnant and was subjected to crude abortions. The second abortion left Pross in great pain . . . "I was begging, hanging on to her feet, and asking for rest," Pross remembered. "She got mad." That's when the woman gouged out Pross's right eye with a piece of metal. (Kristof 2009)

To ensure that readers experienced the full force of Pross's horrifying story, Kristof led off with a compelling picture of the "rescued" young woman's badly scarred face. And, as often happens in antitrafficking human interest stories, the reporter can't resist crossing the line between exposé and activism. For example, in a 2004 series on sexual slavery in Cambodia, Kristof took the dramatic (but hardly unprecedented) step of purchasing two young women from their brothel owners.

The antitrafficking fervor generated by muckrakers such as Landesman and Kirstof is echoed in the rhetoric of prominent political figures, especially from North America and Western Europe.[1] In a 2010 speech declaring January "National Slavery and Human Trafficking Prevention Month," US president Barak Obama observed that:

> As a Nation, we have known moments of great darkness and greater light; and dim years of chattel slavery illuminated and brought to an end by President Lincoln's actions and a painful Civil War. Yet even today, the darkness and inhumanity of enslavement exists. (White House 2010)

And, in an anecdotal vein reminiscent of Kristof, Queen Silvia of Sweden's 2006 speech to concerned EU businessmen included a "true" story about a young Lithuanian girl named Dangoule trafficked into Sweden, "enticed by the man she loved . . . with promises of a better life and a steady job picking vegetables." Once Dangoule arrived in Sweden, however, "her passport was taken from her and she was locked up in an apartment and told that she now had a debt of 20,000 Euros for her travel, passport and accommodation costs . . . [she] was beaten, raped, starved, and humiliated . . . [and] forced . . . to be silent and to suffer several customers per day." A few months later, "in utter despair, Dangoule jumped from a bridge to end her life" (Queen Silva 2006).

With this kind of publicity, human trafficking—especially sex trafficking—has drawn the attention of politicians of all political persuasions, policymakers, law-enforcement agencies, international organizations, and ordinary people throughout the world. Although generally acknowledged to be inaccurate, including by the agencies themselves, often-cited statistics from the US State Department's 2007 *Trafficking in Persons Report* for the number of trafficking victims worldwide (4 to 27 million) and for the number of people trafficked across international borders each year (800 000), coupled with numbers from the International Labor Organization for annual profits from human trafficking (32 billion dollars), have put human trafficking in the same league as illegal arms sales and drug trafficking (US State Department 2007; International Labour Office 2008). The result of this powerful combination of abolitionist rhetoric and alarming statistics is an ongoing *moral panic*—a generalized anxiety about moral threats and social degeneration—over human trafficking in general and sex trafficking in particular that obscures more than it illuminates with regard to the past as well as the present.

Historians of sex trafficking in the modern era confront two serious obstacles. First, sex trafficking has generally been considered a crime so most of its inner workings are hidden, often deliberately, from the prying eyes of police, rivals, journalists, demographers, and historians. As a result, what we see is inevitably distorted by law-enforcement agendas, criminal competition, sensationalistic reporting, misleading statistics, and limited archival materials. Second, sex trafficking has proven quite difficult to define at least until very recently, and even widely accepted definitions are still contested. Sometimes this situation benefits antitrafficking campaigners who have taken political advantage of the vagaries surrounding sex trafficking to link this complex phenomenon to the African slave trade and highlight its most horrific manifestations. More often, inadequate definition has made the crime more difficult to prosecute and the phenomenon more difficult to understand. Indeed, some critics argue that, whatever their intent, the representational strategies of the modern anti-sex-trafficking movement perpetuate a "pornography of suffering" that elicits our empathy and excites our passions without helping trafficked persons in any substantial way (Dean 2003). Pornographic or not, these representational strategies have encouraged law-enforcement solutions to the *crime* of sex trafficking that have had only minimal effect, in part because they fail to adequately address the sociostructural issues that underlie human trafficking and exploitation.

To arrive at a workable definition of trafficking in persons—a crime that includes but is not limited to sex trafficking—Argentina and the United States spearheaded a United Nations push to develop the 2000 *Protocol to Prevent, Suppress, and Punish Trafficking in Persons*.[2] The *Protocol* defined trafficking in persons as:

> The recruitment, transportation, transfer, harbouring or receipt of persons, by means of the threat or use of force or other forms of coercion, of abduction, of fraud, of deception, of the abuse of power or of a position of vulnerability or of the giving or receiving of payments or benefits to achieve the consent of a person having control over another person, for the purpose of exploitation. (United Nations 2000)

As is the case with most UN protocols, the definition aspires to be explicit enough to guide policymakers and police and also comprehensive enough to apply to all member states. In the process, it reveals the range and complexity of the phenomena of sex trafficking. According to the *Protocol*, sex trafficking can range from outright slavery to forced labor, involuntary servitude, and sexual exploitation (i.e. being controlled by a pimp or madam), and can be realized through means as varied as abduction, coercion, fraud, deception, and abuse of a position of vulnerability (i.e. a parent's control over a child or a husband's over a wife). Indeed, contemporary grassroots activists working closely with sex trafficking "victims" have found that most of them understand that they are migrating to do sex work but are deceived about the working conditions they will experience and the debt they will incur once they arrive—a less dire, if still distressing, situation that the worst-case scenarios and statistical manipulations of most antitrafficking campaigners attempt to gloss over. With these complexities firmly in mind, this chapter seeks to navigate the distortions put forth by politicians, law enforcement, journalists, and antitrafficking organizations (including the United Nations) in order to produce a historical overview of sex trafficking in the modern era that is as complicated, perplexing, and disturbing as the phenomenon itself has always been.

This demystification is more than just a matter of historical accuracy. A better understanding of the long-standing structural forces at work in contemporary sex trafficking clarifies some of the problems with current policy. As political scientist Joel Quirk points out, "most recent works have tended to attribute the 'rise' of contemporary slavery to new innovations, such as economic globalization, technological change, Cold War collapse, and demographic trends." While these innovations have indeed influenced contemporary human trafficking, he notes that they can "best be understood as an extension and/or reconfiguration of enduring historical themes rather than as distinctly modern developments" (Quirk 2012, p. 41). Quirk's critique of the focus on new innovations at the expense of historical themes reiterates and expands critics' argument that activists and policymakers have too often ignored the "structural determinants" of human trafficking and have thus developed "inappropriate and disproportionate" policies to combat it (Brysk and Choi-Fitzpatrick 2012, p. 2). To address these concerns, the sections that follow—especially the three case studies—focus on four major historical themes or "structures" that have shaped contemporary sex trafficking: *patriarchy* (the social and cultural forces that reinforce men's domination of women); other forms of *social inequality* within, between, and among different groups (grounded in perceived differences of race, ethnicity, class, and religion); *political asymmetry* within, between, and among different countries and regions of the world (including military conquest and occupation, imperialism, and neocolonial domination); and *economic disparity* within, between, and among various countries and regions of the world (especially the spread of capitalism and its impact on labor migration).

The chapter begins by clarifying some of the definitional issues left unresolved by the UN *Protocol* and providing a concise theoretical framework for understanding sex trafficking as a historical phenomenon. This is followed by a brief history of previous international campaigns to end sex trafficking and then by three exemplary case studies—Nepal to India, the Philippines to South Korea, Eastern Europe to Western Europe and the Americas—intended to provide three distinct sex trafficking scenarios, all of them with deep historical roots and contemporary salience. Each case study deals extensively with the four historical structures outlined in the previous paragraph. The conclusion offers some "lessons" from the history of sex trafficking for scholars, activists, and policymakers.

Clarifications and Frameworks

Discussions of sex trafficking that draw inspiration and impetus from mainstream media and political discourse tend to blur important distinctions between sexual slavery and sex trafficking, sex trafficking and sex work migration, and coerced and uncoerced underage sex workers. In the first case, ubiquitous references to "modern-day slavery" conflate the institution of slavery, which involves the legal ownership of one person by another, with forced labor, indentured servitude, and debt bondage, which are contractual claims to a person's labor that involve varying degrees of exploitation and abuse. While slavery certainly includes claims to labor and forced labor regimes can look a lot like slavery, they are not the same thing. As historical sociologist Orlando Patterson notes,

> standard arguments making the claim that all trafficking in persons and, even more broadly, all forms of coerced labor, constitute forms of slavery are problematic because they embrace too many of the world's migrants— internal and external—and too promiscuously conflate slavery with forms of exploitation not considered slavery in most non-Western societies or in any historically informed and conceptually rigorous use of the term. (Patterson 2012, p. 1)

To avoid confusion, many scholars and activists prefer the term "slavery-like conditions," which acknowledges similarities to the exploitation and abuse of legal slavery without the conceptual muddle. In the second case, neoabolitionists (those who favor the abolition of prostitution) argue that all prostitution is coerced even when the person involved claims to have "chosen" to enter into sex work. They thus refuse to distinguish between sex trafficking, which by definition requires some degree of coercion, and sex work migration (with or without documentation) by "consenting" adults. This distinction often breaks down in practice because illegal activities such as prostitution and undocumented migration put consenting adults at risk of being trafficked, but, since solutions to these specific crimes would involve decriminalization of sex work and immigration reform in receiving countries rather than abolition of sex work migration, it is an important distinction to maintain. Finally, since most legal definitions of trafficking take eighteen as the age of consent, all underage migratory sex workers are technically trafficked regardless of their actual circumstances. This assumption tends to inflate statistics, especially for trafficked children, and further complicate the difficult task of measuring, assessing, and responding to the problem. To be clear: our intention is not to downplay the tragic consequences of sex trafficking—which hardly need distortion and hyperbole to elicit indignation and empathy—but to specify what we mean by the term, especially as we attempt to untangle its history.

A Brief History of Moral Panics over Sex Trafficking

While historians generally trace the first full-fledged international moral panic over sex trafficking back to the so-called White Slavery campaigns of the late nineteenth century in Europe and the Americas, outrage over the sexual aspects of African slavery had played a major role in successful abolitionist efforts to put an end to chattel slavery in most parts of the world. Late eighteenth-century British-Jamaican plantation owner and overseer Thomas Thistlewood, for example, felt no compunction about keeping detailed records of his sexual activities with his female slaves, even as he acknowledged that female slaves who belonged to others were off limits to him. Slave owners such as Thistlewood—and records suggest that he was typical enough—routinely demanded sexual services from their female "property," including access to virgin slaves before they married (Burnard 2004).

As international abolitionist campaigns began to take hold in the nineteenth century, this kind of behavior became unacceptable. Throughout Latin America, "free womb" laws that promised freedom to children born into slavery served as liberal touchstones during the early nineteenth-century wars of independence and entered into legal codes in places as different as Argentina (1813), Paraguay (1842), and Brazil (1871). In this way, the freeing of female wombs came to symbolize not just the emancipation of enslaved peoples but also the independence of nations. It also hinted at some of the complicated ways in which chattel slavery differed from sex trafficking. For example, in 1871, the same year that saw the passage of Brazil's Free Womb Law, a female slave named Honorata went to court to defend her right to be sold to another slave owner because her current owner, a widow, had forced her into prostitution when she was twelve in order to live off her earnings (Graham 1992).

The rise of regulated prostitution in municipalities, nation-states, and empires around the world coincided with the increased migration of people from one place to another. For example, the discovery of gold in places such as the western United States and southern Africa created an instant demand for labor of all kinds, including sex work. Given the difficulties and expense involve in long-distance migration, it also created opportunities for human traffickers, including sex traffickers. And historians have uncovered wide-ranging international networks of pimps who smuggled and trafficked women from European cities to places such as Argentina, Brazil, Chile, and South Africa beginning in the late nineteenth century.

Inspired by the success of mid-nineteenth-century international aboli-tionist movements, the late nineteenth- and early twentieth-century white slavery campaigns brought pressure on countries around the world to put an end to sex trafficking. As the name suggests, racial politics were at the core of these international antitrafficking efforts. The prominence of religious groups and moralistic language helped shape the movement as well, albeit in different ways. Christian groups spearheaded the first anti-slavery and antitrafficking movements, but, as pogroms and anti-Semitic campaigns intensified in Eastern Europe and Russia, European Jewish leaders recognized that "their" women and girls were at increased risk of trafficking (and the temptations of sex work migration). Thus in 1885 elite British Jews founded the Jewish Association for the Protection of Girls and Women for the express purpose of protecting Eastern European Jewish women victimized by political conflicts and inflexible religious laws, espe-cially with regard to the protection of widows. As groups like the Jewish Association intervened on behalf of their constituencies by sending out special investigators and gathering census data on women working as prostitutes in foreign bordellos, they inadvertently contributed to popular misconceptions—fostered by politicians, neoabolitionists, and journalists—that linked specific groups of women and girls (Jewish, Slavic, Irish, etc.) to white slavery and transnational prostitution.

To buttress their moral arguments, neoabolitionists allied themselves with public health officials in the battle against venereal diseases—a topic of considerable interest to national officials, especially in Europe and the Americas. During the nineteenth century, syphilis took a greater toll on soldiers than battlefield casualties. To make matters worse, syphilis and gonorrhea could be transmitted to the unborn, which led to increased rates of infant mortality and blindness. One solution, the legalization and medical inspection of prostitutes, became one of the first public health campaigns linked to moral panics around sexuality. But it also fueled the anger of antiregulationists such as British activist Josephine Baker, who argued that mandatory medical inspections failed to distinguish between respectable and disreputable women either at home or abroad, an argument supported by distressing anecdotes of "decent" English women traveling abroad whom authorities forced to submit to physical examinations by foreign (often dark-skinned) doctors.

Britain, home of the international abolitionist movement, initiated the moral panic around "white slavery" in 1879 with a parliamentary discussion regarding the presence of British women in foreign houses of prostitution. A few years later, investigative journalist William Stead shocked readers all over the English-speaking world by purchasing a thirteen-year-old girl from a procuress as a centerpiece to his *Pall Mall Gazette* exposé of the London white slave trade, "The Maiden Tribute of Modern Babylon." In overwrought language borrowed from the abolition movement and stock-in-trade of muckrakers such as Landesman and Kristof ever since, Stead described the plight of young London girls held against their will by cold-hearted madams and brutalized by sadistic clients:

> "In my house," said a most respectable lady . . . "you can enjoy the screams of the girl with the certainty that no one else hears them but yourself" . . . "Here," said the keeper of a fashionable villa . . . as she showed her visitor over the well-appointed rooms, "Here is a room where you can be perfectly secure . . . You lock the door and then you can do as you please. The girl may scream blue murder, but not a sound will be heard." (Stead 1885)

Although Stead went to prison for purchasing the girl (a crime whatever his intent), neoabolitionists considered him a martyr to the cause, and his gripping account of sex slavery in one of the world's most cosmopolitan cities had a huge impact on the general public and political leaders in Britain and elsewhere. In this way, the rhetorical style of the abolitionist movement, in the hands of a skilled storyteller like Stead, helped neoabolitionists foment a panic around the alleged enslavement and transportation of white women and girls across national borders.

The international moral panic around sex trafficking reached its peak in the years leading up to World War I (1914–18). In 1903 and again in 1908, the US Bureau of Immigration appointed a Hungarian-born Jewish immigrant and investigative journalist, Marcus Braun, as an undercover immigration inspector to report on white slavery in Europe and along the US border. While Braun's earlier report focused on the abuses involved in transnational contract labor including the use of immigrant labor to break strikes, by 1908 his interests had shifted to transnational sex trafficking. "What is the clandestine importation of . . . a gang of men under contract to perform certain labor," he asked, "in comparison to the importation of

the Daughters of Eve, the sex of Mother, Daughter, Wife, Sister for the
purpose of prostitution? . . . Why to me, it seems absolutely insignificant"
(cited in Peck 2011, p. 236). Although his official reports were a bit more
restrained than the salacious accounts of muckrakers such as Stead, Braun
employed many of the same rhetorical stratagems, including the frequent
use of heart-wrenching anecdotes and ubiquitous references to pimps as
"merchants of human flesh." His report and others like it provided the
impetus behind the passage of the 1910 White-Slave Traffic Act (better
known as the Mann Act after its congressional sponsor James Robert
Mann). Advertised as a response to international and interstate sex trafficking, the Mann Act served instead as catch-all legislation for a range of
moral panics and authorities invoked its provisions to persecute interracial
relationships, especially when they involved African American men such
as boxing champion Jack Johnson and rebellious young women who
opposed the marriage choices of their parents. In practice, then, white-
slavery legislation in the United States and Europe worked more often to
enforce racial segregation and domestic patriarchy at home than to combat
sex trafficking across national borders.

International treaties proved no better at stopping sex trafficking, in
large part because they relied on national, state, and local authorities to
enforce them. The 1904 *International Agreement for the Suppression of the
"White Slave Traffic,"* for instance, arranged for

> each of the Contracting Governments . . . to establish or name some author-
> ity charged with the coordination of all information relative to the procuring
> of women or girls for immoral purposes abroad . . . [and] empowered to
> correspond directly with the similar department established in each of the
> other Contracting States.

But, aside from promising to gather data on "the arrival of persons who
clearly appear to be the principals, accomplices in, or victims of, such
traffic" and assisting in repatriation of victims and prosecution of traffickers, the signatories were left to their own devices since the legislation lacked
enforcement provisions (other than "denunciation") to compel compliance
(International Agreement 1904).[3] Moreover, the 1910 *International Convention for the Suppression of the "White Slave Traffic"* focused almost
entirely on the prosecution of traffickers:

> whoever, in order to gratify the passions of another person, has procured,
> enticed, or led away, even with her consent . . . [or] has, by fraud, or by means

of violence, threats, abuse of authority, or any other method of compulsion, procured, enticed, or led away a woman or girl under age, for immoral purposes, shall be punished, notwithstanding that the various acts constituting the offence may have been committed in different countries. (International Convention 1910)

International sex trafficking slowed considerably during World War I, but the cessation of hostilities renewed concerns about the vulnerability of women and girls in the wake of a conflict that claimed the lives of over 10 million soldiers—a lost generation of male protectors. In 1921, the newly formed League of Nations took the lead in international efforts to suppress the "traffic in women and children." Aside from the long-overdue name change (from "white slavery"), the League had no more success than its predecessors at ending sex trafficking, although it did foster increased international awareness and cooperation on the part of humanitarian organizations such as the British-based Association for Moral and Social Hygiene and the International Bureau for the Suppression of the Traffic in Women and Children. It also commissioned a *Report of the Special Body of Experts on Traffic in Women and Children* (1927), based primarily on faulty and often biased data supplied by member states, which further reinforced popular assumptions about the presumed ethnicity of both victims and traffickers.

As happened during the prewar white slavery campaigns, journalists fueled public interest with inflammatory stories about the horrors of the sex trade. In 1927, Albert Londres, a world-famous French investigative journalist who had helped on the League *Report*, published an account of *Le chemin de Buenos Ayres*—published a year later in English as *The Road to Buenos Aires*—a curious mix of bohemian *flaneurie* (slumming) and nationalist anxieties about the traffic in French women and girls to Argentina. According to Londres, his goal was to "go down into the pits where society deposits what it fears or rejects; to look at what the world refuses to see; to pass my own judgment on what the world has condemned" (1928, p. 244). What he reported back from the "pits" of La Boca (Buenos Aires's immigrant ghetto) was a lurid tale of Jewish pimps ("dark Levites" with "filthy skin" and "unwashed corkscrews") and prostitutes ("*polacas*," literally "Polish women") that played to anti-Semitic stereotypes and glossed over the role of French traffickers. Shock at the horrors of Nazi racial "cleansing" during World War II (1939–1945) discouraged blatant anti-Semitism in postwar trafficking discourses, but the figure of the cruel foreign trafficker preying on innocent women has persisted in media representations of ruthless Eastern European and Mexican gangsters who callously sell off "their" women for exorbitant profits.

As concerns about sex trafficking resurfaced after the war, the new United Nations assumed responsibility for coordinating international responses to the problem. Again the principal focus was on prosecuting traffickers rather than helping trafficked women and girls. Cast in the emerging language of human rights, the preamble to the 1949 *Convention for the Suppression of the Traffic in Persons and of the Exploitation of the Prostitution of Others* noted that "prostitution and the accompanying evil of the traffic in persons for the purpose of prostitution are incompatible with the dignity and worth of the human person and endanger the welfare of the individual, the family and the community." With this in mind, the *Convention* urged signatories to help with women's repatriation and "agree to take or to encourage, through their public and private educational, health, social, economic and other related services, measures for the prevention of prostitution and for the rehabilitation and social adjustment of the victims." Nevertheless, the *Convention* still emphasized the punishment of "any person who, to gratify the passions of another . . . procures, entices or leads away, for purposes of prostitution, another person, even with the consent of that person" (United Nations 1949). Although major powers such as the United States, Canada, Britain, and China never signed, the Convention nonetheless provided a basis for international cooperation on sex trafficking through the Cold War era (1946–1991) and until it was superseded by the 2000 *Protocol.*

Understanding Case Studies: An Introduction

Although the term "sex trafficking" comes out of nineteenth-century moral panics over "white slavery," the practices it purports to describe have deep historical roots. The movement of people, cultural practices, raw materials, manufactured goods, technologies, and capital—a process known as globalization—has been around since long before the beginning of recorded history. Despite this impressive genealogy, most observers agree that globalization "took off" during the nineteenth century with the advent of modern transportation and communication technologies and has been growing at leaps and bounds ever since. Indeed the first round of international anti-sex-trafficking conferences coincided with both the development of steamship technology (which brought "floods" of immigrants to ports in Argentina and the United States) and the rise of nationalism (often in response to the "threat" of immigration). Although most official concerns about international migration focused on men and families, unattached migrant women also entered into nationalist discourses: as female citizens at risk of sexual commerce in foreign lands, as potential prostitutes who might pervert or infect the host country's male population, or as innocent victims of international traffickers forced into sexual slavery.

Like most globalization processes, sex trafficking has been characterized by accelerating flows of people, migrations that most often work to reproduce and even exacerbate existing social inequalities. In the vast majority of cases, potential sex workers, whether coerced or voluntary, move from the impoverished, politically unstable margins of the global economy (usually in Global South countries) to its wealthier, more stable centers (usually in Global North countries).[4] As noted in the introduction to this chapter, the three scenarios that follow focus on the deep historical structures—patriarchy, social inequality, geopolitical asymmetry, and economic disparity—that have shaped and continue to shape sex trafficking around the world. Although all three cases share similar structural roots, each scenario is situated in a distinct geographical and historical context with distinct local, regional, national, and transnational dimensions. Taken together, these distinct factors combine with deep structures to shape the general phenomenon of sex trafficking in specific and sometimes very different ways.

Case Study 1: Sex Trafficking from Nepal to India

As is the case with most sex trafficking scenarios outside Europe and the United States, the long history of Nepali migration to India in search of work, including sex work, has often been glossed over or ignored by academic researchers, antitrafficking activists, and policymakers. This historical myopia is understandable given present-day concerns about what by most accounts is a rapidly growing problem. Estimates of the number of Nepali workers in India at any given time range from 1.3 to 3 million, as much as 10 percent of Nepal's national population. Although citizens of the two countries can cross the border without passports, most migrant workers lack official work papers for India, which makes them especially vulnerable to traffickers of all kinds. According to the 2009 *US State Department Human Rights Report* on Nepal, approximately twelve thousand Nepali women and children (almost all of them girls) are trafficked into India each year for sex work—more than double the numbers from ten years earlier. An estimated two hundred thousand Nepali sex workers make up nearly 2 percent of the 3 million or more women and girls who work in India's sex industry, and their numbers are growing just as fast (Mukherjee and Mukherjee 2004, p. 99). A comprehensive 2004 study of Indian prostitution noted a strong correlation between economic development and prostitution: Indian states with the highest levels of trade, business, industry, urbanization, and tourism have the greatest number of sex workers, many of them drawn from poorer states and neighboring countries such as Nepal and Bangladesh (Mukherjee and Mukherjee 2004, pp. 79–80). This migration pattern mirrors the situation in Nepal, where most migrant sex workers—including trafficked women and girls—come from poorer regions close to either the Indian border or Kathmandu, the capital and largest city. As with trafficked sex workers in India, most trafficked Nepali women and girls are unmarried, illiterate, and very young at the time they are trafficked (Hennick and Simkhada 2004, p. 12).

Although Nepali labor migration to India has increased dramatically in recent years, the pattern has deep historical roots. The Kathmandu valley has played a culturally central, if geographically peripheral, role in South Asian civilization since before the birth of Buddha in Lumbini on the Nepali side of the current border with India (c. 563 BCE). Although its peripheral location kept Nepal nominally independent of the various South Asian empires, a steady flow of peoples, religions, and culture into and out of the central valley connected the region to the outside world, especially to India.

As British involvement in the subcontinent intensified in the eighteenth and early nineteenth centuries, this crosscultural exchange took on a new dimension. By the early nineteenth century, the expansionist aims of Nepal's rulers had come into direct conflict with Britain's imperial ambitions. British victory in the Anglo-Nepalese war (1814–16) put an end to Nepali expansion but British military leaders, impressed with the fighting abilities of Gurkha soldiers, began to recruit them into special regiments of the imperial army, first for service in India and later throughout the British empire. Bravery in battle and loyalty to their British commanders during the bloody 1857 Indian Mutiny gave the Gurkha special status as one of South Asia's manly "martial races"—Europeans considered most Asian men effeminate—and they often developed close interregimental ties to their British counterparts.[5]

The widescale recruitment of Nepali men into the British Army coincided with efforts to regulate prostitution in India as imperial governance passed from the East India Company to the Crown in the wake of the Mutiny. Fearful that exposure to "oriental" culture would undermine English morals and morale, British authorities channeled their anxieties into an obsession with the regulation of female sexuality, especially prostitution, which they saw as both a necessary safety valve for the aggressively masculine enterprise of imperial expansion and a dangerous source of disease that threatened to sap the physical strength of its soldiers. Their solution was an elaborate system of regulated brothels attached to military camps and *cantonments* (foreign enclaves built around major military bases) that provided inexpensive, convenient female prostitutes who could be regularly checked for venereal diseases. An official 1886 military order— known to opponents of state-regulated prostitution as the "Infamous Circular Memorandum"—advised base commanders that "it is necessary to have a sufficient number of women, to take care that they are sufficiently attractive, to provide them with proper houses, and, above all, to insist upon means of ablution being always available" (cited in Andrew and Bushnell 1899, p. 10). With no fewer than 60 000 British troops stationed in India at any one time, military prostitution became a prominent part of the imperial sexual landscape (Levine 1994, p. 581). According to opponents, it also provided powerful incentives for sex traffickers. A disapproving British official noted that the "Infamous Circular Memorandum" was:

> faithfully carried out . . . The commanding officer gave orders to his quartermaster . . . to take two policemen (without uniform), and go into the villages and take from the homes of these poor people their daughters from fourteen years and upwards, about twelve or fifteen girls at a time. They were to select the best-looking. (cited in Andrew and Bushnell 1899, p. 11)

This blatant disregard for the sexual propriety of poor "native" women served the instrumental purpose of providing a ready stock of prostitutable women and girls for use by soldiers who, British colonial authorities feared, might otherwise take up more serious relations with local women, which could compromise their political and cultural loyalties, or indulge in sexual relations with each other, which would compromise their manhood. According to historian Philippa Levine, it also worked to

condemn colonized men whose "indifference to the shame of their wom-
enfolk became an index of male brutality" and colonized peoples whose
"unquestioned acceptance of prostitution [was] the mark of coarse and
unfeeling societies" (Levine 2004, p. 160).

Registered prostitutes working in military brothels represented only a
small proportion of sex workers but official tolerance provided the impetus
behind the expansion of the sex industry in major cities such as Delhi,
Bombay (Mumbai), and Calcutta (Kolkata). To contain the problem, colonial authorities pushed sex workers into designated "red-light" districts—
Delhi's G.B. Road, Bombay's Kamathipura, Calcutta's Sonagachi—that drew
locals, soldiers, colonial functionaries, and international sex tourists in
huge numbers. Once established, these districts continued to attract patrons
long after Indian independence in 1947. And, as some of the largest red-
light districts in the world (then and now), they have required regular
infusions of new sex workers to supply ever-growing client demand. Along
with attracting sex work migration from poorer Indian states and neighboring countries, this demand has produced an expanding market for
trafficked women and girls.

Because British authorities were unconcerned about and perhaps even
complicit in the prostitution and trafficking of "native" women, it is difficult
to determine the number of Nepali women and girls who ended up in the
red-light districts of colonial India. Anecdotal evidence, however, suggests
that it might have been quite high. Although Nepal remained nominally
independent, the Rana family, who controlled the country from 1846 to
1953, maintained close ties to the British, supporting their imperial agenda
in South Asia and supplying them with Gurkha soldiers drawn from minority ethnic groups of Tibetan-Mongolian origin from the hill country. Rana
rulers also drew on women from these same groups to serve as household
servants and palace courtesans, allegedly because their skin was fairer than
that of Nepali women of Indian descent—a prejudice Rana elites may well
have acquired from their British allies. The sketchy histories of Nepali
sex trafficking provided by most scholars and antitrafficking activists also
blame the Rana for promoting special castes associated with sex work,
especially the badi, whose original role as itinerant musicians and dancers
shifted almost exclusively to sex work over the course of the twentieth
century—including the regular trafficking of badi women and girls into
Indian brothels (Samarasinghe 2008, pp. 70–1). While a reliable history of
Rana labor practices has yet to be written, it can hardly be a coincidence
that most trafficked Nepali women and girls come from the same ethnic

groups as Gurkha soldiers; Nepali sex workers have a reputation for being whiter (and therefore more desirable) than most Indian sex workers; and most Indian red-light districts have distinct Nepali compounds.[6]

Although the history of sex trafficking from Nepal to India is murky in places, the supply and demand for the labor of Nepali men, women, and children in India clearly has deep roots—as do the conditions that encourage large-scale human trafficking. Academic research corroborated by anecdotal evidence collected by antitrafficking activists supports this conclusion. Both scholars and activists note the role of political violence, most recently a ten-year-old civil war between Maoist insurgents and government forces (1996–2006), in destabilizing the rural areas that supply most trafficked women and girls. But, if political violence in sending areas has been sporadic, most of the other factors that contribute to sex trafficking have been consistent for generations, in particular the insidious combination of widespread poverty and entrenched gender discrimination, clearly manifest in a current 12 percent literacy rate for poor women (UNESCO 2010). Nepali inheritance laws have long favored sons over daughters and Nepali custom requires adult men and their wives to look after the husband's parents. Under these circumstances, many families, especially those with limited resources, have preferred to arrange marriages for their daughters soon after puberty and packed them off to live with their new in-laws. Daughters without good marriage prospects have often been placed as household servants with wealthier (usually urban) families or sent to work in the carpet factories of Kathmandu. Although political instability and rural poverty set the stage, it is family and community pressure to marry at an early age, the placement of young girls in domestic servitude, and labor migration for young women that produce most Nepali sex trafficking scenarios.

A reliance on *dalals* (local marriage and labor brokers), generally known by or related to the young women and their families, links all three situations. In general, *dalals* perform an indispensable social function, connecting relatively isolated villagers with larger networks to help them find everything from suitable marriage partners to work opportunities in other villages, big cities, and neighboring countries. They are paid a commission, sometimes by both the client and the employer, and this pay structure, combined with their access to national and international networks (including police and immigration authorities) gives unscrupulous *dalals* ample incentive, opportunity, and a certain degree of impunity to move from facilitating work migration into labor trafficking of all kinds—and many of

them do. Recent studies indicate that the two principal routes into sex trafficking involve false promises of marriage and labor migration (with or
without a *dalal*'s services) (Hennick and Simkhada 2004; Crawford and
Kaufman 2008).[7] The first route usually takes advantage of social pressures
on young women to marry and a cultural tradition of arranged marriages
between relative strangers, and relies on deliberate fraud on the part of the
prospective husband, who might appeal to a poor family by agreeing to
marry their daughter without the expected dowry. The second route often
begins with a straightforward migration for work, either as a *kaamgarne*
girl (domestic servant) in an urban middle-class household or as a weaver
in a Kathmandu carpet factory—both considered respectable jobs for poor,
unmarried, rural girls (O'Neill 2001, p. 157). Away from prying village
eyes, however, young migrant women are more vulnerable to everything
from abuse at the hands of their employers to the coercive tactics of sex
traffickers.

Families who come to rely on remittances from sex work sometimes
pressure daughters to continue working as prostitutes. A widely circulated
1998 article on the remote village of Ichowk, for example, noted that
according to local sources the new tin roofs on several houses came from
the earnings of daughters working in the Mumbai sex trade—an admission
that suggests that sex work migration and sex trafficking have become a
"normal" part of community life in some parts of Nepal (Newar 1998). At
the same time, strong community sanctions against "fallen" women have
made it difficult for trafficked women and girls to return home even if their
parents agree to take them back despite the damage to the family's reputation, which might inhibit the marriage chances of siblings or the community's willingness to help out a distressed family.

Although outright abductions are relatively rare—as they are in most
trafficking situations—sex trafficking in Nepal seems to involve a higher
degree of deception and coercion than other trafficking scenarios where
women migrate to work as hostesses, entertainers, or prostitutes only to
find themselves deceived about working conditions. While many Nepali
women and girls do migrate for sex work, a disturbing number are indeed
forced into prostitution. And, despite their alleged desirability, most Nepali
sex workers—voluntary or not—experience the worst of the Indian sex
trade, the so-called "pillow houses," which typically require work weeks of
six or seven days, use threats and violence to enforce house rules, regularly
withhold or short wages to pay off unspecified "debts," and do next to
nothing to enforce condom use by clients.

The relative severity of sex trafficking in Nepal has made it easier for authorities and activists to play off the fears of the general public and especially the international community. The sex trafficking issue first drew public attention in 1996 when the Indian government attempted to return two hundred trafficking victims "rescued" in brothel raids. Nepali authorities initially refused them entry because many had tested positive for HIV/ AIDs and relented only after intense lobbying by local activists. A short time later, public furor over the 1998 case of Kani Sherpa, a Nepali domestic worker in Kuwait who committed suicide after authorities threatened to deport her or return her to the employers who had allegedly raped, beaten, and thrown her off a third-story balcony, served to channel public concern about the treatment of Nepali migrant workers, nationalist anxieties about the violation of young Nepalese women, and moralistic

Figure 6.1 US actress Demi Moore (center) poses for a photograph with Anuradha Koirala (left) and children at the end of her six-day visit to Maiti Nepal, an NGO-run Rehabilitation and Orphanage home for HIV-affected children and female victims of trafficking in Kathmandu, Nepal, on April 7, 2011. Moore was in Nepal as a part of CNN's Freedom Project, a worldwide network that works to eliminate trafficking and sex slavery. *Source*: © Narendra Shrestha / EPA / Corbis.

discourses about the "looseness" of ethnic-minority women (O'Neill 2001, pp. 154, 164). The publicity surrounding horror stories such as Kani Sherpa's suicide; documentaries with titles such as *The Sale of Innocents*, in which a father offers to sell his daughter to the filmmaker; and popular Nepalese films such as the melodramatic *Chameli*, the story of a village girl trafficked into a Mumbai brothel by her drug-addict husband and rejected by her community when she returns with AIDS, have helped attract the attention of government bureaucrats and international donors. This support has made it possible for nongovernmental organizations such as the well-known ABC Nepal and Maiti Nepal to raise public awareness about trafficking, rehabilitate and retrain "rescued" women and girls and facilitate their social reintegration into their home communities, and push government officials to prosecute traffickers.[8] But, aside from an occasional dramatic rescue and some anecdotal progress on community attitudes, little has been done to address the underlying structural conditions—cultural and institutional patriarchy, ethnic discrimination, widespread poverty, a long history of labor outmigration produced by economic disparities, and the legacies of British imperialism—that have made Nepalese women and girls vulnerable to traffickers for generations.

Case Study 2: Sex Trafficking from the Philippines to South Korea

At first glance, the trafficking of young women from the Philippines to South Korea to work in the *gijichon* (military camp towns) as "entertainers" for the US soldiers stationed at nearby military bases looks a lot like the trafficking of Nepali women and girls into Indian red-light districts. The shared legacy of imperial occupation and military prostitution in both the Philippines and South Korea is the most obvious point of comparison. The Philippines endured over four centuries of colonial and neocolonial domination as a Spanish colony from 1565 to 1898, a US protectorate from 1898 to 1941, an occupied territory of Japan from 1941 to 1944, a US protectorate again until independence in 1946, and a host to large US overseas military bases from 1946 until 1992. A Japanese colony from 1910 to 1945 and host to a sizable US military presence since the end of the Korean War in 1953, South Korea has been no stranger to foreign occupations either. As happened with the British in South Asia, military prostitution has had a huge impact in both places as a social problem in need of regulation and as a source of national shame (and nationalist diatribes against foreign influences).

It is impossible to tell how much sex trafficking accompanied military prostitution in the two countries before World War II, although US opponents of military prostitution in the Philippines, drawing on British abolitionist efforts in India, insisted that the two were closely linked (Pivar 1981). But recent investigations into the widespread use of "comfort women" to provide sexual services for Japanese soldiers during the war reveal that military officials forced thousands of women and girls into prostitution and regularly posted them to occupied areas against their will. In the expansionist period before the outbreak of World War II, Japanese authorities— concerned about troop morale, homosexual activities among soldiers, and the danger of soldiers raping local women (and fueling local resistance to imperial occupation)—had begun to actively recruit comfort women from the ranks of sex workers in Japan and its colonies. Once the war started, the supply of potential recruits could no longer meet demand so authorities began to "conscript" local women and girls in large numbers or transport them from colonies such as Korea into various war zones. How many of the estimated two hundred thousand comfort women were forced into prostitution and transported without their consent is unknown, but military records on the staffing and regulation of "comfort stations" along with recent testimony of former comfort women seeking redress from the Japanese government suggest that many were trafficked rather than recruited, at least outside Japan proper. But, even in wartime, the line between recruitment and trafficking could be hard to see and easy to cross. For example, a former Korean comfort woman who had fled as a teenager to a friend's house to escape her mother's beatings recounted being approached by an older Korean woman who

> introduced herself as an acquaintance of my mother since they were both "from the North," although I had never met her before. She urged me to go to the *senchi* [battlefield] . . . "for the sake of the country" . . . Without really knowing what the *senchi* was about, I accepted this offer. I naively trusted this woman, who took me to an employment agency in Sinŭiju. Then, Mr. Ko, a Korean, took me and seven or eight girls to Hankow, China. There I worked as a comfort woman. . . . (Soh 2008, pp. 91–2)

After the war, US military commanders—who shared the concerns if not the extreme methods of their Japanese counterparts—worked closely, although rarely openly, with local authorities to ensure a steady supply of sex workers. The construction of major military bases in both the Philippines and Korea prompted the dramatic growth of nearby communities that supplied labor and services of all kinds, including sex for American military personnel.

From 1944 to 1992, the Philippines was the logistical center of US military operations in the South Pacific—a major front in the Cold War against Communist governments in China and North Vietnam—and host to the United States' two largest overseas military bases. With thousands of US military personnel in residence and frequent visits from tens of thousands of soldiers and sailors on "R and R" (rest and recreation), local communities such as Angeles City (near Clark Air Force Base) and Olongapo City (near Subic Naval Base) developed sizable sex industries. Military prostitution in the Philippines "took off" in 1965 with the first US deployments of combat troops to Vietnam and continued for almost twenty years after the war ended in 1973. By the time US bases closed in 1992, there were an estimated three hundred thousand sex workers in the Philippines, as many as a third of them under the age of eighteen, and the country had become a major sex tourist destination to rival Thailand, another former R and R site for the three million American troops sent to Vietnam during the war. Because international law considers all underage sex workers to be trafficked regardless of how they got into prostitution, the shocking statistics circulated in government documents, academic reports, and media stories suggest a human trafficking crisis of the first order. Inflated statistics or not, the legacy of over a century of large-scale military prostitution and the inevitable demands of a huge sex tourism industry guarantee that a significant number of Filipinos, most of them women and girls, were and continue to be trafficked into prostitution.

The post-World War II situation in Korea followed a similar trajectory. The Korean War (1950–3), one of the earliest and bloodiest conflicts of the Cold War era, divided the peninsula into Communist North Korea and (nominally at first) democratic South Korea. To safeguard against a North Korean invasion, the South Korean government has allowed the United States to permanently station tens of thousands of American soldiers to dozens of military bases throughout the country.[9] As happened in the Philippines, camp towns (known to Koreans as *gijichon*) quickly sprang up to provide labor and services for nearby US military bases. Anxious to contain the social problems associated with military prostitution, US military commanders and Korean authorities colluded to ensure that GIs had access to safe, convenient, and inexpensive sex workers—despite the fact that prostitution has been illegal in South Korea since the end of the war. Among other things, they required *gijichon* "entertainers" to register and carry health certificates, and by the 1960s as many as thirty thousand women a year had complied. Again, as in the Philippines, military prostitution provided a stable foundation for the development of a much larger sex industry that has catered primarily to Korean men and international sex tourists. By 2003, government statistics estimated that the nation's sex industry was producing revenues of $22 billion (5 percent of GDP) and employing as many 260,000 South Korean women (one woman in twenty-five)—and these figures did not include over 240,000 "call girls" (Moon 2003).

Until the mid-1990s economic boom, most *gijichon* entertainers were Korean, but, as relatively well-paid jobs opened up in the manufacturing and service sectors (including nonmilitary prostitution), the supply of South Korean women willing to work in camp towns providing sexual services for poorly paid American GIs dwindled rapidly. To address this labor shortage, club owners banded together under the auspices of the Korean Special Tourism Association and began to recruit foreign women—especially Filipinas and Russians—offering yearlong work contracts and pressuring the government into issuing them E-6 "entertainer" visas. Taking advantage of the economic downturn produced by the 1992 closure of US military bases in the Philippines, Korean recruiters sought out motivated young Filipinas whose presumed familiarity with camp town culture, American soldiers, and the English language made them especially desirable entertainers. By 2000, an average of 1500 Filipinas were working in *gijichon* clubs in South Korea as "juicy girls" (after the juice drinks that soldiers purchase in exchange for twenty to thirty minutes of conversation). And, although their work contracts make no mention of sex work, nearly all the clubs include private VIP rooms where women can perform sexual services for money and allow men who pay "bar fines" to take women on unsupervised dates outside the club.

Although similar in many respects to sex trafficking from Nepal to India, the trafficking of young women from the Philippines to South Korea to entertain American soldiers differs in several important ways. While the ethnicity and alleged promiscuity of Nepali sex workers in India is part of their appeal, at least to some clients, the racial, linguistic, and cultural differences in Indian brothels are much less pronounced than in the camp towns. For the most part, American GIs are far from wealthy and come from diverse ethnic, race, and class backgrounds; and Filipina juicy girls (like their Korean predecessors) are often aggressively entrepreneurial, even when they play to American fantasies of docile, delicate, sensual Asian women in order to attract customers or appeal to the chivalrous instincts of a "boyfriend" or potential husband. Nevertheless, GIs' access to the "imperial" privileges that come with membership in the world's most powerful military (including the ability to move freely across national borders) and access to its largest economy give them a distinct advantage over Filipina entertainers.

Opponents of military prostitution in the Philippines, South Korea, and the United States see official (albeit covert) tolerance of *gijichon* juicy clubs as setting the stage for international sex trafficking. For example, an article in *Stars and Stripes*, a semiofficial magazine sponsored by the US Defense Department, on accusations of sex trafficking against juicy-club owners in the US State Department's annual human trafficking report cited a concerned US congressman reminding base commanders (and their bosses) that "the U.S. military has a responsibility and a role to play in enforcing the zero tolerance policy [on sex trafficking]. If it is our servicemen who are creating the demand, we have to ensure that they stop exploiting the women" (Rabiroff 2010). Despite these concerns, the State Department continues to give South Korea (but not the Philippines) the highest ranking

Figure 6.2   US soldiers and Filipina "entertainers" in Dongducheon, South Korea. Photo by Jon Rabiroff published in *Stars and Stripes*, a quasi-official news and information service for US troops. *Source*: © *Stars and Stripes*.

(Tier 1) for its efforts to combat human trafficking and military command-ers routinely refuse requests that they declare *gijichon* juicy clubs off limits to American soldiers.

While sex trafficking certainly occurs in South Korea's camp towns, the informal regulation of the *gijichon* entertainment industry by local and military authorities has discouraged the worst abuses, such as abduction, rape, and beatings. However, it has done little to prevent less overt forms of coercion, such as confiscation of work papers and passports, garnish-ment of wages to repay debts, and threats to bring in police or immigration officers. Although these labor abuses open employers to charges of traf-ficking, recent ethnographic work among Filipina *gijichon* entertainers reveals a much more complex situation in which women, clients, and employers regularly negotiate over everything from working conditions to personal relationships. As might be expected, migrant entertainers, finan-cially dependent on clients and employers, negotiate from a position of relative weakness. But most women retain some measure of self-respect and control over their lives by skipping out on abusive managers, taking charge of their sexual activities (paid and otherwise), and playing off their "boyfriends" against management and each other, usually with the goal of regular financial support for themselves and their families, and sometimes even romance, marriage, and a life in the United States (Cheng 2010). This kind of "entertainment" might still fall within the parameters of trafficking according to the UN *Protocol* but it bears scant resemblance to the worst-case scenarios proffered by neoabolitionists, muckraking journalists, and their political allies. Despite greater opportunities for personal agency and less overt abuse from employers, Filipina trafficked entertainers none-theless experience many of the same structural oppressions suffered by their Nepalese counterparts, including patriarchal attitudes (in this case from Filipino, Korean, and American men and their respective govern-ments), racial/ethnic discrimination (as objects of oppression and desire), imperial/neocolonial legacies (including military occupation), and the geo-political disadvantages of citizenship in the impoverished Global South.

Case Study 3: Sex Trafficking from Eastern Europe to Western Europe and the Americas

If there were a paradigmatic case for the complex history of sex trafficking, it would be the mass migration of Eastern European women and girls into

Western Europe and the Americas. As we have seen, fears of immigration and "white slavery" in the West drove the first wave of moral panics over sex trafficking in the late nineteenth and early twentieth centuries. The 1991 breakup of the Soviet Union and the subsequent economic convulsions produced by the transition from a state-run economy to free market capitalism has produced a similar effect, one that is just beginning to wane as economic troubles (and a subsequent decline in immigration rates) in the European Union and United States turn the public's attention to other matters. This most recent of moral panics looks very much like its predecessor, with the histrionic voices of muckrakers, experts, and politicians obscuring a complex set of interrelated phenomena in an effort to rally support for a second crusade against "modern-day slavery." For example, in a 2010 television documentary, Victor Malarek, a prominent Canadian broadcast journalist and author of a popular exposé on the Eastern and Central European sex trade, related a story about purchasing women from an alleged sex trafficker that could have come straight out of William Stead's "Maiden Tribute of Modern Babylon":

> I wanted to find out just how easy it would be to purchase women from Moscow or Kiev, whatever, and get them into Canada . . . And [I] met this guy, Ludwig Feinberg, also known as Tarzan, real reprobate, real Neanderthal knuckle-dragger, beats up women, thinks he's something else, you know. He had all of the connections ready for me within a week. He would bring in 6, 7, 12, whatever I needed, women and guaranteeing me absolutely no problems with them . . . Now I understand what he means by that. These young women have been taken to the "breaking grounds," where they have been gang raped, where they've been pressured, gang pressured, into this so-called profession, never to speak out. And they're going to come to this country not even speaking a word of English. So who are they going to run to? (Hope for the Sold 2010)

As often happens in the throes of a moral panic, the line between muckraking and academic research becomes blurred. In a widely cited 2001 article titled "The 'Natasha' Trade: Transnational Sex Trafficking" for the *National Institute of Justice Journal*, Professor Donna Hughes—who has testified several times before the US Congress, Russian Duma, and Czech Parliament on sex trafficking issues—cited a horrific story from *Le Monde* in which an eighteen-year-old Ukrainian girl answers a newspaper advertisement for a training course in Berlin and ends up in Brussels, where her traffickers insist that she repay her transportation costs, confiscate her passport, sell her to a series of pimps, and then threaten, beat, rape, and torture her with cigarette burns to keep her in line (Paringaux 1998; Hughes 2001). The even more tragic case of Dangoule's suicide, related by Queen Silvia in the introduction to this chapter, testifies to the power of these widely circulating media stories to shape and distort public perception and political action around complex phenomena such as sex migration and sex trafficking. Moreover, the sense of immediacy generated by the heart-wrenching travails of sex trafficking "victims" tends to dehistoricize the problem, except perhaps to reference a reoccurring primal urge that humanity has yet to outgrow (witness Malarek's reference to Neanderthals). The refusal of sustained historical analysis makes the problem—despite its distressing tendency to resurface every few decades—seem more like a question of human depravity than the inevitable consequence of persistent structural inequalities in the global political economy.

Although often eclipsed in the Western imagination by the African slave trade, the first wave of human trafficking came out of what is now Eastern Europe and mostly involved people of Slavic origin. By the thirteenth century, the association of slavery with Slavic peoples was so strong in Medieval Western Europe that some variant of *slav* had entered all the major vernacular languages (but not Latin) as the common word for slave. This was possibly a result of Holy Roman Emperor Otto the Great's tenth-century expansion into Eastern Europe, which involved the large-scale enslavement of conquered Slavic peoples; it may also have been related to Viking raiders' active participation in the slave trade from Eastern Europe into the Byzantine empire and the Muslim world during the same period. More than three centuries of human trafficking out of the region—a process its perpetrators called "harvesting the steppes"—through the Black Sea port of Koffa into the Ottoman Empire during the heyday of the Crimean Khanate (1441–1783) further consolidated the association of Slavic peoples with slavery in the Western European imagination, especially since Venetian and Genoese merchants controlled much of the slave trade from Crimea into Egypt, the Near East, and North Africa.

How much of this medieval and early modern slave trade involved sex trafficking or sexual slavery is impossible to determine but, as with the African trade, the number of slaves expected to provide sexual services to masters or their clients was probably high. We do know that the Ottoman sultans kept dozens of concubines and eunuchs (castrated males), most of them Christian slaves of Slavic descent taken from the Balkan territories. The image of sequestered harem women and their eunuch guards—an obsession with Western European writers and painters, especially during the eighteenth and nineteenth centuries—added an explicitly erotic element to the traffic in Eastern European women. Although untangling the racial politics of desire is always tricky, a recent study of contemporary Eastern European sex workers in Greece notes the formation of new racial/cultural hierarchies that rank white Russian and Ukrainian women at the top (at least in terms of fees for service), followed by Poles and Bulgarians, Latin Americans and Africans, and Albanians (Lazaridis 2001). While participant observers such as Albert Londres—comparing women and prices in early twentieth-century Buenos Aires—might have preferred French prostitutes to their *polaca* competitors, one of the principal attractions of Eastern European women for European and American men has been the (to them) compelling combination of exotic origins and "Caucasian" features.

This potent mix of erotic obsession and racial prejudice provided the cultural backdrop against which Western Europeans and European-Americans understood the late nineteenth and early twentieth-century influx of Eastern European immigrants into Europe and especially into the Americas to meet labor demands in the boom economies of Argentina, Brazil, Canada, and the United States. The immediate causes of this mass migration were political instability and economic turmoil produced by the competing territorial ambitions of four powerful imperial states—the Russian, German (Prussian), Austro-Hungarian, and Ottoman Empires—coupled with violent anti-Semitic riots and pogroms in the eastern borderlands of the Russian empire, the notorious "Pale of Settlement" (which included much of present-day Belarus, Lithuania, Moldova, Poland, and the Ukraine) where Russian rulers beginning with Catherine the Great had attempted to confine the empire's sizable Jewish population.

For many Europeans and Americans, the millions of Jewish and Slavic migrants who sought asylum and economic opportunity in the West represented a threat to Western civilization not unlike the barbarian hordes that brought down the Roman empire. While statistics on this mass migration to Western Europe and the Americas are unreliable, they do give some sense of scale. From 1880 until the outbreak of World War I in 1914, most major destination countries—England and Germany in Europe; the United States, Argentina, and Canada in the Americas—received tens of thousands of Eastern European immigrants, as many as half of them Jewish. As the preferred destination, the United States took in approximately 7.5 million Eastern Europeans, among them over 2 million Yiddish-speaking Ashkenazi

Jews (about one third of Russia's Jewish population) between 1880 and the passage of the 1924 Immigration Act, which set national origin quotas designed specifically to restrict immigration by less desirable populations. Although much fewer in absolute numbers, Eastern European immigrants to cities such as London, Berlin, Vienna, Montreal, and Buenos Aires (where by 1895 more than half the population was foreign born) had a dramatic impact on everything from politics to culture.

Regardless of their actual numbers, Eastern European immigrant populations, especially Jews, were often singled out as particularly dangerous. One reason was the prominence of Russian-born Jewish intellectuals such as Rosa Luxemburg and Emma Goldman in the Marxist and anarchist movements—the principal sources of the pre-World War II moral panic over international terrorism. Another was deep-seated anti-Semitism dating back to the European Middle Ages, which associated Jews with sexual transgression and blood sacrifice. In late nineteenth-century London, these fears led to widespread speculation that Jack the Ripper, the notorious serial killer of prostitutes, was an Eastern European Jew, a story anxious British authorities worked hard to refute (Walkowitz 1992). In Marietta, Georgia (United States), popular anti-Semitism led to the 1915 lynching by an armed mob of a Jewish-American factory manager, Leo Frank, who had been convicted on scant evidence of raping and murdering a thirteen-year-old girl worker, an event credited with reviving the Ku Klux Klan as a political force. Although the Leo Frank case involved a Jewish victim of mob violence, in practice local populations often had trouble distinguishing between different Eastern European groups, as for example in Buenos Aires and New York, where words such as *polaco*, *ruso*, and pollock referred to all immigrants from the region regardless of religion or ethnicity.

On the surface, the most recent moral panic over sex trafficking looks rather different: today, Muslims are seen as the terrorists and media attention focuses on Russian, Ukrainian, and Balkan mobsters rather than Jews. At the same, the widespread circulation of anti-Semitic and anti-Eastern European stereotypes in various guises—the swarthy, hook-nosed Middle Easterner, the ruthless mobster with the Slavic accent, discrimination against Romanian gypsies in Buenos Aires, and even the atavistic Jewish-Canadian procurer in Victor Malarek's story—remind us of the power of these deep-rooted images to shape our understanding of contemporary phenomena.

The principal cause behind the most recent mass migration of Eastern Europeans was the official dissolution of the Soviet Union in 1991, which granted formal independence to fifteen republics and freedom from Soviet political domination to the seven Warsaw Pact nations and the former Yugoslavia. Political instability in the region and the end to "Iron Curtain" restrictions on immigration to the West laid the groundwork for increased migration out of Eastern Europe and Russia. But it was the economic "shock" produced by the sudden shift from a state-directed economy with a sizable (if inefficient and corrupt) social welfare system to a free market economy that provided the decisive push for most migrants, especially young women. Communist systems in the Soviet Union and Eastern Europe had offered women state-subsidized higher education and job opportunities, especially in education and medicine. As the free market doctrines of Western advisors prompted leaders such as Russian president Boris Yeltsin to reduce government expenditures by cutting social programs and state bureaucracies, public sector jobs in education and medicine, where women made up over 80 percent of the workforce, began to disappear. By the mid-1990s, the gap between men's and women's wages in Russia had shrunk from 70 percent to 40 percent; women represented anywhere from 65 percent to 90 percent of the unemployed; and employed women—more than half of them single mothers with children—made up nearly 90 percent of the working poor, approximately 25 percent of the Russian workforce (Farr 2005, p. 11). Figures for other major sending countries such as the Ukraine were even worse. The precipitous "feminization of poverty" in these places pushed young women to seek opportunities abroad as students, workers, entertainers, and even mail-order/cyber brides. And their desperation to migrate under extremely adverse circumstances put them at serious risk of being trafficked, including into sex work.

As media stories about sex trafficking atrocities began to attract public outcry and political attention, policymakers in the European Union and United States worked diligently to translate indignation and empathy into effective antitrafficking laws, practices, and institutions. From the start, EU efforts to deal with the sex trafficking problem have confronted major legal, institutional, and cultural barriers that hinder the development and implementation of uniform standards and practices for the different member states. Barriers or not, the European Union has made regular efforts to address the problem. Perhaps because the 1993 Maastricht Treaty, which created the European Union, came at a time when immigration into Western Europe was on the rise (and of growing concern to constituents), EU politicians and policymakers have produced a dizzying array of commissions, recommendations, resolutions, declarations, and programs to counter the sex trafficking problem—most of them focused explicitly on

Figure 6.3   US government antitrafficking "Look Beneath the Surface" poster with an Eastern European girl. *Source*: National Human Trafficking Resource Center, funded under a grant from the Administration for Children and Families, US Department of Health and Human Services.

women and children. For example, a 1997 Council of Europe, Parliamentary Assembly recommendation defined trafficking in women as "any legal or illegal transporting of women and/or trade in them, with or without their initial consent, for economic gain, with the purpose of subsequent forced prostitution, forced marriage, or other forms of forced sexual exploitation," clarifying that, "the use of force may be physical, sexual and/or psychological, and includes intimidation, rape, abuse of authority or a situation of dependence" (Council of Europe 1997).[10] To combat this crime, the parliamentary recommendation advocated public awareness programs, increased police cooperation, and victim services. It also gave impetus to the STOP (and later DAPHNE) programs, which helped fund member states' efforts against human trafficking and sexual exploitation.[11]

Despite the proliferation of antitrafficking initiatives, the problem of sex trafficking has continued to haunt EU policymakers. In 2009, for example, the Council of the European Union adopted the Stockholm Programme, designed to ensure "an open and secure Europe serving and protecting the citizens." Along with standardizing and tightening restrictions on immigration, the Programme's Article 4.4.2 on human trafficking called yet again for better data collection, development and enforcement of more uniform antitrafficking laws and policing, increased cooperation among member states, and provision of better services for trafficking victims. It also recommended the creation of an antitrafficking commissioner to monitor, facilitate, and coordinate the antitrafficking efforts of member states (Council of the European Union 2009). The European Parliament's 2010 "Resolution on Preventing Trafficking in Human Beings" provided the latest iteration of ongoing European antitrafficking efforts, noting that "trafficking in human beings is a modern form of slavery, a serious crime and a severe violation of fundamental human rights and reduces people to a state of dependency via threats, violence and humiliation." Like its predecessors, the resolution lamented the lack of reliable statistics (while nonetheless reporting that human trafficking involved "several hundred thousands of people into and within Europe" and generated "many millions of euros/dollars a year" for traffickers) and insisted that antitrafficking efforts focus on prevention, prosecution, and protection—the three Ps approach borrowed from the US State Department (European Parliament 2010). The seemingly endless proliferation of antitrafficking initiatives in the face of the European Union's evident failure to make any serious dent in the actual problem suggests that—as was the case at the turn of the previous century—the principal effects of the antitrafficking campaign have been to reinforce the moral, cultural, and institutional superiority of Western Europe vis-à-vis the European Union's Southern and Eastern Europe member states; to justify meddling in the affairs of its less enlightened neighbors; and to provide ethical cover for increasingly draconian immigration policies.

Efforts in the United States may represent a more focused attempt to tackle the sex trafficking problem, but their ideological effects are nearly identical and no less deliberate. The concerted US push to address the problem may well be related to the increasingly contentious nature of domestic politics, a circumstance in which the media-driven moral panic over sex trafficking represents one of the few arenas of bipartisan political consensus. The prime mover behind the passage of major US antitrafficking legislation was a liberal senator from Minnesota, Paul Wellstone, the son of Jewish immigrants from Russia and the Ukraine, who denounced international human trafficking on the floor of the Senate after reading a series of news reports about the mistreatment of trafficked women in the United

States at the hands of traffickers, brothel owners, police, and immigration officials (DeStefano 2008, pp. 13–15). Wellstone's proposed legislation received a boost from a widely circulated 1999 report by State Department analyst Amy O'Neill Richard under the eye-catching title "International Trafficking in Women to the United States: A Contemporary Manifestation of Slavery and Organized Crime." In her report Richard alleged that "an estimated 45,000 to 50,000 women and children are trafficked annually to the United States" and provided several anecdotes culled from news sources to illustrate the nature of the problem (DeStefano 2008, pp. 32–3).[12] Congress was prodded into action by the combination of Wellstone's advocacy, Richard's report, and compelling testimony by experts such as Laura Lederer, founder of Harvard School of Government's Protection Project, who presented senators with a composite portrait of a sixteen-year-old Eastern European girl named "Lydia" who gets invited out for dinner by a sophisticated older woman and is drugged and trafficked unconscious into a receiver country such as the United States, confined in a brothel, and forced to prostitute herself with up to twenty men a day. The Victims of Trafficking and Violence Protection Act of 2000 (TVPA) passed 371 to 1 in the House and 95 to 0 in the Senate (DeStefano 2008, pp. 32–9). Among its findings, the TVPA noted that each year as many as 700,000 people were trafficked worldwide:

> Many [of them] . . . into the international sex trade, often by force, fraud, or coercion. The sex industry has rapidly expanded over the past several decades. It involves sexual exploitation of persons, predominantly women and girls, involving activities related to prostitution, pornography, sex tourism, and other commercial sexual services. The low status of women in many parts of the world has contributed to a burgeoning of the trafficking industry.[13]

In addition to describing the problem and bemoaning the "low status of women in many parts of the world," the TVPA developed the three Ps (prevention, prosecution, protection) approach to trafficking, provided special T visas for victims who "helped law enforcement *and* would suffer extreme hardship if expelled from the country," and set up sanctions for "countries that fail to comply with minimum standards for the elimination of trafficking" (DeStefano 2008, pp. 44–5). Drawing on previous experience with a tier system for measuring other countries' progress against drug trafficking, the State Department began sending an annual report to

Congress that ranks countries into four "tiers" according to their antitrafficking legislation and practices: tier-one countries comply with US standards, tier-two countries are making significant efforts to comply, tier-two "watch list" countries are at risk of failure to comply, and tier-three countries do not comply. In 2003, the George W. Bush administration decided that international "shaming" was insufficient and sanctioned select tier-three countries by denying them access to nonhumanitarian aid, including development loans from the nominally independent World Bank and International Monetary Fund. From the start, the tier system has provoked resentment among allies and accusations of political bias from US "enemies" such as Cuba and North Korea (DeStefano 2008, pp. 118–27).

As happened in the European Union, initiatives such as the TVPA and its successors have successfully promoted antitrafficking legislation and improved antitrafficking practices in many countries, but they have had little measurable effect on sex trafficking itself. At the same time, however, the TVPA findings, provisions, and rankings set up a moral calculus that put the United States at the forefront of the world's nations—despite its admitted failings—and empowered the US State Department to police the behavior of other countries, including that of its former Cold War adversaries. Taken in conjunction with ever tightening immigration policies and the militarization of the United States–Mexico border, antitrafficking initiatives represent a concerted bipartisan effort to reclaim the moral high ground in the struggle to overcome the pernicious effects of globalization.

Sex trafficking out of Eastern Europe has decreased somewhat in recent years but more likely as a result of improving economic conditions in energy-rich countries such as Russia than because of Western antitrafficking campaigns. Regardless, the basic contours of the traffic into Western Europe and the Americas have remained more or less the same. According to analysts, a significant majority of Eastern European women, perhaps as many as 70 percent, are trafficked into the European Union, while only an estimated 3–5 percent are trafficked into the Americas, despite their high profile in recent Argentine, Canadian, and US antitrafficking campaigns. (A significant percentage of these women end up in places such as China, Japan, and South Korea—a relatively new trafficking pattern outside the scope of this case study.) One reason for this imbalance—which reverses the percentages from the previous mass migration—is that trafficking women and girls from Eastern Europe into the European Union is simpler and cheaper than transporting them across the Atlantic, thanks to shorter distances, easily obtained tourist visas, and the presence of established transportation corridors into and through peripheral countries just inside or adjacent to the European Union such as the Balkans, Greece, Romania, and Turkey, which tend to have laxer immigration standards and long histories of smuggling. While US and Canadian visas are harder to obtain, at least for people from "developing" countries, smuggling Eastern European women through Mexico into the United States with the help of Mexican traffickers and coyotes has proven a viable, if still risky, option.

Various laws around prostitution appear to affect trafficking patterns as well. Neoabolitionists, for example, note that countries with relatively liberal prostitution policies, such as Germany, Greece, the Netherlands, and Turkey (which has applied to join the European Union), have bigger trafficking problems than countries where prostitution is illegal for clients, such as Norway (which is not an EU member) and Sweden. At the same time, however, countries such as the Czech Republic, where brothels and pimping are illegal but prostitution is not, have huge sex tourism industries, including along the notorious Highway E55 near the Czech–German border town of Dubi. According to Czech government reports, 25–30 percent of the prostitutes working in the country are from the Ukraine— most of them controlled by pimps and many of them trafficked to some degree (Stastna 1999). Certainly, laws against organized prostitution (brothels, pimping, public solicitation, and so on) have not discouraged traffickers from bringing women into Argentina and Canada, or into the United States, where prostitution itself is still illegal (except in a few rural Nevada counties).

As we have seen in the two previous case studies, trafficked women are "recruited" into sex work in a variety of different way, ranging from abduction to fraud to deception with regard to working conditions but not the work itself. Despite their sensational tone, media stories (including those related previously in this chapter) have helped expose the worst abuses. Outright abduction is rare, probably because most traffickers fear the public exposure and police response that kidnappings typically elicit even in "developing" countries. In 2004, for example, residents of a working-class Mexico City neighborhood, San Juan Ixtayopan, publicly lynched two undercover police officers suspected of abetting traffickers in the kidnapping of two schoolchildren (Davis 2006, pp. 56–7). While abductions certainly occur, most often in places such as the Balkans and Mexico, where traffickers' strong ties to law enforcement allow them to operate with a certain impunity, the number of actual cases bears little relation to its centrality to antitrafficking campaigns.

Much more common and nearly as well publicized are deceptive recruitment practices. In some of the more egregious cases, recruiters scour Eastern European orphanages for potential recruits, paying finder's fees to complicit staff. More often, women are seduced by promises of romance and marriage; answer advertisements for overseas positions as nannies, waitresses, models, hostesses, and entertainers; join international Internet dating services that offer the chance to hook up with and even marry foreign men; or simply put themselves in the hands of an unscrupulous smuggler who pushes them into sex work to repay the costs of their transportation. The previously cited case of Dangoule provides an exemplary story about the tragic consequences of misplaced trust in friends, lovers, and prospective employers. But most Eastern European women who consider migration are not naïve about the potential dangers of accepting recruiters' pitches at face value, responding to vaguely worded job advertisements, or trying to meet foreign husbands through marriage brokers or over the Internet. And, like most migrant workers, they make extensive use of networks of family and friends to facilitate their migration. Moreover, the circulation of horror stories both informally and in the media along with extensive public education campaigns by concerned governments and nongovernmental organizations ensure that very few women walk blindly into a trafficker's beckoning arms (Johnson 2007, pp. 88–9).

Although less widely publicized than cases of abduction and fraud, the most common recruitment strategy involves Eastern European women who agree to be smuggled into the European Union, United States, Canada, and Argentina for sex work. More often than not, these women have engaged in some form of sex work in their home countries and see work abroad as a chance to improve their circumstances. Because they enter the country illegally or overstay visas and lack proper work papers, migrant sex workers run a high risk of being trafficked. For example, the Los Angeles Police Department's Operation White Lace—frequently cited by academic experts as proof of organized crime's involvement in transnational trafficking—led to the arrest of six Eastern European "ringleaders," four of them women, who were charged with conspiracy, pimping, pandering, and money laundering but *not* with trafficking (Los Angeles Police Department 2002). In this instance, the sex workers had been "call girls" in their home countries prior to their recruitment and had entered the

United States under a variety of false pretenses. Although US courts determined that some of them were "trafficking victims because they had been deceived as to the conditions of their transport [several were smuggled in from Mexico] and of their employment," their trafficking had more to do with the women's vulnerability as undocumented migrant workers (and possibly their desire to take advantage of the T visa program in exchange for testifying against their former employers) than it did with the popular image of naïve young women tricked into sex work by cruel traffickers (Shelley 2010, p. 96). Important and common as they are, these labor-related issues lack the visceral punch of the horror stories preferred by reporters, antitrafficking activists, academic experts, and politicians, in no small part because they expose the shaky foundations of a "war" on sex trafficking based on inflated statistics, fungible categories, and denial about the central role of immigration policies in producing the problem in the first place.

The defining characteristic of international human trafficking is the transportation of the "victim" from one country (usually in the "developing" world) to another (usually in the "developed" world). Because the borders of Global North countries are heavily policed and immigration policies highly restrictive, prospective migrants without proper work papers are forced to rely on visa fraud or smugglers to gain entry, and this makes them vulnerable to traffickers while they are in transit and after they arrive. Worst-case scenarios involve the systematic rape and beating of reluctant women to prepare them for sex work. For example, one of Victor Malarek's informants gave the following description of a "breaking ground" in Serbia where "very mean and ugly men came in and dragged girls into rooms . . . raped girls in front of us . . . ordering them to move in certain ways . . . to pretend excitement . . . to moan" (Malarek 2004, p. 33). Once she was "broken in," this informant was sold to an Albanian pimp who transported her to the Arizona Market in Bosnia to service UN peacekeepers and international aid workers along with local clients. As with abductions, extreme actions like these are risky even in conflict zones such as the Balkans. More typical trafficker tactics include confiscating passports, demanding repayment of travel expenses, threatening exposure back home and in the host country, using intimidation and violence to bully women into turning over more money, forcing women to service more clients than they expected, and exposing them to unhealthy working conditions. For women working illegally in countries where they do not speak the language and cannot report abuses to the police for fear of arrest, deportation, or worse, these slightly less abusive forms of trafficking are routine—and not all that different from the experiences of other types of undocumented workers.

As with the other case studies, sex trafficking from Eastern and Central Europe into the European Union and the Americas has been shaped by persistent structural inequalities grounded in patriarchal attitudes toward women, racial and ethnic prejudices, legacies of military conquests and political upheavals, and long-standing labor migration patterns prompted by geopolitical and economic asymmetries. Seen in historical perspective, then, recent events such as the breakup of the Soviet Union and the "shock" of transitioning to a free market economy (especially for women), which most accounts blame for the dramatic rise in sex trafficking from Eastern and Central Europe, can "best be understood as an extension and/or reconfiguration of enduring historical themes rather than as distinctly modern developments" (Quirk 2012, p. 41).

Conclusion

The history of sex trafficking provides several important "lessons" for scholars, activists, and policymakers. First, despite the sense of immediacy generated by periodic moral panics, sex trafficking in some form or other has been around for a very long time—although it has taken very different forms in different places and at different times in history. Second, moral panics around sex trafficking reoccur because they provide an intensely meaningful (if distorted) outlet for any number of social anxieties, including generalized fears of degeneration, dissolution, and pollution. Third, it is impossible for the historian to separate out moral panics around sex trafficking from the phenomena itself: indeed, sex trafficking becomes a recognizable category only through the discourses that bring it our collective attention. Fourth, sex trafficking has played a central role in large-scale human labor migrations for centuries and is often a result of "voluntary" migration in search of economic opportunity, including through sex work, rather than enslavement. Finally, historical analysis of specific sex trafficking scenarios exposes the deep structures—patriarchy, social inequality, geopolitical asymmetry, economic disparity—that have shaped and continue to shape sex trafficking around the world. Historical analysis thus has important implications for scholars, activists, and policymakers because it forces them (us) to confront sex trafficking not just as an exploding crime problem in desperate need of law-enforcement solutions but as an abiding structural problem that engages a broad range of human rights concerns from relatively straightforward (albeit politically volatile) issues such as immigration reform and improved working conditions (in both the Global North and Global South) to profound social changes such as gender equality, an end to racial/ethnic discrimination, and a more equitable global political economy. Any serious attempt to correct even the simplest of these structural problems is certain to seem naïve, misguided, and even foolhardy, at least to self-proclaimed political realists. Refusal to address them ensures that sex trafficking will continue to thrive into the twenty-first century and beyond.

Acknowledgments

Special thanks to Eithne Luibhéid and to participants at the University of Colorado Boulder Women and Gender Studies Works-in-Progress group on May 6, 2013 for their help with this chapter.

Notes

1   For a historical analysis of political and media discourses on sex trafficking, see Doezema (2010).

2   Argentina and the United States received millions of European immigrants in the late nineteenth and early twentieth centuries. Argentina in particular figured prominently in the first international moral panics around white slavery as an alleged major hub for foreign traffickers.

3   Although often amended, subsequent international legislation to combat sex trafficking has struggled to produce viable enforcement mechanisms. Links to various treaties and amendments are available at www1.umn.edu/humanrts/instree/auof.htm (accessed August 7, 2013).

4   It is important to keep in mind that this movement from poorer margins to wealthier centers also occurs within regions and even within countries.

5   According to one Gurkha officer who served during the Indian Mutiny, British and Gurkha soldiers "called one another 'brother.' They shared their grog with each other and smoked their pipes together" (cited in Streets 2011, p. 79). The British and Indian armies still include several Gurkha regiments.

6   In addition to their whiteness, Nepali sex workers are seen as cleaner, slimmer, better dressed, and more willing to engage in anal sex than their Indian

counterparts (Samarasinghe 2008, p. 79). Allegations of deviant sexual practices by foreign prostitutes are common all over the world.

7   Both studies are based on relatively small samples of "rescued" women and girls but their findings are consistent with each other and with the claims of Nepali antitrafficking activists.

8   Maiti Nepal's website (Maitinepal.org) provides an overview of its various projects and tracks recent busts and trafficking convictions in Nepal.

9   At the end of the Korean War, the United States had over three hundred thousand troops in South Korea. During the 1960s and 1970s, troop numbers ranged from fifty to sixty thousand but diminished somewhat in subsequent decades. The current agreement calls for 28,500 US troops at any one time.

10 For a synopsis of various EU antitrafficking initiatives see www1.umn.edu/humanrts/svaw/trafficking/law/regional.htm (accessed August 7, 2013).

11 For a history of the DAPHNE program see http://ec.europa.eu/justice_home/daphnetoolkit/html/welcome/dpt_welcome_en.html# (accessed August 7, 2013).

12 Subsequent studies suggest that Richard's figures were too high.

13 The 2000 Victims of Trafficking and Violence Protection Act is available online at www.state.gov/g/tip/laws/61124.htm (accessed August 7, 2013).

References

Andrew, E.W. and Bushnell, K.C. (1899) *The Queen's Daughters in India*. Morgan & Scott, London. www.godswordtowomen.org/queensdaughters.pdf (accessed July 30, 2013).

Brysk, A. and Choi-Fitzpatrick, A. (2012) Introduction: Rethinking trafficking, in *From Human Trafficking to Human Rights: Reframing Contemporary Slavery*. University of Pennsylvania Press, Philadelphia, pp. 1–10.

Burnard, T. (2004) *Mastery, Tyranny, and Desire: Thomas Thistlewood and His Slaves in the Anglo-Jamaican World*. University of North Carolina Press, Chapel Hill.

Cheng, S. (2010) *On the Move for Love: Migrant Entertainers and the U.S. Military in South Korea*. University of Pennsylvania Press, Philadelphia.

Council of Europe (1997) Parliamentary Assembly Recommendation 1325. http://assembly.coe.int/Main.asp?link=http%3A//assembly.coe.int/Documents/AdoptedText/TA97/EREC1325.HTM (accessed July 30, 2013).

Council of the European Union (2009) The Stockholm Programme: An Open and Secure Europe Serving and Protecting the Citizens, December 2. http://ec.europa.eu/anti-trafficking/entity.action?path=%2FEU+Policy%2FThe+Stockholm+Programme (accessed August 8, 2013).

Crawford, M. and Kaufman, M.R. (2008) Sex trafficking in Nepal: Survivor characteristics and long-term outcomes. *Violence Against Women*, 14, 905–16.

Davis, D.E. (2006) Undermining the rule of law: Democratization and the dark side of police reform. *Latin American Politics and Society*, 48 (1), 55–86.

Dean, C.J. (2003) Empathy, pornography, and suffering. *differences: A Journal of Feminist Cultural Studies*, 14 (1), 88–124.

DeStefano, A.M. (2008) *The War on Human Trafficking: U.S. Policy Assessed.* Rutgers University Press, New Brunswick, NJ.

Doezema, J. (2010) *Sex Slaves and Discourse Masters: The Construction of Trafficking.* Zed Books, New York.

European Parliament (2010) Resolution on Preventing Trafficking in Human Beings, February 10. http://ec.europa.eu/anti-trafficking/entity.action;jsessionid=TF QLRhhhmnJ2Z6VWj71RL5Dkht87hS9fKqJMpJYvn2sK1KwwMXl1!1142670 905?path=EU+Policy%2FEuropean+Parliament+resolution+on+preventing +trafficking+in+human+beings (accessed August 8, 2013).

Farr, K. (2005) *Sex Trafficking: The Global Market in Women and Children.* Worth Publishers, New York.

Graham, S.L. (1992) *House and Street: The Domestic World of Servants and Masters in Nineteenth-Century Rio de Janeiro.* University of Texas Press, Austin.

Hennick, M. and Simkhada, P. (2004) Sex Trafficking in Nepal: Context and Process. Opportunities and Choices Working Paper 11.

Hope for the Sold (2010) *Enslaved and Exploited: The Story of Sex Trafficking in Canada*, March 23. http://vimeo.com/9829336 (accessed July 30, 2013).

Hughes, D.M. (2001) The "Natasha" trade: Transnational sex trafficking. *National Institute of Justice Journal*, January. https://www.ncjrs.gov/pdffiles1/jr000246c .pdf (accessed August 8, 2013).

International Agreement (1904) International Agreement for the Suppression of the "White Slave Traffic," 18 May 1904, 35 Stat. 1979, 1 L.N.T.S. 83, *entered into force* 18 July 1905. www1.umn.edu/humanrts/instree/whiteslavetraffic1904 .html (accessed July 30, 2013).

International Convention (1910) International Convention for the Suppression of the "White Slave Traffic," May 4, 1910, 211 Consol. T.S. 45, 1912 GR. Brit. T.S. No. 20, *as amended by* Protocol Amending the International Agreement for the Suppression of the White Slave Traffic, and Amending the International Convention for the Suppression of the White Slave Traffic, May 4, 1949, 2 U.S.T. 1999, 30 U.N.T.S. 23, *entered into force* June 21, 1951. www1.umn.edu/ humanrts/instree/whiteslavetraffic1910.html (accessed July 30, 2013).

International Labour Office (2008) ILO Action against Trafficking in Human Beings. www.ilo.org/wcmsp5/groups/public/@ed_norm/@declaration/documents/ publication/wcms_090356.pdf (accessed July 30, 2013).

Johnson, E. (2007) *Dreaming of a Mail-Order Husband: Russian–American Internet Romance.* Duke University Press, Durham, NC.

Kristof, N.D. (2004) Bargaining for freedom. *New York Times*, January 21. www.nytimes.com/2004/01/21/opinion/bargaining-for-freedom.html?ref =nicholasdkristof (accessed July 30, 2013).

Kristof, N.D. (2009) If this isn't slavery, what is? *New York Times*, January 3. www.nytimes.com/2009/01/04/opinion/04kristof.html?ref=nicholasdkristof (accessed July 30, 2013).

Landesman, P. (2004) The girls next door. *New York Times*, January 25. www .nytimes.com/2004/01/25/magazine/the-girls-next-door.html (accessed July 30, 2013).

Lazaridis, G. (2001) Trafficking and prostitution: The growing exploitation of migrant women in Greece. *European Journal of Women's Studies*, 8, 67–102.

Levine, P. (1994) Venereal disease, prostitution, and the politics of empire: The case of British India. *Journal of the History of Sexuality*, 4 (4), 579–602.

Levine, P. (2004) "A multitude of unchaste women": Prostitution in the British Empire. *Journal of Women's History*, 15 (4), 159–63.

Londres, A. (1928) *The Road to Buenos Ayres* (trans. E. Sutton). Blue Ribbon Books, New York.

Los Angeles Police Department (2002) News Release, December 5. www.lapdonline .org/january_2003/news_view/21690 (accessed July 30, 2013).

Malarek, V. (2004) *The Natashas: Inside the New Global Sex Trade*. Arcade Publishing, New York.

Moon, K.-R. (2003) Korea's sex industry is major money earner. *Korea JoongAng Daily*, February 6. http://koreajoongangdaily.joinsmsn.com/news/article/article.aspx?aid=1930662 (accessed July 30, 2013).

Mukherjee, K.K. and Mukherjee, S. (2004) Girls/Women in Prostitution in India: A National Study. Department of Women and Child Development, November.

Newar, N. (1998) My sister next? *Himal: The South Asian Magazine*, 11 (10). www .himalmag.com/component/content/article/2545-My-sister-next?.html (accessed January 7, 2013).

O'Neill, T. (2001) "Selling girls in Kuwait": Domestic labour and trafficking discourse in Nepal. *Anthropologica*, 43, 153–64.

Paringaux, R.-P. (1998) Prostitution takes a turn for the West, *Le Monde*, May 24.

Patterson, O. (2012) Trafficking, gender, and slavery: Past and present, in *The Legal Understanding of Slavery: From the Historical to the Contemporary* (ed. J. Allain). Oxford University Press, Oxford, pp. 322–59.

Peck, G. (2011) Feminizing white slavery in the United States: Marcus Braun and the transnational traffic in white bodies, 1890–1910, in *Workers across the Americas: The Transnational Turn in Labor History* (ed. L. Fink). Oxford University Press, Oxford, pp. 221–44.

Pivar, D.J. (1981) The military, prostitution, and colonial peoples: India and the Philippines, 1885–1917. *Journal of Sex Research*, 17, 256–69.

Queen Silva of Sweden (2006) Address by Her Majesty Queen Silvia of Sweden at the Round Table of Business Community against the Trafficking of

Human Beings. www.interpol.int/News-and-media/News-media-releases/ 2006/N20060124 (accessed July 30, 2013).

Quirk, J. (2012) Uncomfortable silences: Contemporary slavery and the "lessons" of history, in *From Human Trafficking to Human Rights: Reframing Contemporary Slavery* (ed. A. Brysk and A. Choi-Fitzpatrick). University of Pennsylvania Press, Philadelphia, pp. 25–43.

Rabiroff, J. (2010) Report on human trafficking cites South Korean juicy bars. *Stars and Stripes*, June 10. www.stripes.com/news/pacific/report-on -human-trafficking-cites-south-korean-juicy-bars-1.107610 (accessed July 30, 2013).

Samarasinghe, V. (2008) Nepal: Young, female and vulnerable, in *Female Sex Trafficking in Asia: The Resilience of Patriarchy in a Changing World*. New York: Routledge, New York, pp. 59–88.

Shelley, L. (2010) *Human Trafficking: A Global Perspective*. Cambridge University Press, New York.

Soh, S.C. (2008) *The Comfort Women: Sexual Violence and Postcolonial Memory in Korea and Japan*. University of Chicago Press, Chicago.

Stastna, K. (1999) Czech Republic: Taxing the professionals. *Eastern European Review*, 1 (22). www.ce-review.org/99/22/stastna22.html (accessed July 30, 2013).

Stead, W. (1885) The maiden tribute of modern Babylon. *Pall Mall Gazette*, July 6–10. www.attackingthedevil.co.uk/pmg/tribute/index.php (accessed July 30, 2013).

Streets, H. (2011) *The Martial Races: The Military, Race, and Masculinity in British Imperial Culture, 1857–1914*. Manchester University Press, Manchester.

UNESCO (United Nations Educational, Scientific, and Cultural Organization) (2010) Nepal: UNESCO and Japan Support Innovative Efforts to Increase Literacy in Rural Areas, March 29. http://reliefweb.int/report/nepal/nepal -unesco-and-japan-support-innovative-efforts-increase-literacy-rural-areas (accessed July 30, 2013).

United Nations (1949) Convention for the Suppression of the Traffic in Persons and of the Exploitation of the Prostitution of Others. Approved by General Assembly Resolution 317 (IV) of 2 December 1949. Entry into force: 25 July 1951, in accordance with article 24. www1.umn.edu/humanrts/instree/ trafficinperson.htm (accessed July 30, 2013).

United Nations (2000) Protocol to Prevent, Suppress and Punish Trafficking in Persons, Especially Women and Children, Supplementing the United Stations Convention against Transnational Organized Crime. www.uncjin.org/ Documents/Conventions/dcatoc/final_documents_2/convention_%20traff _eng.pdf (accessed July 30, 2013).

US State Department (2007) Trafficking in Persons Report 2007. www.state.gov/j/ tip/rls/tiprpt/2007 (accessed July 30, 2013).

Walkowitz, J.R. (1992) *City of Dreadful Delights: Narratives of Sexual Danger in Late-Victorian London*. University of Chicago Press, Chicago.
White House (2010) Presidential Proclamation—National Slavery and Human Trafficking Prevention Month. www.whitehouse.gov/the-press-office/presidential-proclamation-national-slavery-and-human-trafficking-prevention-month (accessed July 30, 2013).

Suggested Reading

Agustín, L.M. (2007) *Sex at the Margins: Migration, Labour Markets, and the Rescue Industry*. Zed Books, London.
Andrijasevic, R. (2010) *Migration, Agency, and Citizenship in Sex Trafficking*. Palgrave McMillan, New York.
Brysk, A. and Choi-Fitzpatrick, A. (eds) (2012) *From Human Trafficking to Human Rights: Reframing Contemporary Slavery*. University of Pennsylvania Press, Philadelphia.
Doezema, J. (2010) *Sex Slaves and Discourse Masters: The Construction of Trafficking*. Zed Books, New York.
Kempadoo, K., Sanghera, J., and Pattanaik, B. (eds) (2012) *Trafficking and Prostitution Reconsidered: New Perspectives on Migration, Sex Work, and Human Rights*, 2nd edn. Paradigm Publishers, Boulder, CO.
Soderland, G. (2013) *Sex Trafficking, Scandal, and the Transformation of Journalism, 1885–1917*. University of Chicago Press, Chicago.
United Nations Office on Drugs and Crime (2012) Global Report on Trafficking in Persons. www.unodc.org/documents/data-and-analysis/glotip/Trafficking_in_Persons_2012_web.pdf (accessed July 30, 2013).
US State Department (2012) Trafficking in Persons Report 2012. www.state.gov/j/tip/rls/tiprpt/2012 (accessed July 30, 2013).
US State Department (2013) Trafficking in Persons Report 2013. www.state.gov/j/tip/rls/tiprpt/2013 (accessed September 18, 2013).

7

Sexuality and Mass Media

Hai Ren

Sexuality has been a mainstay of mass culture from the rise of print media and theater in the early modern era to its globalization through popular music, film, television, Internet, and the smartphone. At times the effects of this intimate link between sexuality and mass culture have been obvious. For example, sexual scandals disseminated through the media have dogged government officials from Marie Antoinette to Bill Clinton, Silvio Berlusconi, and Anthony D. Weiner. These stories amuse ordinary people, shape public opinions, and change political landscapes, sometimes in dramatic ways. Even more important in the long run is the significant role mass media—as entertainment, leisure, and consumption—has played in shaping the meanings of everyday life, whether through films from Hollywood to Bollywood, advertisements for "modern girls" from Asia to the Americas and Europe, or shopping centers from Mall of America (Minneapolis) to the New South China Mall (Dongguan) and the Dubai Mall.

This chapter analyzes four distinct cases that highlight the links between sexuality and mass media: representations of the "modern girl" in advertisements for cosmetics and toiletries that appeared all over the world from the 1920s to the 1950s; the proliferation of sexual discourses in US-based mass media, especially newspaper advice columns, since the 1950s; the development of media-driven youth culture in Japan centered around the figure of the *otaku* (geek) since the 1960s; and media activism in China that utilizes the Internet, sexting, and blogs in the early twenty-first century.

A Global History of Sexuality: The Modern Era, First Edition.
Edited by Robert M. Buffington, Eithne Luibhéid, and Donna J. Guy.
© 2014 Robert M. Buffington, Eithne Luibhéid, and Donna J. Guy.
Published 2014 by Blackwell Publishing Ltd.

These cases enable us to understand three major aspects of the relationship between sexuality and mass culture: how media and its development shape the ways sexuality is talked about and understood by peoples around the world; how information and knowledge about sex are tied to the ways in which power operates to regulate sexuality as normal or abnormal, permissible or prohibited, and pleasurable or risky; and how powerful links between sexuality and mass culture on a global scale work to affirm some sexual norms and moralities while challenging others. We begin by providing a theoretical framework for understanding the cases.

Sexuality and Power

In many societies, sex and sexuality are uncomfortable topics, especially between parents and children, teachers and students, and bosses and employees. For this reason, conventional wisdom holds that a powerful array of social forces—family, religious authorities, the state, and so on—have worked hard to repress sex and sexuality except in the direct service of social reproduction (forming families, producing children, etc.). Pioneer historian of sexuality Michel Foucault argued the opposite, noting that since the eighteenth century sexuality has entered into nearly every domain of society—politics, economics, arts, education, leisure, health, and so on—and has played a central role in shaping human subjectivity, the different ways that we make sense of ourselves and that others make sense of us. For this reason, discourses about sexuality serve not so much to repress dangerous sexual desires but as a "dense transfer point for relations of power: between men and women, young people and older people, parents and offspring, teachers and students, priests and laity, an administration and a population." As a transfer point for relations of power, sexuality is "endowed with the greatest instrumentality: useful for the greatest number of maneuvers and capable of serving as a point of support, as a linchpin, for the most varied strategies" (Foucault 1978, p. 103).

Foucault highlights two strategies that society uses to manage sexuality. The first is what he calls the deployment of alliance, "a system of marriage, of fixation and development of kinship ties, of transmission of names and possessions" (Foucault 1978, p. 106). One of its main objectives is to govern the reproduction of social relations. Thus, the deployment of alliance is firmly tied to the transmission or circulation of wealth and enforced by laws designed to maintain normative sexual relations through the regulation of marriage, adoption, taxes, properties, and inheritance, and the proscription of adultery and incestuous relations with blood relatives. The second strategy, the deployment of sexuality, is concerned "not in reproducing itself, but in proliferating, innovating, annexing, creating, and penetrating bodies in an increasingly detailed way, and in controlling populations in an increasingly comprehensive way" (Foucault 1978, p. 107). As Foucault's suggestive language implies, the deployment of sexuality links sexual desire with the production and consumption of commodities.

The Foucauldian perspective on sexuality is a useful framework for understanding the relationship between sexuality and power in modern societies. On the one hand, it explains how societies regulate sexuality though distinctions between what is legal and illegal, permissible and prohibited, normative and abnormal, and so on. On the other hand, it shows how new dimensions of sexuality—beyond the conventional conjugal couple—are continually produced. One way to grasp the relationship between sexuality and power is to study mass culture, especially the ways in which it shapes sexuality through the regulation and control of individuals and the collective citizenry of the nation-state.

Mass-Mediated Culture

The concept of "mass-mediated culture" addresses both historical changes in mass media and the relationship between mass media and consumers. From the late nineteenth century to the early twentieth century, mass media's influence on culture was tied to the development of new technologies, which ran the gamut from spectacular cinema (famously associated with Thomas Edison and the Lumière brothers) to communicative devices such as the transoceanic cablegram, linotype, typewriter, telephone, phonograph, and wireless and inexpensive photographic equipment. These new media technologies generated a range of media genres with overlapping but distinct implications for mass culture. Focusing on a specific genre such as newspaper, radio, film, television, or the Internet can be useful for understanding the development of a particular media sector or industry but does not allow us to understand an environment or milieu in which several media converge. For instance, although a media company such as Disney is best known for animation films, it has entered into many other media domains, including print media (magazines and books), music, television, video games, retailing, theme parks, and the Internet. Similarly,

Apple was established as a computer company but dropped "computer" from its original name and became one of the leaders in mobile media.

A good way of understanding media's impact on culture is through the concept of "mediasphere," which refers to "the middle ground, setting or environment of the transmission and carrying of message and people" (Debray 1996, p. 26). Media theorist Régis Debray has identified three major types of mediasphere:

> the *logosphere*, when writing functions as the central means of diffusion under the constraints and through the channels of orality; the *graphosphere*, when printed text imposes its rationality on the whole of the symbolic milieu; the *videosphere*, with its devitalization of the book via audiovisual media. (Debray 1996, p. 26)

Since the twentieth century, there has been a general shift in focus from the logosphere (hand-written and oral public communication) via the graphosphere (mechanical reproduction of text) to the videosphere (the recording of audio and visual signs) (Debray 1996, p. 27). Two more mediaspheres have emerged in the twenty-first century: the websphere and the mobilesphere. The websphere is based on the Internet, a digital multimedia and networked form of communication. The mobilesphere is a digital and networked form of communication that operates through the smartphone and other individualized, location-specific multimedia devices.

Because of mass media's close relationship to standardization and mass consumption, scholars have long debated whether mass media work to alienate or liberate their consumers. In the late 1930s and 1940s, members of the Frankfurt School in Germany launched a heated debate over the impact of mass culture on modern society that is still relevant today. On one side, Theodor Adorno and Max Horkheimer developed the concept of "the culture industry" to refer to the industrial production, distribution, and exhibition of cultural products such as movies, music, television shows, advertisements, magazines, and novels. Adorno and Horkheimer used the term to emphasize the way that mass media standardized and rationalized the production of culture (Adorno 1991). For these two scholars, industrialized cultural production undermined the transformative potential of individually produced high art by creating a mass-produced culture of deception that promoted "pseudo individuality" and standardized lifestyles (Horkheimer and Adorno 1995, pp. 124–61). On the other side of the debate, Walter Benjamin stressed the more positive effects of industrialized cultural production, arguing that, although mechanical reproduction undermined the special "aura" of a unique (irreproducible) work of art, it also created opportunities for a new democratic politics by enabling a wider dissemination of culture through the mass production and consumption of commodities (Benjamin 1968). According to Benjamin, this new cultural politics might be detrimental to high art but could just as easily empower as manipulate the masses.

Most contemporary scholars favor a balanced approach to the understanding of mass culture that looks closely at both the positive and negative aspects of media technologies, especially the ways in which media

> permit individuals to effect by their own means or with the help of others a certain number of operations on their own bodies and souls, thoughts, conduct, and way of being, so as to transform themselves in order to attain a certain state of happiness, purity, wisdom, perfection, or immortality. (Foucault 1988, p. 18)

With these considerations in mind, this chapter addresses three important questions about the relationship between sexuality and mass-mediated culture: What roles do mass media play in shaping the sexualities of media consumers? How do media users negotiate the meanings of sexuality communicated through media? What do we learn about these questions when we examine various national and transnational contexts?

Case 1: Advertisements for Cosmetics and Toiletries from the 1920s to the 1950s—The Emergence of the Modern Girl around the World

The rise of mass-mediated culture is closely intertwined with the development of consumer society. Beginning in the 1870s, the sphere of consumption—previously linked to production for the wealthiest consumers—expanded rapidly as more and more people began to enjoy higher living standards. Expanding consumption led quickly to the proliferation of consumer goods, large-scale advertising campaigns, widespread dependence on credit, and the appearance of department stores. Increased leisure time accompanied the rise in disposable income, and growing legions of consumers spent time away from work in music halls, sports stadiums, and tourist resorts.

From the late nineteenth century to the early twentieth century, advertising companies helped drive a rapidly expanding capitalist economy by encouraging citizens to consume through a significant shift in its business practices from promoting products to shaping the needs and desires of consumers themselves. This case study illustrates how advertisements for cosmetics and toiletries in magazines and newspapers from the 1920s to the 1950s constructed images of modern girls all over the world in ways that sought to shape consumers as gendered and sexualized subjects.

In cities from Beijing to Bombay, Tokyo to Berlin, Johannesburg to New York, the modern girl made her sometimes flashy but always fashionable appearance. What identified modern girls was the link between their use of specific commodities and their explicit eroticism. Modern girls were known by a variety of names including flappers, *chica moderna*, *garçonnes*, *moga*, *modeng xiaojie*, schoolgirls, *kallege ladki*, vamps, and *neue Frauen* in North America, Latin America, Europe, and Asia. Actual modern girls worked as café waitresses in Shanghai or Tokyo and as factory girls sporting

Figure 7.1 1930s postcard advertisement for La Florida bar restaurant, "The Cradle of the Daiquiri Cocktail," in Havana, Cuba. The illustration depicts Spanish conquistador Ponce de Léon—who according to legend went off in search of the Fountain of Youth—as he shares a toast with a young flapper at the crowded bar. *Source*: Transcendental Graphics / Getty Images.

bobbed haircuts in Berlin or New York. And images of modern girls circulated around the world in the guise of internationally renowned performers, including the Paris-based African American stage performer Josephine Baker and film stars such as Clara Bow, Louise Brooks, Marlene Dietrich, Greta Garbo, Ri Koran, Pola Negri, Mary Pickford, Devika Rani, Lupe Vélez, Anna May Wong, and Butterfly Wu. The modern girl was the subject of countless films, novels, and social commentaries, and she was endlessly featured in advertisements for cigarettes, cars, and cosmetics (Modern Girl Around the World Research Group 2005, pp. 248–9).

Advertisements for cosmetics and toiletries appeared all over the world during this period (Modern Girl Around the World Research Group 2005, pp. 250–1). For example, in the United States—the world's biggest producer of magazines and print advertising—such ads appeared in magazines such as *Cosmopolitan*, *Ladies' Home Journal*, and *Vogue* (catering to white middle- and working-class readers) as well as *The Crisis* (a journal published by the National Association for the Advancement of Colored People and edited by W.E.B. Du Bois) and the populist *Baltimore Afro-American* (a weekly newspaper). Mexican women had access to magazines such as *Ladies' Home Journal* and *Vogue* as well as weeklies such as *El heraldo ilustrado* and *El tiempo ilustrado* (Herschfield 2008, pp. 39, 51–2). In Germany, the ads appeared in such magazines as *Die Dame*, *Leipziger Illustrirte Zeitung*, and *Die Woche* (all directed at middle- and upper-class audiences). In the Chinese press, they appeared in treaty port newspapers published in English and Chinese (*North China Daily News* and *South China Morning Post*) and illustrated Chinese-language magazines such as *Ladies' Journal* (*Funu zazhi*) and *Young Companion* (*Liangyou*), which addressed an upper- and middle-class clientele. In India, ads appeared in venues such as *The Statesman* (Calcutta) and the *Times of India* (Bombay), major English-language dailies that catered to British colonials and Indian elites. In Africa, ads appeared in the *Cape Times* (Cape Town), a newspaper catering to the white and, to a lesser extent, "colored" populations in the British dominion of South Africa, and in black newspapers such as *Bantu Mirror* (Salisbury), *Bantu World* (Johannesburg), and the *Times of West Africa* (Accra).

Ads for cosmetics and toiletries encouraged young women to become modern girls by using products to cleanse and alter the color and texture of their teeth, hair, and skin and to change the shape and shade of their eyes and lips. This modern-girl aesthetic cut across national and imperial boundaries in ways that implicated and remade female sexuality. Beginning before World War I and lasting into the 1930s, the modern girl appeared

in advertisements with "an elongated, wiry and svelte body . . . [that signi-
fied] the attractions and dangers of androgyny and sexuality outside reproduction." Her body was also depicted as "excessively refined" with individual
body parts "elegantly polished, carefully scrubbed, meticulously sprayed
or, in an astounding variety of ways, cleaned and covered so that lips, teeth,
mouth, hair, skin, armpits, legs and vagina are all stylishly produced"
(Modern Girl Around the World Research Group 2005, p. 256). As this list
suggests, the modern girl's beauty and youthfulness were often linked to
scientific hygiene. Ads also depicted modern girls engaged in activities that
were particularly relevant to their daily lives: as film stars, as outdoor and
sports enthusiasts, in romantic or intimate poses, and in the process of
making up and admiring themselves in front of a vanity or hand-held
mirror (Modern Girl Around the World Research Group 2005, p. 260).

The modern girl's activities were inseparable from her sexuality: a particular brand of sexualized femininity that exhibited modern characteristics such as self-determination, independence, rebellion, and transgression.
The ads also promoted expressions of female sexuality that disregarded the
normative gender and sex roles associated with being a daughter, wife, and
mother. In Mexico, for example, *la flapperista* (or *la flapperesca*), like her
counterpart in North America and Europe, projected the image of a young,
active, independent woman enjoying a modern consumer lifestyle and who
was neither wife nor mother (Herschfield 2008, pp. 58–9). In China, the
figure of the modern girl marked a significant departure from the traditional Confucian image of a woman who submitted to the patriarchal
power of fathers, brothers, and husbands and (later on) from the Communist Party's image of idealistic (as opposed to materialistic), hard-
working, revolutionary women. In all these places, advertising directed at
young women (and their admirers) sought to link the consumption of
beauty products with a new kind of sexualized female subjectivity decou-
pled from traditional gender roles and reproductive sex.

Case 2: From Solitary Sex to Sexual Socialization—Mass-Mediated Sexuality in the United States since the 1950s

While formal discussions of sexuality—in schools, offices, places of worship,
and so on—are strictly regulated, when they are permitted at all, informal
sex talk in mass media has become increasingly vocal and explicit. Masturbation, for example, is rarely discussed openly in school curricula despite

being a common sexual practice and a staple of innuendo, humor, and harassment in everyday life. A historical discussion of media discourses on masturbation shows us how media work to embed sexuality in public debates about social and cultural norms. Mass media address sexual practices such as masturbation in various ways, sometimes as part of its coverage of medical, health, moral, religious, and educational issues and at other times as entertainment.

Social attitudes toward masturbation across cultures and historical eras have ranged from acceptance to reticence to prohibition. Injunctions against masturbation are especially strong in the Judeo-Christian tradition. For example, Jewish and Christian religious authorities have regularly referenced the biblical story of Onan—punished by God with an early death for spilling his seed on the ground rather than impregnating his widowed sister-in-law and ensuring the family line—as proof of masturbation's sinfulness, even though Onan's sin was more likely withdrawal before ejaculation. And, during the medieval period, Catholic Church authorities such as St. Thomas Aquinas taught that masturbation was not only a "sin against nature" but also worthy of condemnation because of the inevitably impure thoughts that precede the sin.

From the eighteenth century on, religious and medical authorities, especially in Europe and the Americas, came to see masturbation as symbolic of the relationship between the individual and the social world and thus as a major social problem tied to control of boundaries between male and female sexuality and between licit and illicit moralities, pleasures, imaginings, and self–other relations (Laqueur 2003, p. 22). On occasion, medical authorities divided on the issue of when and how it was acceptable to evacuate semen for health reasons, for example following overeating and excessive alcohol consumption, but for the most part they viewed the practice with trepidation (Gudelunas 2005, p. 67). In the United States, health reformers—notably Sylvester Graham, who promoted the whole wheat Graham Cracker as a healthy food that helped stifle masturbatory urges due to its lack of spices—endorsed a multifaceted regimen of Christianity, vegetarianism, and athleticism to thwart sexual incontinence, including masturbation. By the 1880s, medical authorities had linked masturbation with serious diseases such as tuberculosis, heart disease, and epilepsy, and recommended medical procedures, including male circumcision, to help curb the practice. For women, masturbation was also linked to psychological disorders such as hysteria and "marital aversion" (Gudelunas 2005, p. 69).

The acceptance of masturbation as a healthy and normal practice has been a long, arduous process, especially in societies influenced by Judeo-Christian norms. In the late 1940s, renowned US sexologist Alfred Kinsey and his associates provided some safety in numbers when they reported that 88 percent of males masturbate by age sixteen and 93 percent by age twenty-five. By 1952, the American Psychiatric Association had removed female hysteria from its list of psychological disorders, thus paving the way for the electric vibrator to move from medical device to consumer item. It is in this historical context that we explore how 1970s and 1980s newspaper advice columns in the United States offered space for discussions about masturbation by presenting themselves as a uniquely "safe" environment for sexual discourse.

One of the most widely read advice columns was "Dear Ann Landers." From 1955 to 2002, writing under the penname "Ann Landers," Esther Pauline Friedman-Lederer, a Jewish housewife from Iowa, became one of the most powerful voices in syndicated newspapers with an engaging blend of expertise (provided by a panel of consultants) and a lively down-to-earth writing style. In 1978, *World Almanac* named her one of the most influential women in the world and by the time of her death in 2002 "Dear Ann Landers" was syndicated in 1200 newspapers worldwide with an estimated readership that exceeded 90 million.

"Masturbation" first appeared in Landers's column in 1970, around the same time as the word "rape." In a time of rapid social change—the rise of post-World War II consumer society, civil rights, the women's movement, antiwar protests, and so on—Ann Landers helped readers to understand their own sexual practices. Throughout the 1970s, for example, she advised readers that masturbation was safe and healthy unless practiced compulsively. By the early 1980s, she was reassuring readers "who were wracked with guilt over their self-pleasuring habits" that a Notre Dame provost had confirmed that even leading theologians within the Catholic Church had modified their views on masturbation (Laqueur 2003, p. 77). By the late 1980s, masturbation in and of itself was no longer seen as problem, and Landers's subsequent discussions of masturbation appeared almost nonchalantly in connection with other taboo issues such as cross-dressing.

When she personally endorsed masturbation as a recommended sexual practice on October 24, 1993, however, Landers anticipated the fallout:

> The sex drive is the strongest human drive after hunger. It is nature's way of perpetuating the human race. Males reach their sexual peak as early as 17.

Figure 7.2 Outdoor Life poster. The poster explains that, while masturbation is not as bad as "ignorant people" claim, persistent self-abuse can "seriously hinder a boy's progress toward a vigorous manhood." *Source*: Courtesy of the Social Welfare History Archives, University of Minnesota Libraries.

There must be an outlet. I am recommending self-gratification or mutual masturbation, whatever it takes to release the sexual energy. This is a sane and safe alternative to intercourse, not only for teenagers, but for older men and women who have lost their partners. I do not want to hear from clergy-men telling me it's a sin. The sin is making people feel guilty about respond-ing to this fundamental human drive. I love my readers, and my mission is to be of service. This could be the most useful column I have written since I started 38 years ago. (cited in Gudelunas 2005, p. 78)

In an effort to represent the full spectrum of debate, she printed readers' objections to her endorsement, including this letter (dated November 28, 1993):

New York: You are a disgusting, sex-crazed old lady. It's time to hang it up. . . . Pasadena, Calif.: The world is in sad shape because of people like you. I am making a pilgrimage to Fatima, Portugal, soon, and I will pray for you and place your name in the petition basket. Rapid City, S.D.: I couldn't believe my eyes. Ann Landers recommending mutual masturbation! What kind of moral swamp did you grow up in? Young people need to be taught to suppress their sex drives until marriage. Stop promoting immorality. (cited in Gudelunas 2005, p. 79)

In fact, Landers had consistently advocated that children be taught about healthy sexual relationships, and had always expressed a special affinity for young people. Sometimes, she printed positive responses from young readers. One boy, for example, had written on November 18, 1974:

This letter is in response to "No fan of yours," the parent who felt your column should be removed from the newspaper because you spoke about such subjects as homosexuality and V.D. I'm a boy, almost 16. I've read your column since I was nine years old. My parents never told me one thing about sex or anything connected with it. It was from reading your column that I learned most of what I know. I want to thank you, Ann, for helping me (and thousands of other kids) to grow up and to be more mature and responsible. God bless you. May you continue to do your good work for many years to come. (cited in Gudelunas 2005, p. 82)

As these responses show, public discussion of sexuality issues such as mas-turbation has been hotly contested in US media, leaving some interlocutors angry and others appreciative. What is important is that Landers's column became a means to channel and distribute information about sexual practices. This case also shows how sexuality is connected to expert knowledge and power through mediated communication. The "Dear Ann Landers" newspaper columns operated within the graphosphere to impose a kind of rationality—associated with Landers as an expert or advised by experts—that represented masturbation as a normal sexual practice. Landers's advice columns thus played an important role in incorporating the topic into the everyday lives of readers around the world.

Beyond the graphosphere, discourses of sexuality have also proliferated in the videosphere, websphere, and mobilesphere, becoming part of the cultural process of sexual socialization. Mainstream entertainment media such as television, film, and magazines have had important influences on American adolescents' sexual formation and sexual decision-making. Adolescents between thirteen and eighteen years of age spend lots of their discretionary time exploring and interacting with mass media that is known to possess sexual content, and adolescents themselves acknowledge that they often turn to the mass media for information about sexuality.

A recent survey found that media directed at young adults represent sexual practices in varied, sometimes contradictory ways (Wright 2009). In terms of television programs, the survey found that popular programs across the entire television landscape—*Family Guy, Lost, That 70s Show*, and *24*—frequently feature casual sex while deemphasizing sexual risk and responsibility. Primetime programs such as *Buffy the Vampire Slayer* and *Dawson's Creek* also tend to portray sex as risk free and recreational, and to characterize male and female sexual roles and preferences in stereotypical ways. In daytime soap operas, sex between new acquaintances is rare and yet sex outside marriage is normal; adultery is a frequent occurrence and yet married partners are happier with their sex lives than unmarried partners. Daytime talk shows feature a variety of guests who engage in deviant sexual behavior, but the predominant response to those behaviors is condemnation. These shows also tend to feature less sexual content and place more emphasis on sexual risk and responsibility. Music videos often feature sexual images and emphasize a hedonistic orientation to sex. And, while they rarely refer to explicit sexual behaviors such as intercourse, they are often sexist and feature very little same-sex sexual behavior.

In contrast to television, feature films generally contain stronger messages about sexual activity, more concrete role models, and more specific examples, and do so in contexts more relevant to adolescents. But, despite frequent references to and depictions of sexual activity, films generally include very few messages about the risks associated with being sexually

active. Moreover, noncommitted sex is typically portrayed as more normative and satisfactory than married sex. In addition, mainstream films are
mostly devoid of same-sex eroticism and tend to depict homosexuality as
the sexual preference of deviants.

Wright's survey divides women's magazines into magazines for women
(*Allure, Cosmopolitan, Glamour, Marie Claire,* etc.) and magazines for adolescent girls (*Seventeen, YM,* etc.). Both genres pay attention to sexual
health issues, contain graphic sexual descriptions, emphasize the insepara-
bility of female physical appearance and female sexuality, and send mixed
sexual messages. There are, however, two major differences between them.
Women's magazines stress that females must develop their sexual repertoire
to keep up with male sexual passions, while teen magazines instruct their
readers on the ways they might resist men's advances or channel men's
sexuality into relational and romantic endeavors. Moreover, while women's
magazines devote significant attention to female sexual desire, teen magazines approach female sexuality primarily from a relational perspective. In
contrast, mainstream magazines read by adolescent males (*FHM, Maxim,
Stuff,* etc.) tend to privilege male sexuality over female sexuality, portray
sex between strangers as normative, and assume that males are not interested sexually in other males. In addition, they contain little information
about sexual risk or responsibility.

This survey of sexual content in contemporary mainstream media
exposes a proliferation of sexual discourses in multiple mediaspheres in
US society and, by extension, in global mass media. While Ann Landers's
advice column focused on masturbation as a physical and psychological
health issue, other venues such as television, film, and magazines have
impacted sexual socialization in different ways. These differences reveal
how the proliferation of media discourses on sex and sexual practices from
masturbation to casual sex have placed sexuality at the heart of modern
subjectivity.

Case 3: Media Fans—The *Otaku* and the "Beautiful
Fighting Girl" in Japan since the 1960s

Mass media ideas, representations, and advice on adolescent sexual identities and practices do not translate directly into the everyday lives of young
people: media consumers make distinctions between fiction and reality and
between information and practices as they attempt to make sense of mass-

mediated representations of sexuality. In the process, they distinguish and define the boundaries between what is meaningful and what is not, often actively appropriating media culture by becoming fans of certain genres (comedy, horror, science fiction), of specific products and companies (Apple, Disney, Star Trek), or of various media technologies and gadgets. All over the world, fans of comics, animation, and video games meet regularly at conventions and online; they share and exchange knowledge, information, and creations (fan fictions and 'zines); and many dress up as comic book characters and reenact video game scenes while documenting their activities through stories, photos, and videos.

In Japan—a country famous since the end of World War II for developing new media technologies, entertainments, and cutting-edge gadgets—consumers have a long tradition of incorporating media into their daily lives. Many Japanese media practices have become influential around the world. For example, the popular US-based technology magazine *Wired* devotes a special section of each issue to the consumption patterns of Japanese girls. And many popular terms and concepts in media consumption and production directed at youth around the world reflect Japanese uses (even when the original words are English): manga (comics), anime (animation), and cosplay (costume play).

At the heart of the consuming practices involving manga, anime, and cosplay is the figure of the *otaku*, a term used to refer to passionate fans of anime, manga, and video games. *Otaku* are known for their skills with and knowledge of computer technology and for their encyclopedic, even fetishistic, knowledge of particular strains of visual culture. *Otaku* first appeared in the 1960s in the historical context of rapid developments in production and consumption in Japan. Azuma Hiroki, in his *Otaku: Japan's Database Animals* (2009), argues that there are three generations of *otaku* (Azuma 2009, pp. 6–7): the first generation was born around 1960 and saw *Space Battleship Yamato* (1974) and *Mobile Suit Gundam* (1979) during their teen years; the second generation was born around 1970 and during their teen years enjoyed the diversified and mature *otaku* culture produced by the previous generation; the third generation was born around 1980 and were junior high-school students at the time the *Neon Genesis Evangelion* media franchise took off in the mid-1990s.[1] Generational differences partly reflect the evolution of media technologies. While the first generation was interested in science fiction and B-grade movies, the third generation is fascinated with mysteries and computer games. The latest generation also experienced the rapid spread of the Internet during their teens and, thus, their main activities tend to take place on websites and they express particular interest in computer-generated graphics.

Mainstream Japanese culture focuses on negative aspects of the *otaku* phenomenon and views its participants as under-socialized, unhealthily obsessive, and unable to distinguish between fiction and reality. Although manga illustrators first used the term *otaku*—which translates into English literally as "you" and figuratively as "geek"—to refer to each other, by the early 1980s it had taken on negative connotations for the general public. These negative connotations were further solidified in 1989 when police apprehended the serial killer of four young girls, Miyazaki Tsutomu, whose penchant for anime and slasher films caused the media to dub him "the Otaku Murderer."

For many scholars, however, the *otaku* have a great deal to teach us about how to survive and flourish in a media-saturated environment. From a media studies perspective, the *otaku* population exploded after the release of the first VCRs and they have become active users of many media-storage technologies including VCR, laser discs, DVD, and computer hard drives. Over the years, *otaku* interests have grown across media genres, their life histories often becoming inseparable from the development of media technologies, especially analog and digital technologies associated with the videosphere, websphere, and mobilesphere. The *otaku* are not simply anime fans; their practices straddle multiple technologies such as film, comics, and videos. In *An Introduction to Otaku Studies* (1996), Okada Toshio (aka the "king of Otaku") argues that *otaku* have three essential traits: an evolved visual sensibility, advanced referencing ability, and indefatigable desire for self-improvement and self-assertion (Okada 1996, cited in Saitō 2011, p. 13). First, they see like an "aesthete" who has "the ability to find one's own kind of beauty in a work and enjoy watching the growth of its creator"; second, they see like a "master" who has "the ability to analyze the work logically and grasp its structure like a scientist while also looking to steal its secrets like a craftsman"; and third, they see like a connoisseur who is able "to get a glimpse into the creator's situation and the fine points of the work" (Okada 1996, cited in Saitō 2011, note 6, pp. 190–1). From Okada's perspective, then, *otaku* are not passive consumers of mass media but effectively combine active media creation and consumption.

Sexuality plays a multilayered, complex role in *otaku*. One example of that complexity is the invention and development of a series of fictional characters grouped together under the name "beautiful fighting girl"—or, as psychiatrist Saitō Tamaki prefers, "the phallic girl" (Saitō 2011, p. 31). A typical beautiful fighting girl has huge vacant eyes, an unusually small mouth, and enormous breasts, and she sometimes dresses in lingerie-like armor and carries a grotesque laser gun (Saitō 2011, p. 31). Since the 1964 serialization of Ishinomori Shōtarō's *Cyborg 009* (*Saibōgu 009*) in the weekly magazine *Shōnen Sunday*—made into an anime in 1968—beautiful fighting girl characters have proliferated in comics, television series, films, and video games. They were originally icons intended for young teenage girls

Figure 7.3 *Sukeban deka.* Cover illustration from the first volume published by Media Factory Inc. The beautiful fighting girl in a sailor suit is brandishing her deadly yo-yo. *Source*: © Shinji Wada / Media Factory Inc.

but gradually caught on with *otaku* consumers. For example, in the manga serialization of Wada Shinji's *Sukeban deka* (Boss Girl Detective), which began in 1976, the legendary girl boss (*sukeban*) Asamiya Suki uses a cherry blossom yo-yo as her weapon against evil while she patrols schoolyards that the police are unable to infiltrate. Although the series was initially targeted at young girls who liked strong heroines, when it was turned into a live-action television drama in the 1980s, starring teen "idols" such as Saitō Yuki, Minamino Yōko, Ōnishi Yuka, and Asaka Yui, producers modified the work to appeal to a broader *otaku* audience. The heroines, who originally appeared as tomboys with short hair, became sweet girl idols in sailor outfits (Saitō 2011, p. 100). The shift in image of the beautiful fighting girl characters for the *otaku* market resulted from a number of important media events: the first comic market in 1975, the first sales of the VCR for home use in 1976, and the 1979 publication of the first anime magazine, *Animage*. By enlarging consumer markets in Japan, these events made the beautiful fighting girl a staple in a world of expanding media genres (comics, animated and live-action television series and films, video games, and online videos).

The parallel between the development of various beautiful fighting girl characters and the evolution of media technologies toward digital and multimedia formats in *otaku* consumption practices shows how *otaku* make sense of their life worlds through the logic of multiplicity rather than linearity. An *otaku* often transforms his or her sexuality through mediated fictional characters, producing multiple sexual realities (with regard to body sensations, enjoyment forms, and pleasurable qualities), which can run contrary to mainstream sexual norms. According to Saitō, for example, an *otaku* is a person with "a strong affinity for fictional contexts" who "makes use of fictionalization as a way to 'possess' the object of his or her love," "who inhabits not just two but multiple orientations," and who is "capable of finding sexual objects in fiction itself" (Saitō 2011, p. 16).

Otaku sexuality is thus tied to the ways in which they take pleasure in multiple levels of fictionality and treat everyday reality itself as a kind of fiction. Through fictionalization, *otaku* turn external objects to their own purposes. In cosplay (*kosupure*) and fan magazines, for example, writers often borrow settings and characters from popular anime stories to populate their own scenarios, which they then upload to online forums (Saitō 2011, p. 20). Despite these online fantasies, Saitō argues that *otaku* sexuality operates differently in real life. *Otaku* may be perverse and transgressive in their fictionalized lives but follow mainstream sexual norms and conventions in real life. For example, a male *otaku* may idolize anime characters but does not insist that real-world women act as stand-ins for his fantasy (Saitō 2011, p. 30). Instead, most *otaku* make clear distinctions between their media-based interactions with fictional characters and their real-life interactions with real people.

The *otaku* phenomenon tells us a lot about the everyday lives of avid media consumers all over the world. Although outsiders often view their relationship with media in negative terms—as unhealthy, obsessive, deviant, and so on—*otaku* and their fellow media "junkies" participate in media culture not just as passive consumers but also as active producers.[2] Recent developments in social media technology by such companies as Facebook, Google, and Amazon involve sharing messages, images, videos, and music and rely heavily on content produced by consumers. In becoming "prosumers" (producer-consumers), media users help generate massive profits for media and technology companies. At the same time, they put many aspects of their lives under public scrutiny, including their sexuality. And the creative responses of *otaku*, prosumers, and others to the mass mediation of their sexuality reveals that human sexuality is far from one-dimensional or fixed at birth, but continuously adapts to cultural changes as we negotiate the boundaries between real and fictional, public and private, and normative and transgressive.

Case 4: Sexting, "Human Flesh Search," and the "Guo Meimei Baby" Incident in Twenty-First-Century China

In the twenty-first century, mediaspheres involving the Internet and the smartphone have emerged as increasingly influential forms of mass media. While *otaku* are active consumers (and producers) who explore their sexuality through anime, manga, and computer games, ordinary users of the Internet and smartphones engage in a less deliberate but no less meaningful way in consuming and producing a wide range of mass-mediated sexual discourses. Among youth who grew up in the contemporary age of webspheres and mobilespheres, especially those born after 1990, one popular practice involves "sexting." To go beyond a simple understanding of sexting as the act of sharing sexually explicit messages or images through mobile devices, we need to examine it in terms of the relationship between sexuality and mass media.

Like other sexuality-related issues such as gender relations, marriage, masturbation, sexual socialization, and cosplay, sexting has become an important aspect of mass-mediated culture because it too marks the boundaries between public and private, normal and abnormal, and legal and illegal. Thus, its impacts are often greater than we would expect from a simple sexual communication between two mobile devices. In many countries, for example, sexting is influenced by celebrity media culture. In tabloid journalism, paparazzi follow a celebrity and try to take photos and videos or hack email accounts that might include sex-related materials. In this context, celebrities' private lives, including their sex lives, are on public display. Like this celebrity-based media practice, sexting is a public display of private life through multimedia text messages that include photographic, video, audio, and textual information.

Unlike celebrity watching, however, sexting refers to a broader set of practices carried out by the individuals or groups themselves. These materials are uploaded to popular Internet and social media sites such as Facebook, Twitter, and YouTube. As sexting materials accumulate on these sites, they become part of a person's life history. Along with many other types of web-based media—such as personal or organizational websites, blogs, and forums—sexting messages are stored online for a long time (if not permanently). Even when messages are deleted, they continue to circulate in some form online. Thus, online materials including sexting materials become part of an individual's personnal dossier. These stored materials can serve to facilitate and enhance communications with others. They can also negatively affect a person's life. For example, in early 2011, married New York Congressman Anthony D. Weiner's camera-phone photos of his crotch—which he sexted to other women—circulated widely online, producing a media-driven scandal that eventually led the congressman to resign.

In China, "netizens," active online users who act as web citizens, have coined the phrase "human flesh search" (*renrou sousuo*) to describe a practice that searches out online sources to reveal information that is unavailable to the general public or intentionally concealed by government authorities.[3] The Chinese "human flesh search" usually targets a particular official or public figure, exposing corrupt government and corporate practices or provoking a celebrity scandal. These searches often include information on the target's sexual activities.

The Guo Meimei case illustrates the role of sexting and blogging in "human flesh search" practices. Guo Meimei, a twenty-year-old Chinese woman who uses the online name "Guo Meimei Baby," regularly posts photos and short messages on her microblog, a Sina Weibo account.[4] One photo, for example, reveals her closetful of Hermès handbags. Another shows her wearing sunglasses and leaning on the hood of a white Maserati, a luxury car with a price tag of over 2.4 million yuan (about US $370,000) in China. Other photos and entries detail her jet-set lifestyle, describing the orange Lamborghini she drives in Shenzhen as "little bull" and the white Maserati in Beijing as "little horse." Among more than a hundred photos widely circulated and shared on the Internet, Guo Meimei typically appears in sexy and fashionable clothes, including bikini swim suits, tube or push-up tops, and short skirts. Like other Internet photos taken by young women, these pictures include self-shot images of Guo in front of a mirror showing her cleavage, various facial expressions, and her eyes with artificial lashes.

On June 21, 2011, someone on the Chinese Internet commented on the photos and on Guo's job title as "Business General Manager of the Red Cross Society," which was marked with a "V," meaning that her identity had been verified by Sina, the company that hosted the microblog. Within two hours, the message was shared over a thousand times and Chinese netizens began to criticize Guo and the Red Cross Society of China. They raised questions about Guo's personal relationship with an older male Red Cross official, Wang Jun, and about the Red Cross Society's lack of transparency regarding public donations and its business operations. Guo initially defended herself by saying that her company was a commercial operation separate from the Red Cross. As public pressure grew, the Red Cross and Guo claimed they had nothing to do with each other. Through human flesh searches, however, netizens discovered the existence of a shady group called the Red Cross of the Commercial Sector, which was in fact authorized by Red Cross Society headquarters.

On June 24, the Red Cross Society asked the police to investigate Guo. Two days later, Guo apologized online for her "stupid and ignorant behavior" and "made-up identity." Paparazzi-style photographs showed her arriving at the Beijing Airport on June 27 and rushing off in a private sedan. The police launched an investigation and announced two weeks later that Guo did not have any relationship with the Red Cross. Throughout the month of July, the Red Cross took a series of damage-control measures: opening a microblog account, hosting news conferences, stopping operations of the Red Cross of the Commercial Sector, and launching a website for donors who wanted to look up their donation records. In early August, Guo and her mother appeared on *Larry Lang Live*, a *Larry King Live*-style television show on financial and economic issues hosted by Larry Lang (Lang Xianping), a famous Chinese economist. On the show, they attempted to address some of the questions raised by netizens, explaining that the source of their wealth was not the Red Cross but the mother's investments (especially in the Chinese stock market in the 1990s) and Wang Jun, whom Guo claimed to be her "adopted father" (*ganba*), a real estate broker in Shenzhen rather than a Red Cross employee. And they explained the expensive cars: Guo had received a Mini Cooper as a seventeenth-birthday gift from her mother and the white Maserati from Wang Jun. Following the show's broadcast, Wang's business partner Wong told the *Nanfang Urban Daily* that Wang denied that he was Guo's adopted father. Later, a widely circulated message claimed that Guo's mother was under pressure to admit that Guo was Wang's daughter and had been born after Wang married another woman. Chinese netizens continued to explore whether Guo was Wang's adopted daughter, actual daughter, or mistress and to discuss the broader implications of the case.

With respect to sexuality and gender, the case raises three issues. First, Guo grew up in a relatively wealthy family. Unlike her mother's generation in Maoist China, she never faced problems of poverty. Public response to her behavior throughout the incident demonstrated that, although Guo is from an economically secure background, she was still considered a "risky" subject in Chinese society because she lacks self-control and fails to behave like a good citizen. Guo thus reinforced popular perceptions of spoiled, wealthy youth who lack any sense of social responsibility.

Second, most observers blamed Guo's life trajectory as the spoiled daughter of a single mother who grew up without the guidance of a proper father for her poor behavior and the potential risk she poses to society. The story her mother told on *Larry Lang Live* implied that Wang Jun was not a "normal" parent (whether or not he was the girl's adopted or actual father) and that his expensive gifts were closely tied to Guo's improper conduct. To further fix the "spoiled daughter of a neglectful parent" image in the public imagination, Guo's upbringing conveniently mirrored a familiar storyline from popular youth-focused television dramas such as *The Three Daughters of the Xia Family* (Hunan Television 2011).

Third, the normative trajectory of a Chinese woman's life should progress from courtship to marriage to the birth of a child. Guo clearly violated this norm. For Chinese netizens, the fact that Guo was connected to wealthy businessmen and government officials raised obvious questions about whether or not her lifestyle depended on her sexual relationship with wealthy, powerful men. In numerous online posts, netizens speculated that Guo was a mistress or "second breast" (*er nai*). Although the Chinese expression "second breast" was first developed in the 1990s to describe young women from the People's Republic of China (mainland China) who got involved with married businessmen from Hong Kong or Taiwan, the term has come to refer broadly to young women who become mistresses of married, usually wealthy businessmen or government officials. As many human flesh searches have revealed, a "second breast" for a powerful, wealthy man can expect to receive expensive gifts or properties such as a car or apartment, in addition to living expenses. Thus, in speculating that Guo was a mistress, netizens sought to expose possible corruption at the highest levels of the Red Cross Society.

Guo Meimei's weblogs displaying her connections to wealth, power, and men brought to light a range of larger issues: corrupt charities, inadequate parenting, the social irresponsibility of children from wealthy families, and the widespread phenomena of government officials and businessmen with mistresses. All of these issues highlight the links between sexuality and media. While some netizens condemned Guo's deceptive claims about her relationship with the Red Cross Society and Wang Jun, others pointed out the positive outcome of the incident—that their response to Guo's weblogs enabled netizens to publically express their frustrations with the ways in which the Red Cross operated. And one of the many computer-generated images by netizens even portrayed the half-naked Guo as the leader of an uprising. Another showed Guo as a cover girl of *Time* magazine with the headline in Chinese: "A Second Breast Helps to Save the Country." As a result of netizen activism, the Red Cross Society was forced to become more transparent, for example by allowing donors to verify the amounts of their donations through an online database. Whether condemned as a symbol of decadent sexuality or lauded as the catalyst of social reform, the Guo Meimei incident reveals the complicated relationship between media activism, sexual practices, and social issues in an age dominated by the Internet and smartphones.[5]

Conclusion

This chapter has discussed four cases that demonstrate various aspects of the relationship between mass media and sexuality. These cases cover a range of topics and mediaspheres: advertising campaigns that promoted the sexuality of the modern girl through print media (graphosphere); discourses about masturbation, sex, and sexual socialization that proliferated across mediaspheres (graphosphere and videosphere); the relationship between sexuality and media consumption and production in the *otaku* subculture (graphosphere, videosphere, websphere); and the production of sexual discourses through online activism (graphosphere, videosphere, websphere, mobilesphere). As these examples demonstrate, it is important and necessary to understand that media and sexuality change historically and across national boundaries. Mass-mediated culture affects the ways in which sexuality is represented, understood, and practiced by peoples. It plays an important role in communicating which aspects of sexuality are considered normal or abnormal, permissible or prohibited, pleasurable or risky. While affirming some sexual norms and moralities, it also challenges others and generates new ones. Thus, studies of the relationship between sexuality and mass media help us to understand broader issues including families, gender relations, citizenship, economics, and politics.

Notes

1 *Neon Genesis Evangelion* is set in a postapocalyptic future in which a group called NERV uses giant humanoid robots piloted by teenagers to battle hostile beings known as "Angels." From the beginning, the franchise generated a impressive array of product spin-offs.
2 See for example Henri Jenkins's 1992 study of avid US television viewers, especially fans of Star Trek.
3 It should be noted that this practice is different from "cyber bullying." On social media sites in the United States, some people publish unauthorized sex-related materials concerning other people, usually sexual minorities and vulnerable young adults, with the intention of embarrassing and harassing them. Cyber bullying is often an extension of bullying in everyday life.
4 Many news organizations have widely reported the incident (e.g. see Wong 2011).
5 This relationship is true of many other cases. In Egypt and Tunisia, for example, some young women used nude (or seminude) photos of themselves as symbols of liberation to protest against their governments during the 2011 Arab Spring. See www.ibtimes.co.uk/articles/261541/20111205/nude-activism-arab-spring-slideshow.htm (accessed August 9, 2013).

References

Adorno, T.W. (1991 [1975]) Culture industry reconsidered, in *The Culture Industry: Selected Essays on Mass Culture* (ed. J.M. Bernstein). Routledge, London, pp. 98–106.

Azuma, H. (2009 [2001]) *Otaku: Japan's Database Animals*. University of Minnesota Press, Minneapolis.

Benjamin, W. (1968) The work of art in the age of mechanical reproduction, in *Illuminations*. Schocken Books, New York, pp. 217–51.

Debray, R. (1996) *Media Manifestos: On the Technological Transmission of Cultural Forms*. Verso, London.

Foucault, M. (1978) *The History of Sexuality, Volume 1: An Introduction* (trans. R. Hurley). Vintage, New York.

Foucault, M. (1988) Technologies of the self, in *Technologies of the Self: A Seminar with Michel Foucault* (ed. L.H. Martin, H. Gutman, and P. Hutton). University of Massachusetts Press, Amherst, pp. 16–49.

Gudelunas, D. (2005) Talking taboo: Newspaper advice columns and sexual discourse. *Sexuality & Culture*, 9 (1), 62–87.

Herschfield, J. (2008) *Imagining la Chica Moderna: Women, Nation, and Visual Culture in Mexico, 1917–1936*. Duke University Press, Durham, NC.

Horkheimer, M. and Adorno, T.W. (1995 [1944]) The culture industry: Enlightenment as mass deception, in *Dialectic of Enlightenment*. Continuum, New York, pp. 120–67.

Jenkins, H. (1992). *Textual Poachers: Television Fans and Participatory Culture*. Routledge, London.

Laqueur, T.W. (2003) *Solitary Sex: A Cultural History of Masturbation*. Zone Books, New York.

Modern Girl Around the World Research Group (Barlow, T.E., Dong, M.Y., Poiger, U.G., et al.) (2005) The modern girl around the world: A research agenda and preliminary findings. *Gender & History*, 17 (2), 245–94.

Okada T. (1996) *Otakugaku nyūmon* [An introduction to otaku studies]. Ōta Shuppan, Tokyo.

Saitō, T. (2011 [2006]) *Beautiful Fighting Girl*. University of Minnesota Press, Minneapolis.

Wong, E. (2011) An online scandal underscores Chinese distrust of state charities. *New York Times*, July 3. www.nytimes.com/2011/07/04/world/asia/04china .html?_r=0&adxnnl=1&pagewanted=all&adxnnlx=1375265167-9Iwkot nAJhaZDXGp2fy5LA (accessed July 31, 2013).

Wright, P.J. (2009) Sexual socialization messages in mainstream entertainment mass media: A review and synthesis. *Sexuality & Culture*, 13, 181–200.

Suggested Reading

Benjamin, W. (1968) The work of art in the age of mechanical reproduction, in *Illuminations*. Schocken Books, New York, pp. 217–51.

Debray, R. (1996) *Media Manifestos: On the Technological Transmission of Cultural Forms.* Verso, London.

Foucault, M. (1978) *The History of Sexuality, Volume 1: An Introduction* (trans. R. Hurley). Vintage, New York.

Foucault, M. (1988) Technologies of the self, in *Technologies of the Self: A Seminar with Michel Foucault* (ed. L.H. Martin, H. Gutman, and P. Hutton). University of Massachusetts Press, Amherst, pp. 16–49.

Gudelunas, D. (2005) Talking taboo: Newspaper advice columns and sexual discourse. *Sexuality & Culture*, 9 (1), 62–87.

Modern Girl Around the World Research Group (Barlow, T.E., Dong, M.Y., Poiger, U.G., et al.) (2005) The modern girl around the world: A research agenda and preliminary findings. *Gender & History*, 17 (2), 245–94.

Wright, P.J. (2009) Sexual socialization messages in mainstream entertainment mass media: A review and synthesis. *Sexuality & Culture*, 13, 181–200.

8

Sexuality and the Contemporary World
Globalization and Sexual Rights

Richard Parker, Jonathan Garcia,
and Robert M. Buffington

*As with other aspects of human behavior, the concrete institutional
forms of sexuality at any given time and place are products of human
activity. They are imbued with conflicts of interest and political maneu-
ver, both deliberate and incidental. In that sense, sex is always political.
But there are also historical periods in which sexuality is more sharply
contested and more overtly politicized. In such periods, the domain of
erotic life is, in effect, renegotiated.* (Rubin 1984, p. 267)

The late twentieth and early twenty-first centuries—perhaps more than
at any other time in history—have been marked by a sharply contested
and overtly politicized approach to sexuality. Indeed, contentious debates
around sexuality are one of the defining qualities of contemporary life. At
the center of these debates is the clash between advocates of freedom of
sexual expression and social conservatives who uphold "traditional" sexual
values: an ongoing tug-of-war among distinct stakeholders for the mention,
definition, and recognition of sexual rights in arenas ranging from the
dinner table to the schoolyard to the United Nations. Effeminate boys are
still picked on during recess, but now there is a global social movement
against bullying. And, if the world has become smaller to the extent that
sexual rights activists, concerned parents, and local educators pay closer
attention to sexuality in order to ensure a child's right to safe schooling; it

A Global History of Sexuality: The Modern Era, First Edition.
Edited by Robert M. Buffington, Eithne Luibhéid, and Donna J. Guy.
© 2014 Robert M. Buffington, Eithne Luibhéid, and Donna J. Guy.
Published 2014 by Blackwell Publishing Ltd.

has also become more expansive as images and ideas circulate in new ways via digital technologies, generating resonant symbols and shockwaves that sometimes go global through blogs, viral Internet videos, and cell-phone text messages. It is hardly surprising then that struggles for sexual rights around the world have changed in important ways, intensifying and mutating in response to the globalization of the social movements that promote them.

Effective activism requires framing concepts in a way that is culturally resonant enough to make sense to a general public and viscerally shocking enough to prompt popular outcry and inspire public support. For this reason, the *right* to free expression has always been a key concept in most political organizing around sexuality, especially in the West. This right draws on a Western liberal democratic tradition derived from the work of thinkers such as John Stuart Mill (1806–73) who emphasize notions of personal autonomy—"liberty" in Mill's terminology—and self-determination: the capacity to think, to decide, and to act freely and independently provided that individual actions cause no serious harm to others. The concept includes the right to control over one's own body, a central tenet of sexual rights movements. The discourse of sexual rights thus encompasses both negative rights that redress harm (e.g. freedom from sexual violation, rape, traffick-ing in persons, and interpartner violence, among other forms of violence) and positive rights that enable action (e.g. equality in marriage laws and the right to comprehensive sex education). This means that sexual rights must be both protected *and* nurtured. These rights are also inextricably tied to political, economic, civil, and other rights, and we would argue that they intersect with each one of these domains, making a comprehensive approach to human rights, including sexual rights, fundamental to social justice (Corrêa et al. 2008).

Although the contemporary language of human rights originates with Western political philosophy, the concept draws much of its moral author-ity and popular appeal from notions of divine or natural laws derived from a wide range of religious traditions. For example, it was evangelical Chris-tians in England and Quakers in the United States who spearheaded the early nineteenth-century drive to abolish slavery—perhaps the first great global human rights movement. A century later, a British-trained lawyer, Mahatma Gandhi, drew on Hindu religious traditions to develop a success-ful strategy of nonviolent civil disobedience that helped end British impe-rial rule in India. Gandhi's strategy, in turn, inspired Martin Luther King, a Southern Baptist minister, in his efforts to defeat segregation in the

United States a few decades later. Another prominent civil rights leader, Malcolm X, a Muslim minister, credited a 1964 visit to Mecca with alerting him to the transformative possibilities of religious community, noting that "we were *truly* all the same (brothers)—because their belief in one God had removed the white from their *minds*, the white from their *behavior*, and the white from their *attitude*" (Malcolm X 1964). In each case, the close links between shared religious principles and secular human rights proved essential to the remarkable success of these three interconnected global liberation movements.

Important as religious principles have been to human rights movements around the world, deeply entrenched religious attitudes toward "immoral" or "sinful" sexual practices have more often encouraged a strong backlash against sexual rights, especially support for abortion and same-sex marriage. As we will see later in this chapter, sexual rights movements, especially in the Global South, continue to espouse religious ideals such as tolerance, compassion, and "brotherly love," but usually as a counterweight to self-proclaimed traditionalists who oppose (sometimes violently) their efforts to challenge the primacy of heterosexual unions and normative sexual practices. This tension in religious-based approaches to human rights, which sometimes operate in support of universal human rights and at other times in opposition to secular challenges to religious moral authority, has become especially fraught in recent years as local groups negotiate their relationship with global sexual rights movements.

The struggle to include sexual freedoms among our essential political, economic, and civil rights has become especially important in the contemporary world because discrimination on the basis of sexuality is increasingly understood to play a central role—along with long-acknowledged discriminations based on gender, race, ethnicity, poverty, and class—in circumscribing human rights around the world. We would argue that the globalization of political economies, ideas, technology, migration, and media has led to a more global (not to say universal) understanding of sexual rights. This "new world order" requires us to think about dislocations of both time and space, for, while sexual rights, especially the delineation of sexual freedom and autonomy, are highly dependent on historical and geographic context, these links also work to merge histories and geographies as local sexual rights movements go global and as global ones go local.

In this chapter, we explore some of the most important dimensions of this realignment of sexual rights movements in the contemporary world.

We note that local activism has taken on global qualities as transnational links facilitate a greater focus on sexual politics in an increasingly interconnected "global village." We also point out how global processes resonate and impact at local levels, changing the way diverse sexual communities understand and experience sexuality as well as transforming their grassroots struggles for sexual rights. At the same time, these grassroots struggles have produced changes in the other direction as local understandings and experiences "trickle up" to the global/transnational level. While we recognize the extent to which these global and local struggles for sexual rights have confronted powerful conservative reactions, usually cast in religious terms, we argue that they have nonetheless made significant gains in the recognition of sexual rights all over the world.

Globalization and Sexuality in the Contemporary World

Addressing the issue of sexuality in the contemporary world, particularly for a volume that focuses more broadly on the global history of sexuality, is a special challenge. In many ways, it involves an exercise in what Michel Foucault described as "the history of the present" (Foucault 1977, p. 31). Foucault's formulation asks us to understand our present condition through an analysis of the historical factors that have been crucial in getting us to where we are. In the early twenty-first century, no matter the phenomenon—sexuality as much as any other—it is impossible to ignore the centrality of the interrelated forces we call globalization in shaping the contemporary world (Giddens 1990; Castells 1996, 1997, 1998; Held et al. 1999).

While scholars initially focused on economic globalization, in recent years they have come to see globalization as a set of multiple intersecting and intertwining processes that also have a profound influence on politics, society, and culture (Waters 1995). Indeed, as awareness of the multiple dimensions of globalization and its impact on all aspects of modern life have deepened (and broadened), scholars have increasingly turned their attention to issues such as human sexuality, previously dismissed as too "personal" or "private" to be of much interest (Aggleton et al. 2012). Globalization has impacted sexuality in contemporary life in various ways, including through language and culture, migration and population movement, technological and social innovation, and political organization (Aggleton et al. 2012).

One particularly useful way to conceptualize the multiple dimensions of globalization, including the globalization of sexualities, is the notion of accelerating global flows or "scapes" developed by anthropologist Arjun Appadurai (1996). Appadurai identifies five principal "scapes"—financescapes, ethnoscapes, technoscapes, mediascapes, and ideoscapes—each of which highlights a particular set of global flows. The idea of financescapes is probably the most accessible to those familiar with globalization, because it emphasizes the flows of capital through stock markets, futures markets, and other components of the global capitalist system. But the key innovation in Appadurai's framework is its emphasis on a range of other things that also flow around the contemporary world. Ethnoscapes refers to the flow of people and population groups through voluntary and forced migration, relocation, diasporas, and so on. Technoscapes refers to the global flow of technologies such as the Internet, cell phones, and other communications and production technologies that characterize the contemporary world and transform our notions of time and space. Mediascapes refers to the flows of media images that digital technologies, in particular, have made possible, permitting us to follow events on the other side of the world in real time and integrating diverse societies into a single interacting media system. Finally, ideoscapes acknowledges that ideas also circulate, including notions of freedom, oppression, human rights, and social justice, often inflected by different political ideologies and religious beliefs. In our increasingly globalized world, these ideas circulate with far greater speed than ever before, providing the foundation for a wide range of transnational links.

Although Appadurai's various scapes never mention sexuality per se, they are nonetheless quite useful for thinking about the ways in which the multiple and transformative processes associated with globalization affect sexualities in the contemporary world. The notion of financescapes, of course, is especially important because it emphasizes how an increasingly integrated global capitalist system commodifies bodies and pleasures in profound new ways, creating sex markets and marketplaces while at the same time transforming all aspects of sexual life (Corrêa et al. 2008). The notion of ethnoscapes, in turn, helps us understand not just migration generally but also sexual migration specifically—patterns of population movement driven by sexual desire, by the search for sexual freedom, or by a range of complex, controversial, and politicized flows associated with sexual slavery or trafficking, many of them embedded in an erotics of racial and ethnic difference with deep roots in colonial histories of domination and exploitation (Luibhéid 2002; Agustín 2007; Thomas et al. 2010). The notions of technoscape and mediascape also call attention to how technology, and especially the development of digital media in the informational economy, quite literally mediate sexual desire and sexual practices in new and quite remarkable ways (Manderson 2012). And the notion of ideoscapes helps us see how concepts such as sexual oppression, sexual rights, and sexual freedom have traveled to countries and cultures around the world with sometimes quite unexpected directionalities, including transformative returns to the "source" (Corrêa et al. 2008). Indeed, while it might be a bit of an exaggeration to suggest that all these various flows may come together in defining distinct sexualscapes, scholars have coined the term homoscapes to help explain sexual migration and flows of capital, bodies, technologies, media, and ideas in relation to gay and bisexual men, while the idea of heteroscapes helps us understand the effects of globalization in relation to the social and historical construction of heterosexualities (Parker 1999).

If Appadurai's notion of "scapes" suggests new ways to consider the circulation and representation of sexualities, sociologist Manuel Castells's work on globalization in the contemporary "information age" offers key insights into the changing shape of sexuality and especially activism around sexual rights (Castells 1996, 1997). Castells argues that late twentieth-century globalization is grounded in a radical restructuring of the world economy and the growth of "informational capitalism," characterized by rapidly accelerating processes of social exclusion and intensified interaction among multiple forms of exclusion (Castells 1996). Among the most vivid processes of exclusion are the feminization of poverty, intensification of racial and ethnic conflicts, and polarization between rich and poor in both the "developed" and "developing" worlds. Within these processes, exclusions and struggles related to sexuality intersect with exclusions and struggles based on gender, race, ethnicity, class, and national citizenship.

Castells's work also calls attention to the growing centrality of identity to contemporary experience. Much recent work on the nature of identity has emphasized its constructed and constantly changing character (Hall 1990). This crucial insight has made it possible to theorize changing constructions of identity in relation to the experience of both oppression and resistance, particularly through the mobilization of social movements (Castells 1997). Castells, for example, has distinguished between *legitimizing identities*, which are "introduced by the dominant institutions of society to extend and rationalize their domination *vis á vis* social actors"; *resistance identities*, which are "generated by those actors that are in positions/ conditions devalued and/or stigmatized by the logic of domination"; and *project identities*, which are formed "when social actors, on the basis of whatever cultural materials are available to them, build a new identity that redefines their position in society and, by so doing, seek the transformation of overall social structure" (Castells 1997, p. 8).

This formulation is especially useful for thinking about the development of sexual rights movements. Precisely because sexuality (in and of itself as well as in relation to gender, race, ethnicity, class, and national citizenship) has become increasingly contested in public culture and debate, it has also become a focus for mobilization by a growing range of social movements that begin at the local level but become increasingly transnational as they get caught up in the global flows described by Appadurai. These movements have evolved in large measure along the lines suggested by Castells, as legitimizing identities become resistance identities aimed at fighting back against the oppression of dominant social norms, which in turn lead to the development of project identities devoted to large-scale social change and an end to discrimination.

While sexuality has been a key target of social control and a focus for struggles over power in all societies and all periods of history—as Gayle Rubin's epigraph indicates—the extent to which it has become the central point of departure for new social movements, based in large part on a sense of shared identity and focused both on resisting oppression and on building new projects for social change, is perhaps unique to the contemporary world. Although gay and lesbian rights movements entered the mainstream in the United States and Europe as early as the 1980s, they have been profoundly affected by the processes of accelerated globalization described here, becoming increasingly transnational and even global since the late 1990s. In the process, they have given rise to a growing range of more focused movements grounded in community-based resistance identities and advocating for the rights of transgender persons (Currah et al. 2006), sex workers (Kempadoo and Doezema 1998), HIV-positive persons (Terto 1999), and, more recently, intersex persons (Cabral and Benzur 2006). In many cases, these emerging movements are closely linked to a range of parallel and intersecting anticolonial movements and racial/ethnic/indigenous rights movements (Alexander and Mohanty 1997). As Gayle Rubin noted years ago about the industrialized West, "sexualities keep marching out of the pages of the *Diagnostic and Statistical Manual* and onto the pages of social history" (Rubin 1984, p. 287).

This growing array of social movements focused on sexual rights has given new meaning to the notion of "sexual diversity." The narrow focus of much identity-based organizing has traditionally posed challenges for activists seeking to build broader alliances and coalitions, but, as many of these new transnational movements have begun to coalesce around the concept of "sexual rights," it has become easier to organize and mobilize across the boundaries of different sexualized identities (Petchesky 2000). By articulating a common set of concerns, the notion of sexual rights has provided a strategic platform not only for social activism but also for advancing a range of sexuality-related issues in official venues ranging from local and national governments to international agencies and the United Nations (Girard 2007).

It is hardly surprising that relatively rapid success in promoting sexual rights around the world has also generated a good deal of resistance. It is important to remember that Castells's conceptualization of social movements as derived from legitimizing, resistance, and project identities is not by nature either progressive or conservative. Projects for social change can be undertaken just as fervently by the moral majority or the pro-family movement as by antipornography activists or the marriage-equality movement (Castells 1997). Conservative opponents of sexual rights have typically grounded their arguments in heteronormative religious traditions that condemn "immoral" sexual practices and "unnatural" gender relations, especially same-sex marriage. In response, sexual rights movements— especially but not exclusively in the Global South—often combine religious counternarratives (alternative interpretations of religious tenets and sacred texts) with secular notions of human rights. Whatever the local strategy, the global struggle over sexual rights has become perhaps the key battleground for the staging of sexual politics in the early twenty-first century. In the next section we provide a Foucauldian "history of the present" that examines some of the ways in which these political battles have evolved.

Sexual Rights and Contested Bodies

In the past few years, the global struggle for sexual rights has enjoyed some stunning successes, most notably an end to bans on the service of gays and lesbians in armed forces around the world and the rapid spread of laws allowing same-sex civil unions and marriage.[1] Despite their sudden appearance, these remarkable successes came out of a long history of sexual rights activism. In this section, we examine several social movements that have played a central role in the global movement for sexual rights. These examples are not exhaustive and we acknowledge that the existence of a range of social movements with global scope that have fought, and continue to fight, for sexual rights—feminist movements, LGBT rights movements, sex workers' rights movements, groups to combat HIV/AIDS, and so on—does not in itself constitute a global sexual rights movement. The proliferation of nongovernmental organizations (NGOs) certainly suggests the globalization of sexual rights agendas, but a true global social movement would involve formal and informal mobilizations at the grassroots level, working in conjunction with organizations and networks that operate on national, regional, and global scales.

Nonetheless, over the past ten to fifteen years, struggles for sexual rights around the world have increasingly taken on the characteristics of a broad-based global social movement. The recent proliferation of sexual rights discourse is an effect of financescapes, technoscapes, ethnoscapes, ideoscapes, and media spaces, which have helped to both spread and at the same time transform it. The mobilization of resources and networks for achieving sexual rights, including changes in everything from cultural attitudes to legal structures, became easier as activists and political leaders in the Global North and South joined forces.

Much of the early attention to global sexual rights was focused less on sexuality per se than on gender equality. Although there are important links between gender and sexuality, there are also key divergences. Sexuality refers to diverse forms of desire, behavior, and identity related to sexual experience in various social and cultural settings. In contrast, gender refers to the ways in which sexual characteristics—generally understood to be biological or physiological—are implicated in the socially constructed roles, practices, and attributes that different societies consider "normal" for men and women, including when these normalized sexual characteristics are transformed through social performance (e.g. butch, femmes, queens) or medical procedure (e.g. male-to-female and female-to-male surgical transitions). For this reason, social constructions of gender and, by extension, social understandings of gender equality depend heavily on the different ways in which any given society makes sense of concepts such as manhood, womanhood, family, community, and reproduction.

Sexual rights movements have deep historical roots in nineteenth- and twentieth-century struggles for gender equality. In the Global North and South, feminists and proponents of sexual liberation have long seen control

Figure 8.1 Sexual rights as human rights. Swiss Amnesty International poster on the back of an ILGA World Map. *Source:* ILGA, International Lesbian, Gay, Bisexual, Trans and Intersex Association / Queeramnesty Schweiz.

over sexuality and reproduction as central to their causes (Jayawardena 1986; Moore 1988; Mikell 1995; Brown et al. 2010). These activist groups have also connected with struggles against colonialism in the Global South and against class oppression and racial/ethnic discrimination in the Global North, showing how control over sexuality has been used to support slavery, colonial domination, and eugenics programs (Stepan 1991; Epprecht 2004; Campbell 2007; Rousseau 2009). Early efforts to expand sexual rights, including for homosexuals, encountered serious resistance all over the world, although conservative attempts at repression often backfired (Churchill 2008). Nonetheless, throughout most of the twentieth century, authoritarian regimes around the world responded to perceived threats to social order by driving gender and sexual liberation movements underground, as happened in the case of Brazil (Jaquette 1989), which we discuss later in this chapter.

During the latter part of the twentieth century, continued efforts to expand sexual rights became harder to repress. Feminist movements in the Global North during the 1960s and 1970s, for example, centered issues of sexual rights as they pushed back against the objectification of women as mothers and wives in nationalist discourses that promoted heterosexual family values and the commodification of women's bodies in commercial advertising (D'Emilio and Freedman 1997). By the 1970s, the influence of feminist groups within civil society had dramatically increased as the legitimizing identities (as theorized by Castells) coalesced into resistance identities that advocated for women's issues and then into project identities that demanded wholesale social transformation. Central to the feminist project was the assertion of women's right to control their own bodies, a right that the US Supreme Court tacitly acknowledged under the guise of respect for privacy in the 1973 *Roe v. Wade* decision (testimony perhaps to women's increased political leverage). These Global North feminist concerns played out in different ways in other parts of the world, especially during the 1980s and 1990s, as social movements reemerged in many countries of the Global South in response to democratization and constitution-building efforts after decades of authoritarian rule. As these new movements—which built on earlier feminist mobilizations in those countries—became more visible, feminist projects around the world began to take on the characteristics of a global movement (Keck and Sikkink 1998).

Increased NGO participation at international human rights and women's rights conferences provides an important indicator of globalized social mobilization. For example, only fifty-three NGOs sent representatives to the 1968 Teheran International Conference on Human Rights; by the 1993 Vienna Conference, the number of NGO representatives had risen to 841, with unofficial NGO representation as high as 1400 (Clark et al. 1998). Other international conferences saw similar increases. Attendance by NGOs at the 1975 Mexico City Conference for International Women's Year was six thousand; by the 1985 Nairobi NGO forum for the United Nations's Decade on Women it had more than doubled to 13,500; and, by the 1995 Beijing NGO forum, attendance had reached three hundred thousand (Clark et al. 1998). The NGOs working in the Global South gained strength during these years, especially in Latin America, Africa, and Asia, as "listeners and observers . . . networking and lobbying for specific issues" forged alliances between activists and organizations in the Global North and Global South (Garcia and Parker 2006, p. 27).

Rising attendance at international conferences and the forging of global alliances did not immediately translate into greater attention to sexual rights. For example, issues of sexual inequality at the 1993 Vienna World Conference on Human Rights and in the United Nations's 1993 Declaration on the Elimination of Violence Against Women focused on gender-based violence rather than sexual rights (Petchesky 2000). Nonetheless, these were crucial meetings that began to articulate the protection of women against violence through the language of human rights, even if they never directly addressed positive sexual rights or mentioned sexual diversity. Issues of sexuality did take center stage at the 1994 Cairo International Conference on Population and Development, which addressed the "right" to sexual satisfaction and healthy interpersonal relations and proposed a Programme of Action that considered family structures beyond the nuclear family and called for adolescent sex education (although it failed to mention nonheterosexual sexualities) (Petchesky 2000, 2003). Although the Cairo conference's conceptualization of sexuality was heteronomative, it did seek to shift policy concerns from population control to reproductive and sexual health. The 1995 Fourth World Women's Conference in Beijing was also crucial for development and expansion of the concept of sexual rights. Activists in Beijing pushed hard to include issues of sexual diversity and sexual orientation in the Platform for Action, but with limited success as conservative delegates insisted on replacing the term "sexual rights" with "human rights of women" (Petchesky 2000). And follow-up meetings, termed Cairo+ or Beijing+, failed to develop more inclusive policy recommendations around issues of sexuality as Muslim and Christian religious conservatives joined forces to help stall production of the Beijing+5 document—after progressive delegates attempted to include the terms "gender-sensitive" and "diversity in women"—on the grounds that the terms were dangerously vague and might fuel women's liberation movements in societies grounded in patriarchal values as an expression of divine will (Corrêa et al. 2008).

Despite opposition from conservative religious groups, the global emphasis on gender and gender equity has expanded in recent years to include issues of sexuality and sexual equality that go beyond long-standing concerns about population control, reproductive rights, and public health. This is an important shift because, as legal scholar Alice Miller explains:

> the conflation of sexual rights with reproductive rights has . . . caused sexual rights to be viewed as a subset of reproductive rights, albeit with a less developed articulation. This subset status has "disappeared" an array of people of varying ages and non-conforming sexual identities, as well as non-reproductive sexual practices, and has often entirely neglected to consider men as rights holders, thus leaving many already marginalized people outside the framework of human rights protection . . . Another result of removing non-heterosexual, non-procreative sexual activities from human rights protection has been the surrender of these activities to moral, religious, or criminal regulation. (Miller 2000, p. 70)

More than anything, it was gay and lesbian movements in the Global North during the 1970s and 1980s that set the stage for widespread acceptance of an expanded view of sexual rights.[2] That process began in the 1970s in the United States as new forms of collective mobilization around civil rights and women's rights encouraged gay and lesbian activists to create organizations such as the Gay Liberation Front and the Gay Activists Alliance, establish gay bars, and march in gay pride parades. Over the course of the 1980s and 1990s, similar broad-based coalition movements began to spring up in countries around the world (MacRae 1990; Cameron and Gevisser 1995; Joseph 1996). By the beginning of the new millennium—which saw the addition of "bi" and "trans" as distinct identities in need of mobilization—it was possible to speak not just of national LGBT movements but of a truly transnational movement for LGBT rights (Adam et al. 1999; Kollman and Waites 2009).

As this transnational LGBT movement became increasingly influential in the early 2000s, international identity-based movements such as feminism, LGBT rights, and HIV/AIDS activism, which for much of the previous thirty years had evolved in quite separate ways, set aside their differences to form visible coalitions around issues of sexual rights (Edelman 2001; Parker 2012). The vibrant transnational sexual rights movement that emerged from these coalitions has continued to push for a presence at international conferences and a chance to include sexual orientation and gender identity in the international policy agenda. Thus, even though documents such as the UN Millennium Development Goals still focus on gender equality, activists at the local level in the Global North and South have lobbied aggressively for a broad spectrum of sexual rights. Their efforts have resulted in a growing range of transnational initiatives that center on issues of sexual orientation and gender identity (SOGI issues), including from global NGOs such as the International Council on Human Rights Policy and Human Rights Watch, which have taken up issues of sexual rights as part of their formal programs (HRW 2009; ICHRP 2009). And, in the past few years, it is not only activists and NGOs that have taken on such issues but also governments from a range of countries—including ones such as the United States with mixed records on sexual rights—as well as official intergovernmental agencies such as the UN Office of the High Commissioner on Human Rights, the United Nations Development Program, UNAIDS, and the World Health Organization (Myers and Cooper 2011; OHCHR 2011).

In opposition to the increased visibility of sexual rights advocates at international conferences, religious conservatives from Muslim countries, the United States, and the Vatican have formed coalitions of their own to deal with sexuality-related issues. In a 2001 debate on "Women and HIV" before a UN General Assembly Special Session, delegates from the US Commission on the Status of Women insisted that abstinence before marriage was the most effective and moral way to prevent HIV transmission. Placing ideology before epidemiology, coalitions of self-proclaimed traditionalists blocked serious discussion of issues related to sex workers, drug users, and men who have sex with men even though these groups are especially vulnerable to HIV/AIDS (Corrêa et al. 2008). As we will see in the following section, the efforts of conservative religious groups to exclude gender equality and sexual rights from the human rights agenda at the local, national, and international levels have pushed grassroots activists to develop religious counternarratives that seek to deny traditionalists the moral high ground in the ongoing struggle for sexual rights. Despite continued opposition and struggle, however, sexual rights have gone from being a relatively neglected piece of the international human rights agenda to a central arena of contemporary debate. How these developments have influenced local struggles for sexual freedom in communities and countries around the world remains an open question—a question we turn to in the next section.

Sexual Rights at the Grassroots

Over the past decade, scholars have explored the growing demands for sexual rights on the part of multiple social movements—feminism, reproductive rights, LGBT rights, AIDS activism, sex workers' rights, etc.—and how these movements have converged into something like a global sexual rights movement (Kempadoo and Doezema 1998; Adam et al. 1999; Petchesky 2003; Parker et al. 2007; Corrêa et al. 2008). Less studied are the ways in which these transnational developments impact local organizing through the construction of alliances and coalitions with the grassroots. In this section, we will look at how local sexual rights activism has flourished through contact with broader social and political movements in four Global South countries: Brazil, South Africa, India, and Mexico.

These developments are evident in the convergence (and divergence) of feminist and LGBT rights and AIDS activism at the global, transnational, and local levels since the 1980s. In many parts of the world, LGBT rights groups emerged only in the mid-1980s as local activists, alarmed at the epidemic's disproportionate impact on the LGBT community, mobilized in support of HIV/AIDS public health campaigns. As a result of this support, public health initiatives began to insert LGB and sometimes T issues into targeted interventions. And, beginning in the early 1990s, opportunities to attract international agency funding for HIV/AIDS treatment and prevention provided additional incentives for diverse international, national, and local groups to work together under the broader sexual rights umbrella.

This coalition-building process has played out in different ways in different parts of the world as local groups work to reconcile—usually with mixed success—international concepts of sexual rights and globalized notions of sexual identity with local cultural logics. In his work on *gay* and *lesbi* subjects in Indonesia, anthropologist Tom Boellstorff notes that "even the most apparently 'remote' communities are caught up in globalizing processes in ways that impact subjectivities as well as social circumstances" (Boellstorff 2003, p. 221). Access to global mass media, in particular, has encouraged many homosexual Indonesians to see themselves not in terms of indigenous identities such as *waria* (women in men's bodies) or *tomboi* (men in women's bodies) but as gay or lesbian Indonesians "linked to a transnational imagined community" (p. 232). Although inspired by global media, *gay* and *lesbi* subjects do not merely imitate imported gay and lesbian identities but remain distinctly Indonesian, including because "to be 'completely Indonesian' requires thinking of one's position in a transnational world" (p. 238). Boellstorff compares this process of subject formation to the mandatory dubbing of imported film and television shows required by the Indonesian government to mitigate the corrupting effects of Western culture:

> A set of fragmented cultural elements are transformed in unexpected ways in the Indonesian context, transforming that context itself in the process. In other words, *lesbi* and *gay* Indonesians "dub" ostensibly "Western" sexual subjectivities. Like a dub, the fusion remains a juxtaposition: the seams show . . . for *lesbi* and *gay* Indonesians . . . this tension is irresolvable; there is no "real" version underneath, where everything fits. (Boellstorff 2003, p. 238)

As we will see, a similar "dubbing" process occurs in the relationship between global and local sexual rights movements. And the irresolvable tensions that result, especially apparent at the local level, reveal hidden biases in global sexual rights discourse, including the predominance of secular over religious notions of human rights and the disjuncture between global mainstream sexual identities (as represented by the acronym LGBT) and indigenous understandings of nonnormative sexualities.

In 1950s Brazil, women began to mobilize in large numbers as modernization and urbanization pressures pushed more and more of them into the formal workforce (Vianna and Carrara 2007). During the three decades that followed, repressive military regimes discouraged mainstream labor and political organizing but showed less concern for community organizations such as the Catholic Comunidades Eclesiais de Base (Ecclesiastic Base Communities), especially when those groups were led by poor women and focused primarily on "women's issues" (Burdick 1993). Women's prominence as community organizers along with the regime's reluctance to repress religious activism in the country with the world's largest Catholic population put women at the center of a very effective antiauthoritarian coalition that brought together activists from sanitary reform campaigns, labor unions, gay rights groups, women's rights groups, the liberation theology movement, and a range of other social movements. The coalition's central role in ending military rule in 1985 and promulgating a new constitution in 1988 ensured the inclusion of a clause that guaranteed gender equality (Pintaguy 2002).

Encouraged by the coalition's interclass, interreligious, and interracial character, and given added impetus by the feminization of the HIV/AIDS epidemic, Brazilian women's mobilization picked up again in the early 1990s (Parker and Galvão 1996). One of the many groups to emerge from this mobilization was Criola, a Rio-based NGO founded in 1992 by poor urban black women, many of them spiritual leaders in Candomblé, a widely practiced if often persecuted Afro-Brazilian religion. Despite its modest beginnings, Criola has become a leader in the struggle "to empower black women, adolescents, and young girls to combat racism, sexism, and lesbophobia, and to improve living standards for the black population" (Criola 2012). As its mission statement suggests, the group has embraced a broad

Figure 8.2 Candomblé practitioners protest against religious intolerance in front of the Brazilian Congress in Brasilia in 2009. *Source*: © HO / Reuters / Corbis.

spectrum of human rights issues of special concern to its constituents: political representation, sexual and reproductive health, LGBT rights, and tolerance for Afro-Brazilian religious practices including special programs to prevent HIV transmission through traditional scarification rituals and to provide support for LGBTQ religious practitioners (Garcia and Parker 2011). The intersectional logic behind the group's mission is reflected in its promotion of distinct "priority groups . . . of women activist leaders of African-origin religions; garbage pickers and domestics; adolescents and youth" and its efforts to promote joint action among these different groups of black women "engaged in the political struggle to garner respect, recognition, and the transformation of their quality of life" (Criola 2012).

In a country often praised as a model of "racial democracy," Afro-Brazilian women's groups such as Criola have developed comprehensive strategies of protest and advocacy that help expose the structural vulnerabilities produced by long-standing social inequalities of race, class, gender, *and* sexuality. As a Criola-sponsored report on interfamilial violence against poor black women explains:

> Brazilian society, over the course of its history, has divided along lines of class, gender, and race . . . This "social geography" organizes and shapes modes of thought and sociability anchored in the notion of the supremacy of the wealthy, of whites, of men, and of heterosexuals . . . This conjuncture produces a complex web of unequal power relations . . . that generate and reproduce social locations of domination and exploitation, while providing justifications for poverty, racism, phallocentrism, and homophobia . . . and that acquire meaning in the historical experiences of living subjects, where determinations of ethnicity/race, class, gender and sexual orientation do not operate in isolation, but instead feed off each other . . .
>
> A society founded on these kinds of determinations becomes a breeding ground where everyday inequalities flourish, laden with prejudice, discrimination and violence, especially against those who deviate from standard patterns of behavior exemplified by the domination of heterosexual white men over black women. And as these determinations intersect, strengthening and increasing their power to oppress . . . the people most victimized by structural violence are black women who belong to the most impoverished classes, and in particular black women who are poor and lesbians. (Criola 2012, p. 3)

This academic-sounding intersectional critique of a Brazilian "social geography" still allegedly mired in its colonial past—slavery in Brazil began in the sixteenth century and lasted until 1888—reveals the extent to which local activists have increasingly and almost seamlessly integrated their sexual rights agendas into a broader discourse of human rights. Moreover, the group's increased political profile marks an important shift from a community constituted around what Castells calls a *legitimizing identity* linked to the historical persecution of Afro-Brazilian cultural and religious practices to a *resistance identity* grounded in community recognition of defined vulnerabilities and finally to a *project identity* that has empowered the community (through Criola) to organize and fight the institutions and structures that perpetuate these vulnerabilities.

At the same time, Criola remains resolutely focused on local concerns, even as it insists on their centrality to "universal" human rights. Chief among these concerns is religious freedom, a cornerstone of liberal human rights intended to protect minority religions from persecution by state-sponsored, "established" churches (although it is doubtful that Enlightenment proponents such as Voltaire and John Locke had "pagan" religions such as Candomblé in mind). Despite the disestablishment of the Brazilian Catholic Church by the liberal 1891 constitution, political and religious authorities continued to persecute Candomblé and other Afro-Brazilian animist religions, which they considered morally suspect for a number of reasons, including popularity among the lower classes (especially blacks) and promotion of nonnormative sexual behaviors. The phenomenal rise, especially among the poor, over the past two decades of notoriously homophobic Pentecostal churches in Brazil, which sell themselves as moral alternatives to demonic cults, has reinvigorated these charges and may well have prompted Criola's emphatic defense of both religious freedom and sexual tolerance.

But, while international human rights advocates—like their Enlightenment predecessors—tend to see religious freedom and sexual tolerance as distinct (if related) issues, most Candomblé practitioners would have difficulty separating one from the other. One reason that Candomblé is more accepting of nonnormative sexualities than most religions is that its central religious practice often involves the medium's possession by an entity (spirit) of the opposite sex, regardless of his or her initial sexual orientation. As anthropologist Patricia Birman explains:

> The religious activity of possession that "produces" mediators for the supernatural sphere affects a person's gendered nature, "feminizing him" in the case of men and "empowering her" in case of women, which provokes inside

> these people an ongoing contentious dialogue between the social norm and
> the possibilities for transgression. (Birman 2005)

The real-life effects of spiritual transgendering account for the perception
that Candomblé embraces gay and lesbian sexualities (as understood in
global mainstream terms), but ethnographic research reveals a much more
complex relationship. Thus, while Criola articulates its demands for sexual
tolerance in readily translatable terms—as "poor, black lesbians," for
example—in order to underscore its project identity status for national and
transnational activist allies, its members are very likely engaged in a
"dubbing" process that helps them negotiate "irresolvable tensions" in their
own lives as well as between local and global understandings of sexual
rights.

A similar trajectory has played out under similar circumstances in South
Africa with a different kind of social movement: the Inner Circle, a queer
Muslim NGO dedicated to the creation of "a global society free from discrimination and violence based on sexual orientation and gender . . . that
includes acceptance and understanding of the different faiths, beliefs,
sexual diversity, and gender" (Inner Circle 2012). As with Criola in Brazil,
Inner Circle has its roots in the solidarity-based social movements that
emerged in response to a repressive authoritarian government, committed
in this case to maintaining the segregationist policies of apartheid—a
period that lasted until the defeat of the National Party by the African
National Congress in the 1993 election. The South African gay rights
groups that emerged in the late 1970s tended to split along color lines with
white-male-dominated organizations such as the Gay Association of South
Africa going so far as to endorse National Party presidential candidates in
an effort to secure gay rights without challenging apartheid. By the late
1980s, however, gay rights activists had formed an umbrella organization,
the Organization of Lesbians and Gays against Oppression, with a broad
human rights agenda that included opposition to apartheid and other
less blatant forms of institutional racism and discrimination (Cameron
1993). Sexual rights crossed over into mainstream human rights discourse
during this time period as major figures in the antiapartheid struggle, such
as Reverend Desmond Tutu, began to point out the similarities between
forms of discrimination based on race and sexual orientation (Garcia
and Parker 2006). Thanks in part to this more comprehensive understanding of human rights, the postapartheid 1996 South African constitution
included specific provisions outlawing discrimination on the grounds of

sex, gender, and sexual orientation despite the protests of groups such as the Congress of Traditional Leaders of South Africa. Subsequent antidiscrimination laws further extended these protections and a landmark 2005 Constitutional Court ruling asserted the right of same-sex couples to marry in civil unions.

Despite legal gains, widespread discrimination against LGBTQ individuals has persisted, especially among more socially conservative groups such as South Africa's sizable Muslim community (approximately 750,000 people or 1.5 percent of the national population). While the constitution, courts, and legislators have recognized the sexual rights of all South African citizens, orthodox Muslim community leaders continue to interpret constitutionally guaranteed religious freedom as their right to regulate internal and community affairs according to Islamic custom. This has meant that, when queer Muslims "come out" voluntarily or are "outed" against their will, they are often ostracized by their families and communities (Kugle 2005, p. 14).

Although very much a product of the opening in civil society and the validation of human rights discourse brought about by the end of apartheid, Inner Circle first emerged in response to a specific local problem—homophobia in South African Muslim communities—rather than as part of a larger national or transnational social movement. Once established, however, the organization moved quickly through Castells's three stages of identity. Promotional material for Inner Circle's most recent Annual Retreat explains the process:

> The Inner Circle started out as early as 1996 when the founder Imam Muhsin Hedricks declared in a local newspaper that he was "Proud to be gay and Muslim." He saw the need to address homo-prejudice in the Muslim community in Cape Town and to give psycho-spiritual support to Muslims who were marginalized based on their sexual orientation and gender.
>
> His work was formalized under the name Al-Fitrah Foundation in 1998.... For the next few years the organization focused on support groups and helping queer Muslims to reconcile Islam with their sexuality by using alternative interpretations of the scripture and teaching a compassionate, all-inclusive Islam.
>
> In 2004, when funding was available through the Atlantic Philanthropies, the organization formed The Inner Circle and established its base in Cape Town. In 2009, the organization developed an international focus and started to work with Muslim organizations and other queer Muslim organizations locally and internationally who shared a similar vision. The form that the

international work took then was through speaking engagements and training on Islam and sexual diversity through educational institutions, and
organizations. Due to years of consistent involvement in the issues of homosexuality and Islam, [Inner Circle] is now recognized by many international
organizations . . . as *the* consultative organization that is able to engage with
the issues of sexual diversity, gender, and Islam through a theological and
sociological framework and the only organization that has managed to successfully start mainstreaming the issue of sexuality and gender in the Muslim
community. (Inner Circle 2012)

As this institutional history indicates, the group that would become Inner
Circle originally developed around a legitimizing identity imposed on
queer Muslims by a disdainful orthodox Muslim community. The transition to a resistance identity came with Imam Hendrick's public declaration,
followed two years later by the creation of a Social Support Group for local
gay Muslim men, and two years after that by the slightly more formal
Al-Fitrah Foundation, which also included local Muslim lesbians. The official 2004 founding of The Inner Circle—made possible by funding from
US-based Atlantic Philanthropies—marks a clear transition from resistance
identity to project identity, and from a local organization seeking local
solutions to local problems to a transnational social movement that uses
available cultural materials to "build a new identity that redefines [the
group's] position in society and, by so doing, seek the transformation of
overall social structure" (Castells 1997, p. 8).

As we saw earlier, although sexual rights play a central role in Criola's
women-centered agenda, it is only one concern (or "intersection") among
many. This is not the case with Inner Circle, which continues to focus
primarily on the needs of LGBTQ Muslims around the world. At the same
time, it too has expanded its scope to include an annual Conference on the
Empowerment of Women, which addresses the special needs of queer
Muslim women *and* also seeks "to form a collective and informed response
to actions such as forced arranged marriages, emotional blackmail, marital
rape and honour killings" (Inner Circle 2010). Moreover, in this rapid
transition from resistance to project identity, Inner Circle has not just
adapted institutional and discursive strategies from the global sexual rights
movement; it has become "*the* consultative organization that is able to
engage with the issues of sexual diversity, gender, and Islam through a
theological and sociological framework and the only organization that has
managed to successfully start mainstreaming the issue of sexuality and
gender in the Muslim community" (Inner Circle 2012).

Along the way, the liberal Western notions of individual autonomy that inspired the transnational human rights movements have been appropriated, reworked, and redeployed by a faith-based Muslim organization from the Global South in order to foster tolerance in a transnational religious community notable for its distrust of Western imperialist ideologies (including secular notions of personal freedoms and human rights). The cultural "dubbing" in this case involves not so much the strategic adoption of global mainstream categories that do not quite mesh with local understandings but an attempt to map those categories onto an Islamic scriptural tradition that predates them by centuries.

A similar process of appropriation and resignification in the shift from resistance identities to project identities is apparent in sex workers' rights movements from the Global South, including the Sonagachi Project in Kolkata, India, which has achieved a degree of notoriety in the controversies surrounding the Oscar-winning documentary *Born into Brothels*, the 2004 Academy Award winner for best documentary. Sex workers have been among the world's most marginalized populations. Because governments (and societies in general) often see sex workers as dangerous vectors for sexually transmitted diseases such as syphilis and HIV/AIDS, they are frequently targeted in public health and morality campaigns, with little attention paid to their human rights. To make matters worse, mainstream gender and sexual rights movements tend to exclude sex workers, whose deviance from societal norms most view as a product of social inequalities rather than "natural" biological variation. In response, some scholars have pointed out that, precisely because sex workers are "perversely integrated" into selling sexual services as the most viable options for coping with poverty and other forms of social inequality, they merit inclusion in mainstream gender and sexual rights movements (Castells 1998, p. 71). This is highly controversial because it implies that a form of work traditionally interpreted as demeaning and depraved should be reframed as an occupation with some degree of human dignity and choice. Controversial or not, this position has gained traction in recent years as HIV/AIDS-prevention campaigns work to halt the spread of the disease by educating sex workers about modes of transmission and empowering them to take charge of their working conditions by insisting on safe sex practices, especially condom use.

While this instrumental approach does little to acknowledge the sexual rights of sex workers, it has encouraged them to exercise agency with regard to their clients and sometimes with government officials as well. This has helped offset the portrayal of sex workers, by everyone from conservative religious reformers to mainstream feminists, as "victims," an apparently sympathetic label that has nonetheless been one of the principal obstacles to recognition of sex workers' rights. Inspired in part by the 1960s sexual revolution, sex workers' rights groups such as San Francisco's Call Off Your Old Tired Ethics (COYOTE) emerged in the 1970s in North America and Western Europe. By the 1980s, the Global North sex workers' rights movement had gone international with the creation of an International Committee for Prostitutes' Rights, sponsorship of two World Whores' Congresses in 1985 (Amsterdam) and 1986 (Brussels), and the formulation of a World Charter of Prostitutes' Rights. These internationalization efforts, however, included only a handful of representatives from Global South countries such as Singapore, Thailand, and Vietnam (Kempadoo et al. 2005). It was thus only in the early 1990s, as governments and international agencies expanded their HIV/AIDS-prevention efforts in the Global South, that the sex workers' rights movement attracted much attention there.

As we saw with Criola in Brazil and Inner Circle in South Africa, civil society openings and progressive legislation (especially on gender equality) have helped lay the groundwork for the recognition of sexual rights. This is especially true for India, which has a long-standing commitment to human rights that dates back to mid-twentieth-century decolonization struggles, including special legislation to address "issues facing religious and ethnic minorities, including slavery, livelihood, and discrimination; exploitation of children; and the rights of women" (Misra et al. 2000, p. 90). With regard to sex work, however, the "legislative framework consists mainly of The Immoral Traffic in Persons Prevention Act, 1986 (ITPA) as well as an entire range of laws that, in reality, tend to be utilized more often in tackling prostitution than the ITPA itself" (Kotiswaran 2001, p. 167). Even through sex work is legal in India, ongoing stigmatization, discrimination, inadequate enforcement, police brutality, judicial backlog, lack of political will, and a "strong nexus between politicians, police and the brothel-keepers" continue to impede meaningful progress on sex workers' rights (Kotiswaran 2001, p. 169; see also Misra et al. 2000). Despite these obstacles, a strong civil society, progressive legislation, and support from international agencies have allowed local NGOs, including sex workers' rights groups, to publicly address problems such as child prostitution, trafficking, exploitation, and exposure to sexually transmitted diseases, especially HIV/AIDS.

The Durbar Mahila Samanwaya Committee—the group that runs the well-known Sonagachi Project—began in 1995 as part of an HIV/AIDS-prevention program sponsored by Kolkata's All India Institute of Hygiene and Public Health. Although its initial goal was to recruit sex workers to promote client condom use in the country's largest red-light district, Durbar quickly expanded its purview to include a range of sex worker concerns such as education for their children and protection from police harassment. By 2012, the organization had grown from twelve founders to 64,000 members in forty-eight branches across the state of Bengal and was sponsoring seventeen schools, two hostels, a consumer cooperative, and a "cultural wing dedicated to dance, drama, mime and music and run by the children" (Mint 2012). Consciousness-raising has been key to Durbar's remarkable success, especially its insistence on framing sex work as legitimate employment. This has helped facilitate the group's move from a socially imposed legitimizing identity to a proactive resistance identity capable of challenging social norms and institutional authorities, as happened, for example, when Durbar members convinced the State Bank of India to permit them to list their official occupation as "sex worker" and when the group's consumer cooperative successfully lobbied Bengal government officials to amend the state's cooperative law to include sex worker cooperatives rather than forcing sex workers' organizations to register as housewife cooperatives (Mint 2012).

These direct challenges to the structural inequalities and oppressive institutions that have marginalized sex workers for years also mark an organizational shift toward a full-fledged project identity that works toward a fundamental transformation in societal attitudes toward sex work around the world (Ghose et al. 2008). Durbar's willingness to take on the international film industry over the negative portrayal of Sonagachi and sex worker parenting in *Born into Brothels* gives some evidence of its status as a voice for sex workers, especially in the Global South, as does the organization's recent sponsorship of a five-day alternative International AIDS Conference in Kolkata—attended by over a thousand sex workers from China, India, Indonesia, Kenya, Mexico, and Uganda—to protest against US immigration restrictions on sex workers, which had prevented many of them from attending the official conference in Washington. The Kolkata conference also gave Global South sex workers a forum to participate in the Washington conference via video link, to promote the legalization/decriminalization of sex work around the world and to discuss HIV/AIDS-related issues such as access to drugs, safe sex strategies, and the shortcomings of current HIV/AIDS policies (Bhalla 2012). As is the case with The Inner Circle in South Africa, Durbar's growing prominence in the transnational struggle for sexual rights, along with its readiness to shame Global North institutions

246   *Richard Parker, Jonathan Garcia, and Robert M. Buffington*

and governments that seek to impede that struggle, suggests that the global flows theorized by Appadurai are far from unidirectional—that Global South sexual rights movements are not just engaging the foundational tropes of Western human rights that equate dignity with personal autonomy and loss of dignity with victimhood but also imbuing them with new and at times radically different meanings.

On the surface, Durbar's evolution from AIDS activism to international sex workers' rights advocacy appears a clear-cut case of a local group drawing direct inspiration and support from Western-based organizations such as the International Committee for Prostitutes' Rights. Certainly, the organization's avowed preference for "sex worker" over "prostitute" (a shift reflected in its consciousness-raising work), its inclusion of male and trangender sex workers, and its use of socialist-inspired concepts such as "collectivization" suggest a unapologetic adoption of imported concepts and none of the "irresolvable tensions" that come with cultural dubbing. Missing

Figure 8.3 Partially nude devadasi women protest in Mumbai, India, to demand INR 2000 (about US $43) per month as a retirement pension. The sign reads: "Maharashtra Destitute and Devadasi Women's Organization. Various Demands, Opposing Maharashtra Government. Nude Rally." *Source*: Rajanish Kakade / AP / Press Association Images.

from the organization's extensive promotional materials, however, is any mention of South Asia's long history of castes associated with sex work, including the devadasi (India and Pakistan), badi (Nepal), and hijra (India and Pakistan)—an understandable omission given the negative association of these groups with child prostitution, caste discrimination, sexual deviance, and religious backwardness.

Durbar's efforts to represent its members as modern, professional "sex workers" who provide an indispensible public service in a responsible way thus serve to distinguish those members, especially for a South Asian audience, from their tradition-bound, "untouchable" counterparts. At the same time, traditional caste affiliations, bolstered by religious practices that "dedicate" young girls to various gods and goddesses, have made it easier for some devadasi and badi women (but not transgender hijra) to maintain family support systems and recognition as family breadwinners (Orchard 2007). This tradition of family support and recognition has carried over into other sex worker communities such as those in Sonagachi, helping to facilitate their rapid and extensive mobilization. In this instance, then, cultural dubbing obscures a complex history of South Asian sex worker communities that function in this case as a symbol of a backward, oppressive past against which contemporary sex worker "collectives" construct themselves as modern human rights organizations and their members as modern rights-bearing citizens entitled to pensions, health care, and education for their children.

Our final case study, dedicated to the prominent Mexican lesbian rights group El Closét de Sor Juana (Sister Juana's Closet), touches on one of the sexual rights movement's greatest success stories, the passage of same-sex civil union and marriage laws all over the world since 2001, including in unexpected places such as Brazil, Mexico City, and South Africa. As with the previous case studies in this section, an opening in civil society—in this instance the political organizing that preceded the 2000 election of an opposition party president after more than eighty years of one-party rule—provided the impetus for previously marginalized activist groups to push more openly for social change. Although the victorious PAN (National Action Party) would prove even more socially conservative than its predecessor (the PRI or Institutional Revolutionary Party), many members of the other major opposition party, the leftist PRD (Democratic Revolutionary Party), openly supported sexual rights. A 2001 PRD-sponsored amendment to Article 1 of the Mexican Constitution prohibited discrimination on the basis of sexual orientation. And a follow-up 2003 Federal Law to

Prohibit and Eliminate Discrimination explicitly outlawed "promoting or indulging in physical or psychological abuse based on physical appearance or dress, talk, mannerisms or for openly acknowledging one's sexual preferences." After 1997, when the PRD won both the Mexico City mayor's office and a majority in the Legislative Assembly, sexual rights activists including openly lesbian congresswomen Patricia Jiménez (cofounder of El Closét) and Enoé Uranga began a successful push for municipal legislation allowing same-sex civil unions in 2006, followed by same-sex marriage in 2009. The 2009 marriage law also permitted same-sex couples to adopt children, inherit from a same-sex partner, take out joint loans, and share insurance policies.[3]

On both occasions, PAN politicians, Catholic Church authorities, and pro-life groups such as Pro-Vida and the Unión Nacional de Padres de Familia (National Parents' Union) protested against what they saw as a deliberate attack on biblical and constitutional requirements that marriage involve a man and woman. Despite his PAN affiliation, President Felipe Calderón took a fairly nonconfrontational approach to the 2009 same-sex marriage law, noting that the Mexican Constitution defined marriage as between a man and woman and promising to respect the ruling of the Supreme Court (which later declared the legislation constitutional). A PAN spokesperson also accused the PRD of perpetrating "an electoral ploy . . . that mocks and abuses the gay community" (González 2009). In contrast to these relatively mild rebukes from politicians, Catholic Church authorities blasted the legislation and the Supreme Court decision to support its constitutionality as an affront to God and a threat to the nation's moral health. Mexico City Archbishop Cardinal Norberto Rivera declared the legislation and court ruling "intrinsically immoral since they contradict the divine plan, [and] undermine the nature of marriage, which Christ elevated to the dignity of a sacrament" (Gaudium 2010). Cardinal Rivera's counterpart in the city of León, Archbishop José Guadalupe Martín Rábago, went still further, adding same-sex marriage laws to a more general list of causes of natural disasters:

> Faced with violence, hate, revenge, and death, *faced with legal initiatives that affect the foundations of society like the family*, faced with insecurity and the suffering of so many people, it is fitting to meditate on the signs of the times and ask ourselves if through earthquakes, torrential rains, floods: Is God speaking to us? What is God trying to tell us with all this? (Proceso 2010, emphasis added)

In response to these accusations of sinful behavior, opponents accused Cardinal Rivera and Archbishop Martín Rábago of complicity in efforts by the Catholic Church and Pope Benedict XVI—who visited Mexico in 2012—to cover up the crimes of "pederast priests," including extensive abuses committed by priests affiliated with the hyperconservative Legion of Christ (Vega 2012).

Founded in the early 1990s by a group of lesbian feminists, El Closét played a central, sometimes controversial, role in these dramatic events. Since its official launch in 1994, the Mexico City group has dedicated itself to "the defense and promotion of the human rights of women, especially those that suffer discrimination because of their sexual orientation" (El Closét de Sor Juana 2011)—a particularly serious concern in a country with the second highest rate of homophobia-related murders in Latin America after Brazil (Vanguardia 2012). As happened with Criola, Inner Circle, and Durbar, El Closét moved quickly through the three stages theorized by Castells: legitimizing identity, resistance identity, and project identity. By 1995, only three years after its founding and one year after its official launch, the group had become a force in national, hemispheric, and international sexual rights movements. In that year alone, El Closét affiliated with a prominent international sexual rights organization—ILGA (International Lesbian, Gay, Bisexual, Trans and Intersex Association)—and actively participated in the Fourth Meeting of Lesbian Feminists from Latin American and the Caribbean in Buenos Aires, the International Conference of Gays and Lesbians in Rio de Janeiro, and the Fourth World Conference on Women in Beijing.

Although still focused on lesbian issues, El Closét includes among its goals a broad range of sexual rights issues, feminist concerns, and human rights issues. The manifesto for the 2003 First Mexican Lesbian March, for example, includes proposals for lesbian rights, LGBTI rights (including same-sex civil unions), women's rights, antidiscrimination legislation, sexual-diversity promotion, antipornography initiatives, and sex education, along with calls for action on the serial murders of young women in Ciudad Juárez, an end to the Mexican government's violent "war" against narcotrafficking, freedom for political prisoners, and a renegotiation of NAFTA (the North American Free Trade Agreement) (Marcha Lésbica 2003). The group's desire to simultaneously promote "strategies of lesbian visibility" and offer a critique "of the dictatorship imposed by heterosexism, religious fundamentalisms, neoliberalism, globalization, capitalism, and consumerism"—a clear indication of its project identity status—has opened

Figure 8.4   Image from the 2011 Mexican Lesbian March on the central plaza (Zócalo) in Mexico City. The sign reads: "Lesbianism is Sexual and Political Rebellion." *Source*: Reuters / Jorge Dan Lopez RTR2K4Z0.

it to criticism, especially from more narrowly focused lesbian rights activists, who accuse the group of advancing a broad LGBT rights agenda allegedly controlled by lesbophobic gay men and heterosexual feminists (Castro 2004).

El Closét's public espousal of a broad transnational social justice agenda might suggest that cultural dubbing has produced few of the irresolvable tensions evident in the previous case studies. Charges of *malinchismo* (selling out) on the part of some lesbian feminists suggest otherwise.[4] Whatever the politics involved, El Closét can hardly be accused of ignoring its Mexican roots. The group's name pays homage to a seventeenth-century Mexican nun, Sor Juana Inés de la Cruz, an international literary star in her lifetime, still renowned for protofeminist poems on the "foolishness" of men and considered by later biographers a martyr to misogynistic Church officials, who convinced her to give up her literary career at the height of her fame. A 1990 feature film by Argentine director María Luisa Bemberg, *I, Worst of All*, even hinted at a closeted lesbian relationship between Sor Juana and her patroness, the wife of the Spanish imperial viceroy, to whom Sor Juana wrote several romantic poems with erotic overtones. The name, El Closét de Sor Juana, and the appropriation of Sor Juana as a closeted lesbian thus put the Catholic Church and Catholic patriarchal culture at the center of long-standing efforts to repress women's independence, creativity, and sexuality.

Moreover, the group's critique of the institutional Catholic Church links it to a long and bloody postindependence (1821) history of Church–state struggles in Mexico that came to an official end only with the restoration of formal diplomatic relations between the Mexican government and the Vatican in 1992, the same year El Closét was founded. This history of strained Church–state relations—which included a ruthless purge of Catholics and a hard-fought revolt by "Cristeros" (soldiers of Christ) against the national government in the two decades following the Mexican Revolution (1910–20)—has long posed a problem in the world's second largest Catholic country. One consequence has been an ongoing struggle over the meaning of major religious symbols, especially the Virgin of Guadalupe, the much beloved "dark-skinned" Virgin who according to the official legend appeared to an Indian man, Juan Diego, in the years immediately following the conquest and who is generally considered the symbolic mother of all Mexicans. Despite serious issues with the official Church, major independence- and revolutionary-era leaders from Fathers Miguel Hidalgo and José María Morelos (both defrocked by the Church prior to their executions) to Emiliano Zapata (assassinated by a government agent) fought under her banner. According to Nobel Prize-winning poet and essayist Octavio Paz—also the author of an anticlerical biography of Sor Juana—Mexicans believe in only two things: the national lottery and the Virgin of Guadalupe. But popular veneration of the Virgin often refuses to align with official dogma, despite the Church's best efforts, including its 1999 canonization of Juan Diego and elevation of Our Lady of Guadalupe to "Patroness of the Americas." This long tradition of imbuing religious symbols with local (often subversive) meanings is evident in El Closét's suggestive alternative lyrics for a popular hymn to the Virgin of Guadalupe, sung during the 2003 Mexican Lesbian March:

> From heaven on a beautiful morning, from heaven on a beautiful morning, Lupe the lesbian, Lupe the lesbian, Lupe the lesbian, came down to Tepeyac. Juana of the Rainbow said to the virgin, Juana of the Rainbow said to the Virgin,
> Let us lie down together, let us lie down together, here in Tepeyac,

We'll take it all off, we'll take it all off, we'll take it all off,
Once we get there.

(Marcha Lésbica 2003)

In transforming Juan Diego into Juana of the Rainbow and having her entice the Virgin of Guadalupe into a lesbian embrace, El Closét contributes to a centuries-old Mexican tradition of cultural dubbing that exposes rather than disguises irresolvable tensions in the Church's official story—even as it enlists the "Patroness of the Americas" in the service of sexual rights.[5] And, if cultural dubbing works here to situate the group firmly within Mexican political and cultural traditions, it also serves to quell concerns that a broad social-justice agenda has diluted El Closét's foundational mission. For example, the group's most recent march manifesto goes out of its way to distinguish its brand of lesbian feminism from that espoused by "queer theorists"—most often US-based academics—whose work allegedly attempts "to destabilize and dismantle all social movements through the negation of identities . . . especially the lesbian feminist movement, which spearheads the fight against patriarchy" (Marcha Lésbica 2013). In this instance, El Closét argues in favor of maintaining (rather than overdubbing) conventional global categories, in opposition to "postmodern" theorists who question the normative power of those categories to construct individuals as lesbian, gay, bisexual, trans, or intersex. Nonetheless, we see again the essential role that the process of cultural dubbing—here in defense of global normative categories—plays in sustaining the legitimacy of local grassroots organizations such as El Closét as they negotiate their complex, potentially delegitimizing relationships with national, transnational, and international sexual rights movements.

The very different NGOs surveyed here—dedicated respectively to religious freedom and women's rights (Criola), LGBTQ rights within Islam (Inner Circle), sex worker rights (Durbar), and lesbian empowerment (El Closét)—are just four examples of recent social mobilization efforts that link the international sexual rights movement with grassroots initiatives. If space permitted, we could easily include a range of others, such as HIV-positive people working to overcome stigma and discrimination, women mobilizing against sexual violence, intersex people protesting involuntary medical interventions, and other as-yet-unidentified sexual rights movements that are taking shape on the ground even as we write. As Castells's work suggests, in almost all such cases in the contemporary world, legitimizing identity formation emerges as marginalized groups become conscious of their shared oppression, organize collectively around resistance identities, and (in many cases) develop project identities that move beyond local concerns to link up with larger transnational movements that seek social transformation. The four case studies also emphasize the importance of claiming existing legal and constitutional rights, the crucial role of civil society projects in helping enforce rights through nongovernmental collective action, and the power of religious counternarratives to promote group cohesion and inspire social justice agendas. And, most importantly, they highlight the paramount role that grassroots activism and community mobilization have come to play in the early twenty-first-century struggle for sexual rights.

Conclusion

Perhaps the single most important quality or characteristic defining sexuality in the contemporary world is the extent to which it has, as the saying goes, come out of the closet—the extent to which sexuality has ceased to be considered an essentially private affair and has entered the public arena as a focus for political organizing and policy debate. Sexuality and power may have always been linked, but never before have sexuality and politics been so intimately intertwined. In this so-called "information age," intense processes of economic, social, cultural and political globalization have enveloped and linked all societies and in only a few decades have profoundly transformed the world as we know it. As a consequence, sexuality, like every other dimension of human experience, has been profoundly transformed. While the basic mechanics and choreography of sexual practice have perhaps changed relatively little, the shape and structure of sexual meanings, the contours and content of sexual cultures, and the dynamics of sexual politics have all undergone amazing transformations. Within this context, whether at the local level of grassroots mobilization or in the jet-setting world of transnational organizing, sexual rights have come to the center of public concern and policy debates, and have thus become one of the defining characteristics of life in the globalized world of the twenty-first century.

Notes

1   It should be noted that allowing gays and lesbians into military service and sanctioning same-sex marriage work to normalize those who seek inclusion in mainstream institutions deemed crucial to social stability and reproduction— two essentially "conservative" functions.

2   Homophile activists and sexual outlaws, especially in the United States and Western Europe, created spaces for resistance against heteronormative oppression—and often deployed a discourse of "rights"—long before US gay rights groups seized on the 1969 Stonewall riots in New York City as the origin myth of the modern LGBT movement (Duberman et al. 1989; Kennedy and Davis 1993; Churchill 2008).

3   Mexico City also passed relatively liberal abortion laws, rare in most of Latin America and other Mexican states. Since 2007, a woman in Mexico City can get an abortion on demand throughout the first trimester of pregnancy.

4   The common use in Mexican popular culture of the word *malinchismo* for "selling out" refers to La Malinche, one of the names for the Indian woman who translated for the Spanish conquistador Hernán Cortes and later bore him a child. Although in recent years feminists have attempted to rehabilitate La Malinche, the word *malinchista* still signifies someone who has betrayed the homeland. Given its connotations (female betrayal in the fashion of the biblical Eve), the phrase itself is seldom used by feminists but is implicit in any accusation that involves the betrayal of the country to foreign invaders.

5   According to the Guadalupe legend, Tepeyac is the place where Juan Diego encountered the Virgin. It has been the site of her shrine since the early colonial era and continues to attract millions of pilgrims and tourists each year. Juan Diego's symbolic transformation into Juana of the Rainbow "queers" Sor Juana by juxtaposing her name with a "rainbow," the international symbol of sexual diversity.

References

Adam, B., Duyvendak, J.W., and André Krouwel, A. (1999) *The Global Emergence of Gay and Lesbian Politics: National Imprints of a Worldwide Movement.* Temple University Press, Philadelphia.

Aggleton, P., Boyce, P., Moore, H.L., and Parker, R. (eds) (2012) *Understanding Global Sexualities: New Frontiers.* Routledge, New York.

Agustín, L. (2007) Introduction to the cultural study of commercial sex. *Sexualities,* 10 (4), 403–7.

Alexander, M.J. and Mohanty, C.T. (1997) *Feminist Genealogies, Colonial Legacies, Democratic Futures.* Routledge, New York.

Appadurai, A. (1996) *Modernity at Large: Cultural Dimensions of Globalization.* University of Minnesota Press, Minneapolis.

Bhalla, N. (2012) U.S. ban unites global sex workers at Indian festival. *Reuters,* July 26. www.reuters.com/article/2012/07/26/us-india-sexworkers-idUSBRE 86P0FH20120726 (accessed July 31, 2013).

Birman, P. (2005) Transas e transes: sexo e gênero nos cultos afro-brasileiros, um sobrevôo ["Transas" and trances: Sex and gender in Afro-Brazilian cults, an overview]. *Revista Estudos Feminista*, 13 (2). www.scielo.br/scielo.php?script =sci_arttext&pid=S0104–026X2005000200014&lng=en&nrm=iso&tlng =pt (accessed July 31, 2013).

Boellstorff, T. (2003) Dubbing culture: Indonesian gay and lesbi subjectivities and ethnography in an already globalized world. *American Ethnologist*, 30 (2), 225–42.

Brown, G., Browne, K., Elmhirst, R., and Hutta, S. (2010) Sexualities in/of the Global South. *Geography Compass*, 4 (10), 1567–79.

Burdick, J. (1993) *Looking for God in Brazil: The Progressive Catholic Church in Urban Brazil's Religious Arena*. University of California Press, Berkeley.

Cabral, M. and Benzur, G. (2006) Cuando digo intersex: Un diálogo introductorio a la Intersexualidad [When I say intersex: Introductory dialogue for intersexuality]. *Cadernos Pagu*, 24, 283–304.

Cameron, E. (1993) Sexual orientation and the constitution: A test case for human rights. *South African Law Journal*, 110, 450–72.

Cameron, E. and Gevisser, M. (1995) *Defiant Desire: Gay and Lesbian Lives in South Africa*. Routledge, New York.

Campbell, C. (2007) *Race and Empire: Eugenics in Colonial Kenya*. Manchester University Press, Manchester.

Castells, M. (1996) *The Rise of the Network Society*. Blackwell, Oxford.

Castells, M. (1997) *The Power of Identity*. Blackwell, Oxford.

Castells, M. (1998) *End of Millennium*. Blackwell, Oxford.

Castro, Y.M.Y. (2004) El movimiento lésbico feminista en México, su independencia respecto a los movimientos feminista heterosexual y gay y su misión histórica [The lesbian feminist movement in Mexico, its independence with respect to the heterosexual feminist and gay movements and its historic mission]. http://infouam.blogspot.com/2005/06/el-movimiento-lsbico-feminista -en.html (accessed July 31, 2013).

Churchill, D.S. (2008) Transnationalism and homophile political culture in the postwar decades. *GLQ*, 15 (10), 31–66.

Clark, A.M., Friedman, E.J., and Hochstetler, K. (1998) The sovereign limits of global civil society: A comparison of NGO participation in UN world conferences on the environment, human rights, and women. *World Politics*, 51 (1), 1–35.

Corrêa, S., Petchesky, R., and Parker, R. (2008) *Sexuality, Health and Human Rights*. Routledge, New York.

Criola (2012) Quem somos [Who we are]. www.criola.org.br/quem_somos.htm (accessed July 31, 2013).

Currah, P., Juang, R.M., and Minter, S.P. (eds) (2006) *Transgender Rights*. Minneapolis, University of Minnesota Press.

D'Emilio, J. and Freedman, E.B. (1997) *Intimate Matters: A History of Sexuality in America*, 2nd edn. University of Chicago Press, Chicago.

Duberman, M.B., Vicinus, M., and Chauncey Jr., G. (eds) (1989) *Hidden from History: Reclaiming the Gay and Lesbian Past*. Meridian, New York.

Edelman, M. (2001) Social movements: Changing paradigms and forms of politics. *Annual Review of Anthropology*, 30, 285–317.

El Clóset de Sor Juana (2011) El Clóset [The closet], February 7. www .elclosetdesorjuana.org.mx/2011/02/hello-world-2 (accessed July 31, 2013).

Epprecht, M. (2004) *Hungochani: The History of a Dissident Sexuality in Southern Africa*. McGill-Queen University Press, Quebec.

Foucault, M. (1977) *Discipline and Punish: The Birth of the Prison* (trans. A. Sheridan). Vintage, New York.

Garcia, J. and Parker, R. (2006) From global discourse to local action: The makings of a sexual rights movement? *Horizontes Antropológicos*, 12 (26), 13–41.

Garcia, J. and Parker, R. (2011) Resource mobilization for health advocacy: Afro-Brazilian religious organizations and HIV prevention and control. *Social Science & Medicine*, 72 (12), 1930–8.

Gaudium (2010) Unión homosexual es intrínscamente inmoral, explica Cardenal Rivera [Homosexual union is intrinsically immoral, explains Cardinal Rivera]. *Gaudium*, August 9. www.gaudium.org.mx/?p=2925 (accessed July 31, 2013).

Ghose, T., Swendeman, D., George, S., and Chowdhury, D. (2008) Mobilizing collective identity to reduce HIV risk among sex workers in Sonagachi, India: The boundaries, consciousness, negotiation framework. *Social Science & Medicine*, 67 (2), 311–20.

Giddens, A. (1990) *The Consequences of Modernity*. Stanford University Press, Stanford, CA.

Girard, F. (2007) Negotiating sexual rights and sexual orientation at the United Nations, in *SexPolitics: Reports from the Front Lines* (ed. R. Parker, R. Petchesky, and R. Sember). Sexuality Policy Watch, Rio de Janeiro, pp. 311–58. www.sxpolitics.org/frontlines/home/index.php (accessed August 9, 2013).

González, J. (2009) Mexico City approves gay marriage. *Agence France-Presse*, December 22. www.google.com/hostednews/afp/article/ALeqM5h4_uOzElZ ivyqR7ZpWRTnJdAJ5dg (accessed July 31, 2013).

Hall, S. (1990) Cultural identity and diaspora, in *Identity: Community, Culture, Difference* (ed. J. Rutherford). Lawrence & Wishart, London, pp. 222–37.

Held, D., McGrew, A., Goldblatt, D., and Perraton, J. (1999) *Global Transformations: Politics, Economics and Culture*. Polity, Cambridge.

HRW (Human Rights Watch) (2009) *Together, Apart: Organizing around Sexual Orientation and Gender Identity Worldwide*. Human Rights Watch, New York.

ICHRP (International Council on Human Rights Policy) (2009) When Legal Worlds Overlap: Human Rights, State and Non-State Law. International

Council on Humans Rights Policy, Versoix, Switzerland. www.ichrp.org/en/projects/135 (accessed August 9, 2013).

Inner Circle, The (2010) Conference for the Empowerment of Women. ICEW Report. http://theinnercircle.org.za/resources (accessed August 9, 2013).

Inner Circle, The (2012) Annual International Retreat. AIR Report. http://theinnercircle.org.za/resources (accessed July 31, 2013).

Jaquette, J.S. (1989) *The Women's Movement in Latin America: Feminism and the Transition to Democracy*. Unwin Hyman, London.

Jayawardena, K. (1986) *Feminism and Nationalism in the Third World*. Kali for Women, New Delhi.

Joseph, S. (1996) Gay and lesbian movement in India. *Economic and Political Weekly*, 31 (33), 2228–33.

Keck, M. and Sikkink, K. (1998) *Activists Beyond Borders*. Cornell University Press, Ithaca.

Kempadoo, K. and Doezema, J. (1998) *Global Sex Workers: Rights, Resistance and Redefinition*. Routledge, New York.

Kempadoo, K., Sanghera, J., and Pattanaik, B. (eds) (2005) *Trafficking and Prostitution Reconsidered*. Paradigm Publishers, Boulder, CO.

Kennedy, E.L. and Davis, M.D. (1993) *Boots of Leather, Slippers of Gold: The History of a Lesbian Community*. Penguin Books, New York.

Kollman, K. and Waites, M. (2009) The global politics of lesbian, gay, bisexual and transgender human rights: An introduction. *Contemporary Politics*, 15 (1), 1–17.

Kotiswaran, P. (2001) Preparing for civil disobedience: Indian sex workers and the law. *Boston College Third World Law Journal*, 21 (2), 161–242.

Kugle, S. (2005) Queer jihad: A view from South Africa. *ISIM Review*, 16, 14–15.

Luibhéid, E. (2002) *Entry Denied: Controlling Sexuality at the Border*. University of Minnesota Press, Minnesota.

MacRae, E. (1990) *A Construção da Igualdade: Identidade Sexual e Política no Brasil da "Abertura"* [The Construction of Equality: Sexual Identity and Politics in Brazil's "Opening"]. Editora da Unicamp, Campinas.

Malcolm X (1964) Letter from Mecca. www.malcolm-x.org/docs/let_mecca.htm (accessed July 31, 2013).

Manderson, L. (ed.) (2012) *Technologies of Sexuality, Identity and Sexual Health*. Routledge, New York.

Marcha Lésbica (2003) Documento central de la 1a y 2a Marcha Lésbica México 2003–2004 [Central document of the 1st and 2nd Lesbian March, Mexico 2003–2004]. www.marchalesbica.com/documento-central/1a-y-2a-marchas-2003-04 (accessed July 31, 2013).

Marcha Lésbica (2013) Documento central y demandas [Central document and demands] www.marchalesbica.com/documento-central/documento (accessed July 31, 2013).

Mikell, G. (1995) African feminism: Toward a new politics of representation. *Feminist Studies*, 21 (2), 405–24.

Miller, A.M. (2000) Sexual but not reproductive: Exploring the junction and disjunction of sexual and reproductive rights. *Health and Human Rights*, 4 (2), 68–109.

Mint (2012) The new rhythms of Sonagachi. *Live Mint & The Wall Street Journal*, February, 24. www.livemint.com/Leisure/zc6wRB1Jmjj9cJKrSCLlWP/The-new -rhythms-of-Sonagachi.html (accessed July 31, 2013).

Misra, G., Mahal, A., and Shah, R. (2000) Protecting the rights of sex workers: The Indian experience. *Health and Human Rights*, 5 (1), 88–115.

Moore, H. (1988) *Feminism and Anthropology*. University of Minnesota Press, Minneapolis.

Myers, S.L. and Cooper, H. (2011) US to aid gay rights abroad, Obama and Clinton say. *New York Times*, December 6. www.nytimes.com/2011/12/07/world/ united-states-to-use-aid-to-promote-gay-rights-abroad.html?pagewanted =all (accessed July 31, 2013).

OHCHR (2011) *Combatting Discrimination Based on Sexual Orientation and Gender Identity*. United Nations Office of the High Commissioner on Human Rights, Geneva. www.ohchr.org/EN/Issues/Discrimination/Pages/ LGBTBrochure.aspx (accessed July 31, 2013).

Orchard, T.R. (2007) Girl, woman, lover, mother: Towards a new understanding of child prostitution among young Devadasi in rural Karnataka, India. *Social Science and Medicine*, 64, 2379–90.

Parker, R. (1999) *Beneath the Equator: Cultures of Desire, Male Homosexuality, and Emerging Gay Communities in Brazil*. Routledge, New York.

Parker, R. (2012) Critical intersections/engagements: Gender, sexuality, health and rights in medical anthropology, in *Medical Anthropology at the Intersections* (ed. M. Inhorn and E. Wentzell). Duke University Press, Durham, NC, pp. 206–38.

Parker, R. and Galvão, J. (eds) (1996) *Quebrando o Silêncio: Mulheres e AIDS no Brasil* [Breaking the Silence: Women and AIDS in Brazil]. Relume-Dumará, Rio de Janeiro.

Parker, R., Petchesky, R., and Sember, R. (eds) (2007) *SexPolitics: Reports from the Front Lines*. Sexuality Policy Watch, Rio de Janeiro. www.sxpolitics.org/ frontlines/home/index.php (accessed July 31, 2013).

Petchesky, R.P. (2000) Sexual rights: Inventing a concept, mapping an international practice, in *Framing the Sexual Subject* (ed. R. Parker, R.M. Barbosa, and P. Aggleton). University of California Press, Berkeley, pp. 81–103.

Petchesky, R.P. (2003) *Global Prescriptions: Gendering Health and Human Rights*. Zed Books, London.

Pintaguy, J. (2002) Bridging the local and the global: Feminism in Brazil and the international human rights agenda. *Social Research*, 69 (3), 805–20.

Proceso (2010) Por mi madre, Bohemios [For my mother, Bohemians]. *Proceso,* March 7. http://hemeroteca.proceso.com.mx/?page_id=278958&a51dc26366 d99bb5fa29cea4747565fec=82139&rl=wh (accessed July 31, 2013).

Rousseau, N. (2009) *Black Woman's Burden: Commodifying Black Reproduction.* Palgrave MacMillan, New York.

Rubin, G. (1984) Thinking sex: Notes for a radical theory of the politics of sexuality, in *Pleasure and Danger: Exploring Female Sexuality* (ed. C. Vance). Routledge & Kegan Paul, Boston, pp. 267–319.

Stepan, N. (1991) *The Hour of Eugenics: Race, Gender, and Nation in Latin America.* Cornell University Press, Ithaca.

Terto Jr., V. (1999) Seropositivity, homosexuality, and identity politics in Brazil. *Culture, Health and Sexuality,* 1 (4), 329–46.

Thomas, F., Haour-Knipe, M., and Aggleton, P. (2010) *Mobility, Sexuality and AIDS.* Routledge, New York.

Vanguardia (2012) Igualdad y aceptación: "México, segundo país en asesinatos por homophobia" [Equality and acceptance: "Mexico, the second [ranked] country for homophobic killings"]. *Vanguardia,* May 16. www.vanguardia.com.mx/ igualdadyaceptacionmexicosegundopaisenasesinatosporhomofobia -1288358.html (accessed July 31, 2013).

Vega, R. (2012) Ante la pederastía, el Papa del desdén [In the face of pederasty, the Pope of disdain]. *Proceso,* March 31. www.sectas.org/notas/pederastia-papa-desden.asp (accessed July 31, 2013).

Vianna, A.R.B. and Carrara, S. (2007) Sexual politics and sexual rights in Brazil: A case study, in *SexPolitics: Reports from the Front Lines* (ed. R. Parker, R. Petchesky, and R. Sember). Sexuality Policy Watch, Rio de Janeiro, pp. 27–52. www.sxpolitics.org/frontlines/home/index.php (accessed July 31, 2013).

Waters, M. (1995) *Globalization.* Routledge, New York.

Suggested Reading

Adam, B., Duyvendak, J.W., and André Krouwel, A. (1999) *The Global Emergence of Gay and Lesbian Politics: National Imprints of a Worldwide Movement.* Temple University Press, Philadelphia.

Aggleton, P. and Parker, R. (2010). *Routledge Handbook of Sexuality, Health and Rights.* Routledge, London and New York.

Cornwall, A., Corrêa, S., and Jolly, S. (2008). *Development with a Body: Sexuality, Human Rights and Development.* Zed Books, London.

Corrêa, S., Petchesky, R., and Parker, R. (2008) *Sexuality, Health and Human Rights.* Routledge, New York.

Currah, P., Juang, R.M., and Minter, S.P. (eds) (2006) *Transgender Rights.* University of Minnesota Press, Minneapolis.

Kempadoo, K. and Doezema, J. (1998) *Global Sex Workers: Rights, Resistance and Redefinition*. Routledge, New York.

Nagel, J. (2003). *Race, Ethnicity, and Sexuality: Intimate Intersections, Forbidden Frontiers*. Oxford University Press, New York.

Wieringa, S. and Sivori, H. (2013). *The Sexual History of the Global South: Sexual Politics in Africa, Asia and Latin America*. Zed Books, London.

Index

Page locators related to figures or figure captions are given in *italic* type.

A Global History of Sexuality: The Modern Era, First Edition.
Edited by Robert M. Buffington, Eithne Luibhéid, and Donna J. Guy.
© 2014 Robert M. Buffington, Eithne Luibhéid, and Donna J. Guy.
Published 2014 by Blackwell Publishing Ltd.